Exotic Memories

EXOTIC MEMORIES

Literature, Colonialism, and the Fin de Siècle

CHRIS BONGIE

Stanford University Press
Stanford, California
1991

Stanford University Press
Stanford, California
© 1991 by the Board of Trustees
of the Leland Stanford Junior University
Printed in the United States of America

Published with the assistance of a
special grant from the Stanford
University Faculty Publication
Fund to help support nonfaculty
work originating at Stanford.

CIP data are at the end of the book

Nostri sogni leggiadri ove son giti
Dell'ignoto ricetto
D'ignoti abitatori, o del diurno
Degli astri albergo, e del rimoto letto
Della giovane Aurora, e del notturno
Occulto sonno del maggior pianeta?
Ecco svaniro a un punto,
E figurato è il mondo in breve carta;
Ecco tutto è simile, e discoprendo,
Solo il nulla s'accresce. A noi ti vieta
Il vero appena è giunto,
O caro immaginar; da te s'apparta
Nostra mente in eterno; allo stupendo
Poter tuo primo ne sottraggon gli anni;
E il conforto perì de' nostri affani.

—Giacomo Leopardi, "Ad Angelo Mai"

(Our errant dreams, where have they gone,
Of the unknown dwelling place
Of unknown peoples, or of the diurnal
Shelter of the stars, and of young Aurora's
Distant bed, and of the largest planet's
Unseen night's repose?
Lo, they vanished all at once,
And the world is figured on the confines of a map;
Lo, all is uniform, and in disclosing,
Alone the void does grow. Once reached,
The real keeps you far from us
O beloved imagining; from you our thoughts
Eternally are parted; the years
Remove us from your stupendous founding power;
And perished is the balm of our uncertain hours.)

Acknowledgments

In the course of writing this book, I have received advice and encouragement from many people. Among those who read and commented on parts of the manuscript, I would especially like to single out the contributions of Edward Hundert, Robert Polhemus, Mary Louise Pratt, Ralph Sarkonak, Jeffrey Schnapp, and Richard Terdiman, as well as the careful editorial work of Helen Tartar and John Ziemer. I have also profited from discussions with more friends than bear listing here; be that as it may, I take this opportunity to acknowledge the particular insights of Rex Bossert, Fraser Easton, Jim English, Stephanie Lysyk, Reg McGinnis, Chris Mooney, Craig Moyes, Paul Nelles, Aruna Srivastava, Stephen Steele, Joanne Yamaguchi, and Gianni Zuliani. A special debt of gratitude is owed to my parents, Laurence and Elizabeth Bongie, as it is to Heesok Chang, Marguerita Chiarenza, David Wellbery—and to Paolo Valesio, for having shed a few glimmers of light in the heart of an academic darkness. Finally, I would like to thank the members of the Izaak Walton Killam Foundation, who, in awarding me a research fellowship at the University of British Columbia, greatly facilitated completion of the manuscript.

Unless otherwise noted, all translations in this work are my own. Parts of Chapters 2, 3, and 6 have previously appeared in print; I am grateful to the editors of the collection *Macropolitics of Nineteenth-Century Literature* and of the journals *Clio*, *Igitur*, and *L'anello che non tiene* both for their support and their permission to use that material here.

Conrad once said that "the permanence of memory" is "the only possible form of permanence in this world of relative values": it is in the spirit of his remark that I have written this book, and that I dedicate it to Alex, Kate, Rowan, and Myles.

C. B.

CONTENTS

Exotic Memories

Chapter 1

AN IDEA WITHOUT A FUTURE

EXOTICISM IN THE AGE OF COLONIAL REPRODUCTION

> Voyages, magic caskets full of dreamlike promises, you will no
> longer hand down your treasures intact. A proliferating and
> overexcited civilization troubles forever the silence of the seas.
> The perfumes of the tropics and the freshness of beings are
> vitiated by a fermentation of questionable scent, which mortifies
> our desires and destines us to gather half-corrupted memories.
> —Claude Lévi-Strauss, *Tristes tropiques*

● In 1861 Captain Harry Grant sets off to explore the islands of the Pacific with the idea of founding "a vast Scottish colony in one of the continents of Oceania." But after a year of reconnoitering he drops out of sight, effectively orphaning the two children he had left behind in England. However, several years later, while yachting off the coast of Scotland, a certain Lord Glenarvan comes across a bottle containing a puzzling and fragmentary message. The contents lead him to believe that Grant and his companions are still alive, either stranded or in captivity at some point along the 37th parallel of the Southern Hemisphere. Glenarvan summons the two children and decides to undertake a rescue mission on their behalf; this voyage in search of the lost father will eventually take him and his troupe through the wilds of Patagonia and then on to Australia and New Zealand.

Although geographically close, these last two territories prove very different in at least one important respect. In Australia, "civilization" is making definitive inroads; the island is coming to resemble nothing so much as another England—distinguished from its model, to be sure, in any number of picturesque yet inconsequential ways (flora, fauna, and so on). One of the most salient results of the British occupation has been the near-total effacement of the island's indigenous peoples; as far as Glenarvan and his band of adventurers are concerned, those who have survived are among the least interesting (and least threatening) of the picturesque elements that make up the Australian landscape. Herded onto reserves, the aborigines form a "sorry spectacle": "These beings, in a state of utter destitution, were repugnant. . . . Never had human creatures presented such an example of animality." Reduced to an animal state, vanquished by the forces of "a homicidal civilization," these "savages" seem on the point of disappearing once and for all.

The same cannot, however, be said about the indigenes of New Zealand. As one of Glenarvan's companions, Monsieur Paganel, explains while their ship is approaching the New Zealand coastline: "We're not dealing here with timid or deadened Australians, but with an intelligent and sanguinary race, with cannibals fond of human flesh, anthropophagi from whom one can expect no pity." The native peoples of these islands have yet to be "tamed"; indeed, they are at present waging a vicious war with the British colonial forces—one whose outcome, we are led to believe, still rests in the balance. These indigenes "are not deadened Australians, who flee in the face of the European invasion: they are resisting and defending themselves; they hate their invaders, and an incurable hatred is at this moment driving them against the English emigrants. The future of these large islands is resting on the throw of a dice. An instant civilization awaits it, or a deep barbarism for long centuries, according to the luck of the weapons." The Maoris are powerful enough to withstand the onslaught of a "civilization" that would push them in the same direction as the hapless Australians. But for how long? How long before the (loaded) dice fall? Before the "luck of the weapons" proves anything but a matter of chance, and the alternative prospect of some distinctly "barbaric" future nothing more than a quixotic vision?

We need go no further along the 37th parallel with Glenarvan and his companions. Their capture by the Maoris, "precisely in that savage part of the island where Christianity has never penetrated," or the manner in which they outwit their bloodthirsty but nonetheless strangely noble adversaries is not (yet) our concern; nor is Captain Grant's eventual rescue, even further along that adventure-laden line of latitude. Those curious enough can procure a copy of Jules Verne's *Les enfants du capitaine Grant* (1867–68) and read onward.[1] For us, the essential points have been raised. In Verne's novel "civilization" and "savagery/barbarism" are at complete odds. This conflict, in turn, anticipates a situation in which the one critically reduces the stature of the other: "savagery/barbarism" becomes a shadow of its former self and is drawn within the boundaries of a "civilization" that negates its very reality. What is at stake in the opposition of these two realms, and when was it established? How and when was the Other, as it were, reduced (in)to the One, and what are we to make of the world that results from this reduction—of a globe without geopolitical alternatives and in which, as Monsieur Paganel remarks, "as far as continents or new worlds go, everything's been seen, recognized, and invented"? These are some of the central questions that I will address in this account of the rise and fall of the (idea of the) *exotic* in our modern, all too modern times.

Some one hundred years after Glenarvan and his band have their run-in with a still autonomous but imperiled indigenous tribe, the Italian writer and film director Pier Paolo Pasolini provides an exceptionally blunt formulation of the issue that will occupy us throughout this study: the "novelistic," he affirms in one of his columns for the magazine *Tempo* (March 1969), is and has always been founded upon "the sense of an *elsewhere*" ("il sentimento dell'*altrove*"). If the novel, and by extension all literature, has reached a crisis point, it is because this "elsewhere" has ceased to exist:

One can now say that there no longer exists an *elsewhere* (or that it is on the point of completely disappearing). . . . The national and particularistic powers are put to rout: industrial power is by now, practically, the whole of humanity. One can no longer go "toward the Horizon" as if it were a matter of an adventure: that is, of the conquest of an *elsewhere*. The mystery of an *elsewhere* has fallen away, and with it the imaginary confrontation with one's own values. . . . We are all *here*. (*Il Caos*, p. 149)

"We" are all here, part of a homogenized world community organized according to the dictates of (post-)industrial, transnational power; "ours" is a world without horizons, essentially lacking in mystery, out of which nothing new can arise. With the disappearance of an "elsewhere" and of those who might formerly have inhabited this alternative space, something essential has been lost—or at least, Pasolini adds, "in theory." "In reality," as he goes on to say, the "novelistic" does remain a vital force in the lives of the vast majority, who are not (yet) fully engaged by the problems facing society in an age of global capitalism. But this continued experience of the "novelistic" can only be a source of nostalgia for those like himself who are part of the cultural elite and "go in airplanes, or at least know that all this is on the point of ending: and how can one act as if one didn't know [*e come si fa a fingere di non sapere*]?" (p. 150)

Pasolini's analysis of the modern condition is not particularly original. Twentieth-century sociology and ethnography abound with likeminded visions of alternative societies on the wane and global homogenization in the works. One thinks especially of Theodor Adorno and the Frankfurt School, but also of Claude Lévi-Strauss, who put the matter very bluntly in *Tristes tropiques* (1955): "Humanity is sinking into monoculture; it is getting ready to produce civilization as it does beetroot—en masse" (p. 27). Dire visions such as these, however, most often resemble each other not only in their pessimism but also in their propensity for deferring the very thing that is being affirmed: although humanity is settling into a "monoculture," it is at the same time still only *in the process of*, or *on the point of*, producing a "beet-like" mass society. "In theory" there are no more horizons, but "in reality" they still exist.

A writer like Pasolini may well find himself drowning in the troubled waters of global capitalism, but he nonetheless affirms the continued existence of what he claims is disappearing: a solid ground upon which others, if not himself, may yet station themselves. This concurrent affirmation and deferral is, clearly, another version, writ small, of the opposition at work in Verne's *Les enfants du capitaine Grant* between a degraded Australia and a still "savage" New Zealand. The story that Pasolini, Lévi-Strauss, and countless others have told in the twentieth century is little more than a repetition of one that was very much on the nineteenth-century mind: the gradual loss of alternative horizons that had to result from the diffusion of "Western civilization" to all corners of the globe. The process of intensive industrialization and urbanization that in Europe begins toward the end of the eighteenth century is, by Verne's time, already seen as having worldwide repercussions. This global vision puts into question the faith in cultural heterogeneity undergirding the ideological project that I refer to here as *exoticism*.

For the purposes of this study, exoticism is defined as a nineteenth-century literary and existential practice that posited another space, the space of an Other, outside or beyond the confines of a "civilization" (and I will henceforth, as much as possible, spare the reader the quotation marks that ought to be placed around this and other such loaded words) that, by virtue of its *modernity*, was perceived by many writers as being incompatible with certain essential values—or, indeed, the realm of value itself. What modernity is in the process of obliterating "here" might still prove a present possibility in this alternative geopolitical space: such is the primary credo of the exoticist project. The initial optimism of this project, however, gives way in the second half of the century to a deep pessimism stemming from the rapid spread of colonial and technological power. How can one recuperate "elsewhere" what civilization is in the process of eliminating if this same process has already taken on global proportions? This is the dilemma that we find at work in Verne's novel and, belatedly, in the writings of Lévi-Strauss and Pasolini. The emergence of this crisis, and various reactions to it, will occupy us in chapters to come. At this point, however, we need to look more closely at my definition of exoticism—at both its methodological presuppositions and its historical trajectory.

I have defined exoticism as a discursive practice intent on recovering "elsewhere" values "lost" with the modernization of European society. This definition clearly begs at least one crucial methodological question: Where do I stand with regard to the historical and ethical judgment (what was *once* present is *now*, alas, absent) that by my account generates the exoticist project? Is there something objectively true about this scenario of loss, or is it nothing more than a retrograde ideological fiction from which we can and must take an absolute critico-historical distance?

The answer to that question, of course, depends upon how one defines "modernity" (or, indeed, if one has any use for the concept at all). There are certainly ample reasons for being wary of this holistic concept; however, as will soon become apparent, I not only make plentiful use of it but have adopted as my own the pessimistic and nostalgic evaluation (or devaluation) of modernity central to exoticism. I will not be describing the exoticist project from some putatively neutral observation post: the story of loss that generates exoticism is also the story of this book, a study that to a certain extent participates in what it purports to analyze. For this reason, exoticist (and, by implication, metaphysical) categories of thought—such as modernity/tradition, civilization/savagery, Same/Other, presence/absence—will retain an objective, or perhaps I should say *quasi* objective, status in my own discussion of them. I have re-inscribed myself within these categories, accrediting what—because of the nature of critical analysis—must at the same time be discredited. Ultimately, what this redeployment of some of the key figures of exoticism has allowed me to do is to develop, alongside my consideration of the exoticist project, an essentially ethico-political argument about coping with(in) "late capitalist" society—an argument that depends upon the *definitive* loss of value(s) and a *real* absence of alternative worlds.

Some of the details of this argument emerge later in this introduction; for now, what needs to be kept in mind are the problems that arise from framing history within the terms of a story—in this case a story about loss (the loss of tradition, the loss of alternatives, the loss of the possibility of an "authentic experience"). Stories can be used to resolve complex issues in oversimplified terms. No one, for instance, would dispute the fact that the French Revolution and the industrialization of European society played an important and transformative role in world history; on the other hand, when such events are given a decisively causal status and cited as key moments in the epochal shift from a traditional to a modern society, one has every right to be suspicious. This is, however, exactly the sort of thinking that structures exoticism, and to the extent that I have adopted its scenario as my own the same suspicions must, from beginning to end, be cast upon what I will be saying about the exoticist project.

At least one signal difference exists, however, between my vision of historical change and that which underwrote (and underwrites) the ideology of exoticism. Both, to be sure, envision material transformations within the narratological terms of loss: modernity has taken the place of tradition; a writing and colonizing society has devastated a primitive oral culture; and so on. But what the critic of exoticism knows and repeatedly brings to the fore—unlike its less self-conscious practitioners—is that such narratives of loss are indeed nothing more (or less) than stories, ex post facto hypotheses that do not, and cannot, correspond to the reality of historical change. And in this knowledge lies the critical difference between my own use of this melancholy (hi)story and the sort of unproblematical belief in cultural decline characteristic of so many nineteenth- and twentieth-century exotic texts.

In order to reinforce what is at stake in a "critical" as opposed to "naive" recourse to this narrativizing strategy, I will turn for a moment to Fredric Jameson's strategic use in *The Political Unconscious* of Max We-

ber's sociological apparatus.[2] In his engaging discussion of Joseph
Conrad (pp. 206–80), Jameson invokes Weber's notion of "rationalization" as a "mediatory code" by which to situate Conrad historically.
For Weber, he explains, "all social institutions describe a fatal trajectory
from the traditional to the rationalized, passing through a crucial transitional stage which is the moment—the vanishing mediation—of so-
called charisma" (p. 249). Conrad's work is, according to Jameson, best
approached as a product of this brief transitional stage—the liminal
moment when, among other things, "value" for the first time becomes
a theoretical object of concern.

In older societies, Jameson explains following Weber, the problem
of value could not arise. The question of what human activities are or
are not worthy of being pursued cannot be posed "in the world of the
traditional village, or even of tribal culture"; each activity there is
"symbolically unique, so that the level of abstraction upon which they
could be compared with one another is never attained" (p. 249). This
level will be reached only with "the secularization of life under capitalism and the breaking up (or, in the current euphemism, the 'modernization') of the older tradition-oriented systems of castes and inherited professions, as the combined result of the French Revolution
and the spread of the market system." Once this happens and a "least
common denominator"—equivalent labor-power—has become available by which to compare various forms of activity, the relative value
of these activities can begin to be thought. With the reorganization of
what had once seemed "qualitatively different forms of concrete work
or productive activity" into "more efficient systems which function according to an instrumental, or binary, means/ends logic" (p. 227), the
realm of values becomes, "for the first time in any general and irreversible way . . . problematical, with the result that it can, for the first
time, be isolated as a realm in itself and contemplated as a separate
object of study" (p. 249).

We are, Jameson continues, thus able to think the concept of value
only because we have been engaged by a historical process (rationalization) that is, in point of fact, drawing all activities and institutions
together onto a single plane of equivalence and thereby erasing whatever qualitative differences might once have distinguished them. In
speaking of value(s), then, we are necessarily operating in a hypothetical mode—be it one of nostalgic reconstruction or of utopic projection. To consider the notion of value critically is to see it as a posthumous creation—as that which has been, from the beginning, put

inside quotation marks: it "becomes visible as abstraction and as a strange afterimage on the retina, only at the moment in which it has ceased to exist as such" (p. 250). In the passage from the traditional to the rationalized, value is at once lost (as reality) and gained (as abstraction); the precondition of our every idea of value turns out to be "the systematic exclusion of 'value' by the new logic of capitalist social organization" (p. 252).

Value is thus, by Jameson's account, hollow at the core: recuperable only as a hypothesis—that is to say, in the largest sense of the word, as fiction. It can be argued that Weber himself was well aware of the necessarily ex post facto and hence fabulatory ("ideo-typical") nature of the object that he was analyzing; for Jameson, the abstracted status of a concept like "value" is glaringly apparent, although he will nonetheless grant the story of its loss a limited heuristic validity in his discussion of Conrad's "charismatic moment." Jameson, in other words, will stage the scenario of lost values as if those values really had existed at some point in the past, as if we were able truly to speak of "traditional institutions and social relations" that have undergone a "wholesale dissolution" (p. 227) in the objective process of rationalization.

It is this same strategy of staging that will engage me here in my examination of the ideology of exoticism, but with one crucial difference. As a Marxist critic, Jameson resituates a narrative like Weber's within the terms of a more encompassing master narrative of dialectical redemption that purports to conform, however indirectly, to the true unfolding of events. It might well be argued that Jameson's belief in this master narrative is at odds with his insight into the abstract, hypothetical nature of value in capitalist society. If value is for us what can be grasped only in its unreality, "at the moment in which it has ceased to exist as such," is it theoretically coherent, or politically interesting, to assert, as he does, that we must work toward its future real-ization in the form of a "genuine community" (p. 261)? If the idea of value and the realm of traditional *communitas* become apparent only in the wake of their "wholesale dissolution," then might it not be no more than a complacent gesture of bad faith to posit their dialectical recuperation at some more or less distant point in the future? To think our time, a time of dissolution, should, rather, be to broach a thinking without solutions, a thinking that forgoes resolute endings of the sort Jameson proposes. Faced with the (hypothetical) loss of values under global capitalism, perhaps it is more urgent to confront the unreality of what we have lost than to continue to invest in the reality of its future.

I will pursue this irresolute, and non-futural, line of thought later in the introduction; for now, having considered some of the methodological difficulties raised by my definition of exoticism, we need to flesh that definition out a little. I will start by discussing two of the central concerns of the exoticist project: "authentic experience" and "sovereign individuality."

According to Lévi-Strauss, "our relations with one another are now only occasionally and fragmentarily based upon global experience, *the concrete 'apprehension' of one person by another*."[3] The underlying project of exoticism is to recover the possibility of this total "experience," this concrete apprehension of others that is (or so the critics of modernity hypothesize) typical of traditional communities but has been, or is being, eliminated from our own world. Walter Benjamin, for instance, consistently stressed that the modern era was a time constituted by "the increasing atrophy of experience" ("die zunehmende Verkümmerung der Erfahrung").[4] To be sure, opinions vary greatly as to when this decline set in. Benjamin himself at times dated the loss of a capacity for experience from the First World War, as in this familiar passage from his essay "The Storyteller" (1936):

With the World War a process began to become apparent which has not halted since then. Was it not noticeable at the end of the war that men returned from the battlefield grown silent—not richer, but poorer in communicable experience? . . . A generation that had gone to school on a horse-drawn streetcar now stood under the open sky in a countryside in which nothing remained unchanged but the clouds, and beneath these clouds, in a field of force of destructive torrents and explosions, was the tiny, fragile human body.

(*Illuminations*, p. 88)

In Benjamin's essays on Baudelaire, on the other hand, the "atrophy of experience," and the consequent disappearance of what he termed "aura," is pushed back a half-century to the time of Haussmann's Paris, if not before. The choice of a date and a place depends largely upon which version of modernity, or which reaction against it, is under consideration. As far as the exoticist project is concerned, I will argue that the relevant historical coordinates are the political and technological revolutions of the late-eighteenth and early-nineteenth centuries.

To raise the question of experience is also necessarily to open up the problem of just who it is that does—or, rather, does not—do the ex-periencing. I say "not" because Benjamin's notion of experience has, arguably, the same posthumous status that Jameson identifies with Weber's idea of value: in other words, that such a thing as experience *was* possible can become visible to us only once it has been radically problematized. The old subject of experience, the one who (in Lévi-Strauss's words) would have been able to apprehend others concretely, can have no place in the age of mechanical reproduction—a modern age in which, paradoxically, it first becomes possible to conceptualize what this non-alienated form of subjectivity might have been like. What arises in compensation for and as a reaction against the disap-pearance of the old subject is its phantasmic afterimage: the modern (Romantic) *individual*, a subject who, desirous of experience, is none-theless constituted by the impossibility of that experience. The indi-vidual is, from the beginning, a posthumous figure of and in crisis, an afterimage in search of what is itself no more than an afterimage.

In asserting this, of course, I am speaking of the Romantic individual from a critical perspective that is not immediately apparent to him; al-though aware of his own alienation and in search of a remedy for it, the individual cannot admit that this alienation is what actually con-stitutes him. (The grammatical convention according to which an un-gendered subject/object is referred to by the masculine pronoun is, I suspect, rather appropriate in this particular case; the extent to which modern individualism and masculist ideology feed into each other is not, however, an issue that I will be considering here.) That his very being depends upon the absence of a solid ground is the insight to which the individual would remain blind. He will thus devise strate-gies—or what René Girard has dubbed *mensonges romantiques* ("ro-mantic lies")—by which he hopes to overcome his alienation, to re-cuperate a wholeness from which he was separated at birth. Exoticism is one such individualistic strategy designed to maintain "the illusion of spontaneous desire and of a subjectivity almost divine in its auton-omy."[5] In seeking out a realm of experience beyond the confines of a modernity that denies him the possibility of self-realization, the "exotic subject" averts his gaze from the essential hollowness of his own phan-tasmic subjectivity—an evasive operation that, as we will see in the discussion of Jules Verne and Pierre Loti in Chapters 2 and 3, becomes increasingly difficult as the nineteenth century draws to a close.

Near the beginning of our own century, the French writer Victor Se-galen gave a succinct formulation of this vital connection between individualism and the exoticist project: "Exoticism can only be *singular*, individualistic. It does not admit plurality."[6] This plurality that exoticism cannot admit (to) proves synonymous with such ominous abstractions as Society or the State and often has its most vivid figural embodiment in the modern crowd—the "huge fermenting mass of human-kind," as Wordsworth put it, that played such a crucial role in the political and cultural life of revolutionary Europe. Paolo Valesio has argued that "individualism . . . was (re)born as a revolt against the mass rebellion that erupted into history as the French Revolution":[7] the figure of the modern individual and that of the masses are inseparable, the latter arising as a sort of alienated (and alienating) afterimage of the traditional *communitas* in which the old (hypothetical) subject of experience might once have found a home. Alexis de Tocqueville, for one, gave a clear description of this situation in 1840: "Everything was different in the old societies. There unity and uniformity were nowhere to be found. In our day everything threatens to become so much alike that the particular features of each individual may soon be entirely lost in the common physiognomy."[8] As one of the privileged modes of recuperating this lost individuality,* the exoticist project attempts to defuse the supposed threat of homogenization that mass society poses—a threat that for the exotic imaginary proves indissociable from the specifically modern form of territorial expansion that I will refer to as *colonialism*.

This dynamic antagonism between the individual and a noxious plurality is a commonplace of many Romantic texts. The hero of Ugo Foscolo's *Ultime lettere di Iacopo Ortis* (1802), set in post-revolutionary northern Italy, provides us, for instance, with an extremely blunt formulation of this novel conflict between the individual and the world in which he finds himself: "Every individual is a born enemy of Society, because Society is necessarily the enemy of individuals" (p. 382). What needs to be stressed is both the modernity of the hero's dilemma (the *individuo* counterpoised against an essentially plural *Società*) and the fact that, as a consequence of this dilemma, he comes to pose the exoticist question par excellence. Exiled from his native Venice, Iacopo

---

*As Steven Lukes points out, many nineteenth-century writers "stressed the opposition between *individualism*, implying anarchy and social atomization, and *individualité*, implying personal independence and self-realization" (p. 8). Thus, for Tocqueville, assimilation of "the particular features of each individual" was contemporaneous with the emergence of an egotistical "individualism" that he found to be sadly characteristic of modern democracies. It is to this positive *individualité* that I refer whenever I use the terms "individual" or "individualism" in this study.

Ortis will ask himself: "In what faraway lands might I go and lose my-self? Wherever shall I find men who are different from men?" (p. 387) Ortis, of course, will eventually answer this question in the negative, committing suicide rather than attempting to lose (and thereby pos-sibly recover) himself in some "faraway land." His suicide is an essen-tially modernist response to the problem of modernity; as Walter Ben-jamin has stated, "Modernism must be under the sign of suicide, an act which seals a heroic will that makes no concessions to a mentality inimical towards this will."[9] By contrast to this nascent modernism, it is precisely a willingness to create the grounds for some sort of working compromise with modern "Society" that at the turn of the nineteenth century generates one of the most vital literary responses to the prob-lem of modernity: the bildungsroman.

Franco Moretti has given a convincing explanation of the origin of this quintessentially modern novelistic genre: "Industrial and political convulsions acted simultaneously over European culture, forcing it to redraw the territory of individual expectations, to define anew its 'sense of history,' and its attitude toward the values of modernity." The bildungsroman, Moretti argues, came to "dominate the narrative universe of the [nineteenth] century" because it was the symbolic form best suited to the task of redrawing expectations and adapting readers to the (alienating) conditions of modern society.[10] Most other eighteenth-century novelistic genres (the epistolary, lyric, satirical, and so on) perished at this time because they were less adequate to such a task. Significantly enough, however, one branch of the novel that does carry over from the previous century is the adventure novel, where what is at stake is neither compromise nor (real or spiritual) sui-cide but, rather, the evasion of a now ineluctably modern, technolog-ical, and democratizing civilization.

The novel of adventure, which we may take as originating with Dan-iel Defoe, emerges in the nineteenth century as the polar opposite of the domestic novel (and notably the bildungsroman). By the time of the French Revolution, as Martin Green has argued, it had been ex-cluded from the realm of "serious literature" in England.[11] Notwith-standing, or, rather, precisely because of, this exclusion, a Romantic writer like Walter Scott (and later, Captain Marryat and R. M. Ballan-tyne) would redeploy it as a symbolic form uniquely suited for pre-serving, in a (spatially or temporally) distant locale, whatever seemed no longer to have a place in the rapidly changing world of the Industrial Revolution. This invocation of geographical or historical distance was

also, to be sure, at work in an earlier novel like *Robinson Crusoe*, but
there is a significant difference in approach between the eighteenth-
century adventure novel and its nineteenth-century successor: the
anxiety about modernity that generates the exoticist project is relatively absent from Defoe. We can see this, for instance, in his use of the
word "adventure" itself: for Crusoe, as Peter Hulme has noted, the
word is "replete with what, for us, have become two separate meanings"—(economic) "investment" and (heroic) "action." These two
meanings will, in later writers, come to be treated as mutually exclu-
sive: the nineteenth-century hero's adventures will be more or less cor-
doned off from the economic world; "the larger the degree of *financial*
involvement in the non-European world, the more determinedly *non-*
financial European adventure stories become."[12]

Still, the problematic of modernity, individualism, and the exotic is
already present in a work like Defoe's. My portrayal of modern individualism as issuing out of the twin revolutions at the turn of the nineteenth century thus needs clarifying, since it is indisputable that something like the figure of the individual can be traced all the way back to
Descartes, if not further (as too can the Benjaminian notion of "the
atrophy of experience"—a task that Giorgio Agamben carries out in his
essay "Infanzia e storia"). If the post-revolutionary individual is in his
very essence an afterimage, always alienated from experience and tradition, what are we to make of an earlier manifestation of the bourgeois
individual such as Crusoe? Is he somehow more solid, any less of an
afterimage? No. Or, rather, he only seems more solid from a perspective, such as my own or that of the exoticist project itself, that takes as
its starting point a later date. The individual has never been anything
more than a figure of and in crisis, but the moments of this crisis can
and must be distinguished. As Valesio says, individualism was *reborn*
at the turn of the nineteenth century, specifically as part of an agonistic
response to the emergence of mass society. It is this rebirth that gives
birth to what I have been calling the exoticist project. (However necessary it may be in grounding my own argument, a genealogical prehistory of the nineteenth century's "new individualism," to use Georg
Simmel's term,[13] remains outside the limited scope of this book.)

The second major discursive source of the exoticist project, alongside the novel of adventure (and its biographical counterpart, the *récit
de voyage*), is Enlightenment anthropology. The meditations upon cultural alterity in both the *conte philosophique* (for example, Voltaire's *Zadig*
or Johnson's *Rasselas*) and the more theoretical considerations of such

writers as Montesquieu, Rousseau, and Diderot provide nineteenth-century exoticism with much of its conceptual apparatus (the "noble savage," the evolutionary dichotomy between "primitive" and "civilized" societies, and so on). Although a discussion of the specific ways in which Enlightenment thought theorized the exotic is not within my purview here,[14] even a brief mention of this second lineage makes clear the necessity of one last methodological caveat, which concerns my comparatist treatment of nineteenth-century exoticism as an essentially *transnational* phenomenon.

In the eighteenth century, the novel of adventure is a predominantly English form, whereas the thinkers of the Enlightenment are in large part French. The greater continuity between, say, Defoe and Scott than between Voltaire and Stendhal can to a certain extent be explained by the fact that the trauma of the Revolution, and the perceived rupture of tradition by modernity, was less strongly felt in England than in France or on the Continent in general. England, whose own pre-Enlightenment revolution had occurred a hundred years before, was, as Moretti puts it, "perhaps the only European nation for which 1789 did not seem like year one of modernity."[15] Already present to some extent in eighteenth-century England, the problem of a hegemonic modernity was for that reason felt rather less acutely there during the following century (hence both the precocious role of the bourgeois individual in a writer like Defoe and the relative continuity between *Robinson Crusoe* and later adventure novels). In other words, nineteenth-century exoticism will take particular forms that depend in large part on the different national literature traditions that feed into it and continue to shape it—be that to a greater (England) or lesser (France) extent. As should be evident from the table of contents, I am most concerned here with French literature and thus tend to privilege the more radical experience of modernity that characterizes it.

While not wishing to downplay these national differences, I will seldom take them into account in the course of this book; it is, rather, as a transnational phenomenon that I approach the exoticist project. If nineteenth-century exoticism can be spoken of in such comprehensive terms, and more or less sharply distinguished from the genealogical precursors that I have just mentioned, this is due precisely to the fact that it is above all a *project*, "a fragment of the future" (in Friedrich Schlegel's words).[16] As Moretti argues in his *Way of the World*, modernity, unlike the traditional society that it has come to replace, "seeks its meaning in the *future* rather than in the past" (p. 5); it is structured

around a "new image of time linked to the French Revolution: a promise without limits, a beginning without end, a perennial uncertainty"
(p. 60). This absorbing concern with, and fundamental grounding in,
the future-oriented time of secular history, which characterizes modernity, is the common thread joining all forms of nineteenth-century
exoticism.

As a project, exoticism necessarily presumes that, at some point in
the future, what has been lost will be attained "elsewhere," in a realm
of ad-venture that bypasses the sort of contemporary present that a
symbolic form such as the bildungsroman, by contrast, prepares us for.
But if exoticism partakes of modernity and its promise, what the future
promises—and here, of course, is the central irony of this particular
project—is a recovery of the past and of all that a triumphant modernity has effaced. Indeed, the very emergence of this project is unthinkable without such a triumph. Because of this vicious circle that draws
the future and the past together, the exoticist project is, from its very
beginnings, short-circuited: it can never keep its promise. And therein,
I will eventually suggest, lies the promise that it holds out to us.

Although it is not my purpose to discuss at any length the beginnings of nineteenth-century exoticism, it will be useful here to sketch
the case history of an early, and exemplary, instance of a modern individual attempting to recover in exotic locales a once and future way
of life that appears to have been ruled out of his own "busy and pur-
blind" world. Wordsworth's portrait of the Solitary in Book Three of *The
Excursion* (1814) exemplifies the break between the essentially utopian
mode of Enlightenment thinking about alternative cultures and the
post-revolutionary meditation on lost values that developed out of it.
At first inspired by the coming of the Revolution (a time when "crowds
in the open air / Expressed the tumult of their minds"), the Solitary
quickly becomes disillusioned, both at the spread of violent zealotry
and the odious counterrevolutionary tactics adopted by the British
government. Unwilling merely to retire into himself, he resolves, unlike Foscolo's Ortis, "To fly, for safeguard, to some foreign shore, / Remote from Europe; from her blasted hopes; / Her fields of carnage, and
polluted air."[17] He sets sail to the United States; yet even in the new
republic he finds himself "in the very centre of the crowd," bearing
"the secret of a poignant scorn" for everything there that resembles the
old (yet unbearably modern) world he has left behind. He thus goes
even further west, seeking out the place where "Man" still abides—

where he might yet witness "Primeval Nature's child," the savage yet noble figure that he would like to showcase in reaction against the post-revolutionary Society from which he has become estranged.

The Solitary expects that the exotic locale will offer him dominating vistas, and in this at least he is not disappointed; from the top

> Of some commanding eminence, which yet
> Intruder ne'er beheld, he there surveys
> Regions of wood and wide savannah, vast
> Expanse of unappropriated earth,
> With mind that sheds a light on what he sees.
>
> (ll. 936–40)

If, in his westward wanderings, the Solitary comes across his fair share of "unviolated woods," he nonetheless fails to find "that pure archetype of human greatness" which he had, spurred on no doubt by his readings of the *philosophes*, expected to see. In his stead appears "a creature, squalid, vengeful, and impure; / Remorseless, and submissive to no law / But superstitious fear, and abject sloth" (ll. 953–55). Perturbed by the disjunction between his utopian dreams and ethnographic "reality," the Solitary eventually returns to England, all options but a certain languid despondency exhausted. Having beat a retreat from the world of the Revolution and the city only to be disappointed by (the fiction of) alternative cultures, the Solitary returns home, there to live a sullen, hermit-like existence in the far reaches of the English countryside—that is, in the very place that Wordsworthian ideology continually proposes as a viable alternative to the modern world. This insertion of the hollowed-out figure of the Solitary in the heart of rural Britain, of course, seriously puts into question the poet's own pastoral resolution to the dilemma that industrial society posed the individual.

Wordsworth's attempt to found a "new world" upon the ground of the old, by valorizing the country over the city, is in many ways a peculiarly English response to the onset of modernity. Although intimately connected with the exoticist project, this valorization of the rural can be of only peripheral concern to us here; rather, we must return to the Solitary's encounter with both the territory and the person of the primeval Other. In this encounter we can discern what I will identify as the two modes of nineteenth-century exoticism. That which the Solitary envisioned and yet would ultimately turn away from, *imperialist* and *exoticizing* exoticism actively embrace: on the one hand, an imperial conquest of all the "unappropriated earth" that the Solitary had surveyed from his commanding eminence—a drawing up of this world

into the (logocentric) realm of "mind"; on the other hand, an erotic attachment to both the Other "creature" and his/her world—a personal
connection that the Solitary peremptorily rejects. Whereas imperialist
exoticism affirms the hegemony of modern civilization over less developed, savage territories, exoticizing exoticism privileges those very
territories and their peoples, figuring them as a possible refuge from
an overbearing modernity. I will examine these two distinct modes of
exoticism in the chapters on Verne and Loti, respectively. What needs
underlining here, however, is that they are both grounded in a common belief: namely, that there still exist places on this earth that are
Other than those in which modernity has come to hold sway. The autonomy of alternative cultures and territories, their fundamental difference from what we might call "the realm of the Same," is the one
requisite condition of exoticism: only given this difference can the individual hope to exercise—be it for imperialist or exoticizing ends—
that heroic sovereignty denied him in post-revolutionary Europe.

As I have said, this book is not a study of the exoticist project in its
beginnings; nor, I should now add, is it a consideration of exoticism in
its prime. I will pass over in silence such mid-nineteenth-century writers as Captain Marryat, Benjamin Disraeli, and Richard Burton, or Victor Hugo, Gérard de Nerval, and Théophile Gautier—the immediate
and, for our purposes, unproblematical predecessors of the writers
who interest me here.[18] Since, as I have argued, exoticism is an essentially posthumous project and thus precluded from ever truly realizing
what it sets out to achieve, a close textual analysis of these "primary"
works of nineteenth-century exoticism would result in an exposition of
their hollowness similar to the sort that I will perform on later, "secondary" writers: the exoticist project is no less problematical in Disraeli
or Hugo than in the fin de siècle writers I consider in this book. What
distinguishes the latter from the former, however, is that they were
forced to confront openly what earlier writers could more easily ignore:
namely, the end of the exotic—that end which from the beginning
haunts it and which, toward the close of the nineteenth century, would
become ever more glaringly apparent.

The initial optimism of the exoticist project gives way, in the last decades of the century, to a pessimistic vision in which the exotic comes
to seem less a space of possibility than one of impossibility. This critical
transformation of the exotic imaginary, which we begin to see at work
in writers like Verne and Loti, is conterminous with the phase of acute
geopolitical expansion initiated by the European nation-states during

the last decades of the nineteenth century and commonly referred to as the New Imperialism. Most frequently associated with the Scramble for Africa, this unprecedented period of expansion marks the moment when nineteenth-century colonialism, and with it the immeasurable problematic of modernity, first asserts itself as a *global* phenomenon— one that inevitably, and irreparably, puts into question the Other's autonomy, absorbing this Other into the body of the Same and thereby effacing the very ground of exoticism.

What were the central features of this New Imperialism? Annexation of land was pursued with a new sense of urgency, and the State came to play a much more important role in organizing this geopolitical takeover: "The Scramble involved the *rapid* acquisition of large peripheral areas to be ruled on a *formal* basis."[19] By 1880 the age of exploration was largely over: the globe had been mapped to such an extent that little or no territory was beyond the pale of Euro-American knowledge and techniques of control and communication. This new awareness of the world's finitude in turn partially accounts for the intensity of what, in New Imperialist parlance, had become a territorial steeplechase. Those lands not yet under the control of a Great Power had nonetheless been identified and transformed into objects of a colonial desire.

As one justification for the continued expansion of the British Empire, the then–foreign secretary Lord Rosebery—leading advocate of the so-called Liberal Imperialism—drew attention in 1893 to the fact that the world was not "elastic" and that for this reason Britain needed to "peg out" as many claims for the future as possible. "We have to consider," he went on, "that countries must be developed either by ourselves or some other nation."[20] This revelation of global inelasticity is the moment when colonialism, as it were, comes into the presence of its own, quintessentially modern, "truth." And the continued relevance for us today of fin de siècle thinking resides, I would argue, in the fact that this "truth" is still with us. For all that the dimensions of the capitalist world-economy have, in our own "post-colonial" age of multinational corporations, undergone a significant transformation from the days of the New Imperialism,[21] this change may indeed be no more than an exacerbation of the problem of a global modernity that first surfaced toward the end of the nineteenth century.

Faced with the complete dissolution of exotic horizons, the fin de siècle imagination envisions a world given entirely, and hopelessly, over to modernity. At one point in his influential *Du sang, de la volupté et de la mort* (1894), the novelist Maurice Barrès, looking out from the

Iberian peninsula onto the bleak Atlantic, perfectly captures this mood of exhaustion: "Nothing in front of us but the limitless Ocean. We heard some cries out to sea. It was, in the evening mist, the signal of ships doubling the cape and leaving for over there [*là-bas*]. But *over there* no longer has any unknown lands, nothing but repetitions of our Europe" (p. 116). Although Barrès seems to be thinking here specifically of the Americas, no part of the world will be exempt from this fin de siècle insight into the dissolution of "unknown" alternative worlds and the repetitive appearance in their place of "our" world, which for the decadentist imagination seems caught up in a process of irreparable decline. The last-gasp enclaves of difference that we see later writers like Lévi-Strauss and Pasolini belatedly, and almost despite themselves, conjuring up have no place in the world of colonial reproduction that Barrès confronts. What is there (or what remains) to be done in the face of this world in which little more than the simulacrum of "individual sovereignty" and "authentic experience" appears possible?

As the young Victor Segalen makes clear in his Tahiti journal (1905), the dissolution of exotic horizons that Barrès envisaged has an equally critical effect on the *writing* of exoticism. With the onset of global colonialism, the prospective exotic writer is faced with a dilemma: either to chronicle the "new" world of colonialism (that is, the Same old world) or to persevere in what was clearly an exhausted vein, relying on the by-now clichéd visions of the exotic that his precursors, with the benefit of their more immediate "experience" of it, had already set down in print. The exotic was no longer that which could be written; it was now no more than a matter for *rewriting*. "The completely unforeseen," Segalen comments, "no longer exists in exoticism since the 'perfecting' of voyages, and above all of *récits de voyage*: a series of garish watercolors toned down with sun, two or three cadences of [Flaubert's] *Tentation*, and then, through an immediate transposition, what one 'could milk out of' the things seen and recognized, and there you have everything written, everything sensed, everything grasped [*et voilà tout écrit, tout flairé, tout étreint*]."[22] There is, to be sure, something outrageous about this remark if we take it as being more than a merely empirical observation on Segalen's part about the literary inadequacy of many of his contemporaries. After all, surely "everything" has not yet been written! Outrageous as it may be, however, it is precisely such a claim that I will attempt to pursue in this book.

In Chapters 4 and 5, I will sketch out a portrait of two writers, Victor

Segalen and Joseph Conrad, coming to grips with the dissolution of their belief in the reality of the exotic and of the individual. In responding to the finite world of the New Imperialism, Conrad will only say of himself, in his best fin de siècle French: "Moi je regarde l'avenir du fond d'un passé très noir et je trouve que rien ne m'est permis hormis la fidélité à une cause absolument perdue, à une idée sans avenir" ("For myself, I look at the future from the depths of a very dark past, and I find I am allowed nothing but fidelity to an absolutely lost cause, to an idea without a future").[23] Where, I will ask, does this sort of negative thinking lead, and what, if anything, does this "idea without a future" promise? Is this decision to inhabit the scene of decadence, to renounce the future for a present that is conditioned by an absolutely lost cause, merely a nihilistic gesture? I will eventually argue that something more than a sterile nostalgia is at stake in this attachment to a cause that has once and for all been lost. Only after the cause of the individual has been abandoned as a real possibility does it (again) become a vital concern: once Segalen and Conrad have registered the impossibility of the ideological project that they "naively" advocated in the time of their youth, they choose not to abandon this empty project but rather to re-inscribe themselves within what they know to be no more (yet no less) than a dream.

This rhetorical gesture of re-valorizing what has been definitively devalued is, I will suggest, an ethically interesting response to Pasolini's question: *E come si fa a fingere di non sapere?* This response is not, of course, available to those who, like Pasolini, remain belatedly committed to the real existence of what they cannot help but see as at an end or, in their covertly optimistic terms, "on the point of ending." It is beyond this point, a beyond in which the beyond no longer has a place, that fin de siècle writers like Segalen and Conrad take us. The details of how they get there must wait; for now, however, and by way of drawing this introduction to a close, a few additional, and rather more theoretical, remarks about their (and my own) enterprise are in order.

In a recent and curiously irenic account of Rudyard Kipling's *Kim* (1901), Edward Said sums up the book's underlying motivation as follows. The world that the late-nineteenth-century novel figured forth was one in which a dire pessimism held sway; according to Said, the imperialist vision of a Kipling functioned as a positive counter to the disbelief and cynicism prevalent in the domestic novel. The buoyant presence of a Kim serves to overturn the obscurity of a character like

Hardy's Jude who, try as he might, fails to go forward in the world: "What one cannot do in one's own Western environment—where to try to live out the grand dream of a successful quest is only to keep coming up against one's own mediocrity and the world's corruption and degradation—one can do abroad. Isn't it possible in India to do everything? be anything? go anywhere with impunity?"[24] The imperialist vision shapes public opinion, offering it the possibility of boundless horizons as compensation for the dismal prospects of industrial society. Although Said's remarks hold true not only during the age of the New Imperialism but well into our own century,[25] one cannot help but argue against making such an acute and self-conscious writer as Kipling an unproblematical spokesperson for this vision. Perhaps Kipling's open-ended portrayal of India in *Kim* ought, rather, to be read as a willfully utopic response to an India that had, as far as he was concerned, turned into something rather less than the scene of a *possible* heroism. Kipling could no longer overlook the modernity of India; the Indian subcontinent could never (again) satisfy his exoticist need for a real alternative space—for an India that, as Ashis Nandy says in his incisive portrait of Kipling, "in its hard masculine valour, would be an equal competitor or opponent of the West that had humiliated, disowned and despised his authentic self."[26]

The will to escape the "world's corruption and degradation," to go elsewhere and thereby transform the constitutive mediocrity of the modern subject: Said is talking here, of course, about the central aims of nineteenth-century exoticism. But for many writers, this project had by the turn of the century become ineluctably caught up in a colonial enterprise that was strictly incompatible with exoticism as originally conceived. The "grand dream of a successful quest" could not, under these conditions, be lived out. But strictly speaking, a "quest" is never geared to success; its (etymological) essence lies in "seeking"—not in attaining at some point in the future that which is being sought. In this sense, as Giorgio Agamben has noted, a quest is the very contrary of an adventure (which, as the word itself tells us, is unthinkable without a future).

For the modern age, Agamben states in *Infanzia e storia* (pp. 23–24), the realm of adventure appears as "the last refuge of experience": "Adventure presupposes that there is a path for experience and that this path leads through the extraordinary and the exotic (as opposed to the familiar and the common)." By contrast, this positing of a "way out" is not at issue in the world of the *quête*, where it is a given that the object one desires can never be fully experienced. The object is never present, or present only at an insuperable distance: here, then, is a "recognition that the absence of a path (aporia) is the only experience possible for man." What for the adventurer holds out the promise of a positive resolution takes on a very different meaning for the subject of the quest, to whom "the exotic and the extraordinary are only ciphers for the essential aporia of every experience." As far as Said is concerned, Kipling has written a novel of adventure, in the relatively unproblematical mode of what I earlier called "imperialist exoticism"; I, on the other hand, would tend to read *Kim* as signaling Kipling's awareness of the impossibility of that "authentic experience" that he nonetheless continued to desire.

In the age of the New Imperialism, the exotic necessarily becomes, for those who persist in search of it, the sign of an aporia—of a constitutional absence at the heart of what had been projected as a possible alternative to modernity. All the writers studied here give voice to this sign (be it inadvertently or strategically); they register the exotic as a space of absence, a dream already given over to the past. This is one half of the decadentist intuition that provides so much of fin de siècle writing with its largely unheard resonance; that such dreams can be followed up on, and traced back, albeit posthumously, is the second half of this intuition, one whose literary and political consequences I will be emphasizing.

This duplicitous act of simultaneously renouncing and, as it were, re-announcing the exotic, affirming and negating it, is an example of what Walter Benjamin called "allegory" (literally, other-talk, or in our particular case, talk of the Other). For Benjamin, allegory is a central feature of modernity: *die Armatur der Moderne*, he terms it—that is, not only the protective armor of modernity but also its very framework. As the following passage from his unfinished commentary on Baudelaire, *Zentralpark* (1938–39), makes clear, the allegorical intention is profoundly ambivalent. That which this intention has stricken "finds itself separated from the ordinary correlations of life: it is at once smashed to pieces and conserved. Allegory adheres to ruins. It offers the image of frozen unrest [*sie bietet das Bild der erstarrten Unruhe*]."[27] In order to posit its object, allegory removes it from the realm of everyday life and transforms it into a ruin—an act of shattering that at the same time nonetheless serves to conserve the object. The image of the object is fixed, immobilized, and yet continues to convey a sense of motion and unrest; it is an image that has become inseparable from memory (*An-denken*)—and memory, we are told in another *Zentralpark* fragment (p. 681), is that which has its origin in "the corpse of experience" ("das Andenken [kommt] von der abgestorbenen Erfahrung her"). What allegory remembers (and rewrites) can have no real place in the degraded time of the present; it has already come to terms with the essentially memorial, commemorative nature of our relation to what precedes us.

Whereas Verne and Loti occlude the historical disjunction between the exotic world they wish to portray and the colonial present in which they must write, Segalen and Conrad take as their starting point the exotic's divergence from the time span of modernity, from the domain of what Benjamin negatively referred to as "lived experience" (*Erlebnis*: that is, the atomized successor of that integrated experience, or *Erfahrung*, whose loss he never ceases to lament). Verne and Loti create allegories despite themselves: everywhere their texts reveal the groundlessness of what they continue to posit as present in the world. For Segalen and Conrad, exoticism has been exhausted as an *ideology*, that is, as a discursive practice that still produces itself in the register of belief; yet, by means of the duplicitous strategy of allegory, they *rhetorically* conserve the exotic, engaging in a renewed, and strategic, dreaming of what they know to be no more (but no less) than a dream.[28] It is precisely this resort to rhetoric that the subject of my final chapter, Pasolini, rejects in his attempt at portraying the "Third World" as the abode of positive alternatives to (neo-)capitalist society; Pasolini's commitment to a decolonized Other, however, only leads (back) to the same ideological dead end that Verne and Loti come up against and that Segalen and Conrad take as their point of departure.

The inadequacy of ideological thinking to our time(s) is one of the foundation stones of current analyses of the postmodern condition, which is characterized, in the words of Jean-François Lyotard, by an "incredulity toward metanarratives"—toward those "big" stories (idealism, illuminism, Marxism) that since the time of the French Revolution have served to legitimate science, thought, and political action.[29] Because my own enterprise shares several of the assumptions of such analyses (including, one might add, the "big" story about the end of "big" stories!), I find it useful to conclude this introduction with a brief discussion of one vision of postmodernity that has been of particular relevance to me in writing this book; the following discussion of Gianni

Vattimo's *The End of Modernity*, in turn, inevitably raises the problem of how my own work fits in with the recent spate of literary and historiographical studies of colonial discourse.

In *The End of Modernity*, Gianni Vattimo, standard-bearer of what in Italy is called *pensiero debole* ("weak thought"),[30] rehearses a by-now familiar distinction between the modern and the postmodern: modernity is characterized by the idea of history, an idea that grounds the great nineteenth-century narratives of progress and overcoming. In the following century, this idea becomes ever more "secularized," ever less providential. Yet, notwithstanding this decline, the futuristic orientation that constitutes modernity remains a vital force, be it in philosophy (Sartre, for instance), art (the avant-garde), or the politics of emancipation—all of which in one way or another "seem ever more insistently to locate the value of an action in the fact of its making possible other choices and other actions, thus opening up a future." The modern is that time in which "the pathos of the future is still accompanied by an appeal to the authentic"; it is a time of alienation in which we continue to posit the future as the space of a possible renewal and a return to those conditions of "originary authenticity" that have been marginalized in the "forward" march of humanity (p. 100).

The postmodern critically disengages itself from the future that modernity considers its place of arrival: the postmodern displays, "as its most common and most imposing trait, an effort to free itself from the logic of overcoming, development, and innovation" that grounds modern ways of thinking about the world (p. 105). However, this effort is, strictly speaking, possible only if modernity has *not* come to an end: postmodernity cannot itself be the overcoming of the logic of overcoming because any such definitive emancipation from modernity would, ironically enough, serve only to confirm the very logic of progress from which the postmodern wishes to be free. For this reason, even as it registers the dissolution of modernity and its futuristic projects, the postmodern remains contained within the boundaries of the modern. As a philosopher, Vattimo's discussions of the modern and the postmodern are inseparable from a meditation on the end(s) of metaphysics, and it is from Heidegger's attempts at preparing us for a postmetaphysical kind of thought that he derives two of the central terms of his analysis: *Verwindung* (overcoming) and *Andenken* (remembering).

The first term captures the ambiguous relation between the modern and the postmodern. Like the more familiar *Überwindung*, it means

"overcoming," but not in a "strong" sense (the strength, say, of He-
gelian or Marxist thinking). The overcoming envisaged here is a fundamentally "weak" one: "The term *Verwindung*," Vattimo remarks, "indicates a sort of improper *Überwindung*, an overcoming which is an
overcoming neither in the usual sense nor in the sense of a dialectical
Aufhebung" (p. 171). What is to be overcome (in this case, metaphysics)
cannot be abandoned for some new and improved doctrine: "Rather,
it is something which stays in us as do the traces of an illness or a kind
of pain to which we are resigned" (pp. 172–73). In other words, the
strong categories by means of which we once hoped to effect real
change remain with us even as their total inadequacy to the present
makes itself felt everywhere and in everything. No new categories arise
to take the place of those that, weakened and hollowed out, continue
to linger on in our time. Modernity, to shift the terms of discussion
from the philosophical to the political, stays with us even when we
have become "critical" of it; because it will not go away, we must learn
to resign ourselves to it.

This resignation also, and inevitably, involves a re-signing of oneself
to the strong "truths" that are being weakly overcome. Divested of
their pretension to Truth, revealed as "a mobile army of metaphors,
metonyms, and anthropomorphisms" (Nietzsche), these "truths" remain the only ones we have and for that reason we cannot avoid making use of them—although this use will henceforth be shaped by our
awareness of their purely rhetorical nature. Vattimo goes on to insist,
though here energumens of the postmodern will hardly wish to follow
him, that our attitude toward these hollowed-out "truths" be one of
piety. Once the categories of metaphysics have been vacated of their
pretended access to Truth, he notes, "their only 'value' is as monu-
ments, a legacy to which one shows the *pietas* that is owing the traces
of what has lived."[31] In a world without a (strongly conceived) future,
all that has come before us gains a monumental significance: caught
up in a process of decline that cannot be undone but to which one cannot help attending (be it piously or not), the traces of the past become,
as it were, signposts in the labyrinth of our postmodernity.

Andenken, the second of Vattimo's key terms in *The End of Modernity*,
is the recollective form of thought that attends to, instead of neglect-
ing, this monumental past. It does not pursue a direct contact with the
past, but, rather, establishes itself in the abyss that forever separates
us from that which we are remembering—first and foremost, Being itself. In its attempts at rendering Being present (at re-presenting it) tra-

ditional metaphysics—so the familiar Heideggerian critique goes—
forgets Being; it forgets that Being, in its original difference, can never
really be thought of as a presence. *Andenken*, by contrast, remembers
Being—that is to say, acknowledges the irremediable absence of Being:
"The thought that does not forget [Being] is only that which remembers it or, in other words, already thinks of Being as absent, vanished,
or gone away" (p. 120). In remembering Being, we do no more than
follow the trace of what is immemorial. Indeed, *Andenken* pursues the
traces of this immemorial trace: the original absence of Being is doubly
removed from us inasmuch as we remember it, Heidegger and Vattimo
insist, only through a (re)consideration of those very texts—the clas-
sics of the metaphysical tradition—which, in attempting to re-present
Being, show that they have forgotten it.

This recollective form of thought is central to my own discussion of
exoticism (although one must be cautious in applying what is, after all,
a primarily ontological category to the social problematic of modernity
that concerns us here). The exoticist project, similar in this respect to
the metaphysical tradition, attempts to re-present what has "always-
already" been lost and forgotten; only once this project has been exhausted does the possibility of truly remembering the exotic arise—of
remembering it, that is, as what can never be truly remembered, as
what is absent, vanished.[32] This act of recollection does not take us any
further along the road of history, for it is possible only once the end of
that particular road has been reached. As Vattimo says, "The re-col-
lection of the spiritual forms of the past, their coming to fruition (their
being relived), understood also in an 'aesthetic' sense, does not serve
as a preparation for something else, but has an emancipatory effect
in itself."[33] We come to understand the past as that which "destines"
us, and with this understanding we are absolved from the tyrannical
specter of that "something else" our modernity insistently demands.

In bringing the past into the light of memory, we inevitably distort
it; returning to the (absent) ground of *tradition*, of that which is handed
down to us and at the same time betrayed, thus also forces us to turn
our attention to the transformations it is now undergoing. This is the
other side of the *Verwindung* coin: on the one hand, it precludes us from
a radically Other future, consigning us to a life lived within the global
boundaries of the world of modern technology; on the other hand, it
also includes us in a present that is radically different from our past,
revealing to us a world of hybridity. The two moments are inseparable
though in some ways deeply contradictory. In this introduction and in

everything that follows, I have chosen to emphasize the former, and with it the importance that memory holds out to us. I do so in part because too often in contemporary theory the undeniably central fact of hybridity appears to function as an unproblematically dialectical form of (ir)resolution that will deliver us from our present condition. The hybrid becomes valorized as a good in itself, as that which will burst the bounds of the present and start the wheels of historical prog-ress rolling again; surely, so goes the argument, postmodernity is not just an (essentially convalescent) condition but the prelude to an en-tirely "new" epoch?

At times, in *The End of Modernity*, Vattimo himself seems to be ar-guing toward such a position, as when he preaches the need for em-bracing "the poverty of the inapparent and the marginal, or of contam-ination lived as the only possible *Ausweg* from the dreams of meta-physics, no matter how they may be disguised" (p. 161). Postmodern impoverishment here blossoms into our *"chance"* for laying the foun-dations of what he calls an "ultra-metaphysical humanity." In making this sanguine nod to contamination, Vattimo indeed confirms the cri-tique that Giorgio Agamben levels against the whole idea of postmod-ernity. Agamben points out that "concepts like those of the postmod-ern, of a new renaissance, of an 'ultra-metaphysical humanity,' betray the grain of progressivism hidden in every thinking of decadence and even in nihilism: the essential thing, for every one of these, is not to miss the new epoch that has already arrived or will arrive, or at least could arrive, the signs of which are all around us and only in need of our deciphering."[34]

I do not, however, believe that "weak thinking" must inevitably re-introduce this futural (epochal) dimension. As I have described it, such thinking can do no more than resign/re-sign itself to the labyrinth of dreams from which there is no exit—or rather, in which this exit is only present to us as that from which we have been pre-cluded. Weakness cannot persist if the idea of strength is not still with us in some form; hence my own insistence on a "thinking of decadence." *Decadentism,* as I will use the term, refers to a form of nostalgia that in no way hopes to recuperate the object it contemplates (for then it, too, would be sub-ject to Agamben's critique) but, rather, probes—rhetorically, hypocrit-ically—the past away from which we have, from the beginning, de-clined.

The question of whether the postmodern is a preparation for some-thing else or merely an endless commentary on modernity aside, however, one central assumption of theories of postmodernity needs to be commented on here: namely, their global pretensions. Typical of these theories is a willingness to assert that modernity is everywhere and in everything: the scientific-technological unification of the world has been more or less completely effected—or so the story goes. Vattimo makes his allegiance to this story especially clear in an essay from *The End of Modernity* entitled "Hermeneutics and Anthropology." His account of these two intimately linked disciplines takes off from the assertion of one anthropologist (Remo Guidieri) that "the Westernization of the world has now reached its end" (p. 151). The rule of what Heidegger called "enframing" (*Gestell*) is worldwide, and for that very reason we are unable to come across any radical alternative to it: "The hermeneutic—but also anthropological—illusion of encountering the other, with all its theoretical grandiosity, finds itself faced with a mixed reality in which alterity is entirely exhausted" (p. 159).

But although alterity has been entirely exhausted, the "mixed reality" that appears in its place forces us, Vattimo notes, to rethink the apocalyptic idea of a global "homologation" that might seem the logical result of this exhaustion. The "Westernization" of the earth, far from resulting in the "total organization of the world in rigid technological schemes," produces a hybrid situation typified by constantly shifting political and economic inequalities and the survival, in a distorted form, of pre- or non-modern ways of life (as occurs, for instance, with cargo cults). To confront a world unified by science and technology, Vattimo argues, is at the same time to envision this world as, in Guidieri's words, "an immense construction site of traces and residues, in conditions which have still to be analysed" (p. 158). The postmodern poetics, and politics, of "survival" that I am arguing for in this book has as its end a taking-into-consideration of these traces and residues, and of the past in whose absence they emerge.

In its recognition of the universal imposition and provocation of the technical world, this global vision—however nuanced, however attuned to the praxis of survival—cannot fail to strike those who put their faith in the continued existence of radical cultural alterity as unconvincing at best and totalitarian at worst. Kumkum Sangari has put the case well, in an article entitled, significantly enough, "The Politics of the Possible," in which she derides at length the tendency of postmodernism "to universalize its epistemological preoccupations." By this account, analyses of postmodernism are guilty on two fronts. First, they bring to bear a specifically Eurocentric perspective on the rest of the world—namely, skepticism: "The postmodern problematic becomes *the* frame through which the cultural products of the rest of the world are seen." Second, they depend upon that "master narrative" in which "the West expands into the world; late capitalism muffles the globe and homogenizes (or threatens to) all cultural production." Such a narrative, Sangari insists, continues to privilege the "West" as an "engulfing 'center'" against which everything else must be read as peripheral (p. 183).

These are, of course, powerful—might I say "strong"—objections to the spirit of postmodernity, and I have no wish to dissolve them away. In making the second point, however, Sangari has given the "master narrative" of so-called Western expansion an ideological edge that it does not necessarily possess (although for a late-blossoming champion of "Third World" literature like Fredric Jameson, who gets taken to task here, it may well function in this way).[35] Whether or not one agrees with this "master narrative," let us at least do justice to its ending. The end result of this expansion to all corners of the globe is not, as Sangari goes on to claim, a perpetuation of "the notion of the 'Third World' as a residue and as a 'periphery' that must eternally palpitate the [Western] center"; rather, the story ends with the "residualization" of both the "West" and the "non-West" as differential categories. The center-periphery perspective has, in essence, dissolved (for all that it continues to play its masking role in discourses of both oppression and dissension). The very real political, economic, and cultural differences that separate the peoples of this planet from each other have now taken their place in one world whose global ending, indifferent to geographical distance, we must begin to read. This world, in all its heterogeneity, is governed by one fundamental tendency, which is nothing more and nothing less than technology and the "will to power"—the will to create and destroy—that this technology enacts.[36]

This, to my mind, is a rather more just account of the story that Sangari rejects—a story that allows us to begin to think *in* and not *beyond* the ending. Ultimately, of course, to engage in this endgame does mean adopting a skeptical position—although one that does not necessarily involve, as she seems to assume, singing the praises of "decentered subjects" who have kicked themselves free of the ground of political praxis. What such skepticism does preclude, however, is the unquestioning adoption of strong ideological positions. The skeptic proceeds cautiously and with an awareness of the purely rhetorical nature of his or her encounter with those ostensibly viable alternatives that inevitably present themselves as definitive solutions to a global problem that, like any aporia, has none.

Gayatri Spivak, in an argument that bears a tenuous similarity to my own, has insisted on the "catachrestic" nature of our relation to the "subaltern"—to the voice(s) and world(s) silenced by the "epistemic violence" indissociable from what she calls "imperialism."[37] The subaltern is one of those valuable "properties" that we hold on to in the face of capitalist—or, better, technological—hegemony. But the very essence of the subaltern, Spivak argues, is that we cannot speak of it truly; the subaltern's "truth" is forever absent and can be reached only by means of an untrue, disfiguring representation—a catachresis. Our distance from the place and time of the subaltern is "always-already" inscribed in our attempts at representing it. Historiographical work that takes the subaltern as its object of study, for instance, goes badly astray when it treats the subaltern as a full-bodied entity, sovereign in the face of the hegemonic force that oppresses it: if "the restoration of the subaltern's subject-position in history is seen by the historian as the establishment of an inalienable and final truth of things, then any emphasis on sovereignty, consistency, and logic will . . . inevitably objectify the subaltern and be caught in the game of knowledge as power." But, Spivak counters, we may nonetheless practice a sort of "affirmative deconstruction" that carefully, and strategically, re-inscribes the very notion whose vacancy is its precondition; in this case, "knowing that such an emphasis is theoretically non-viable, the historian then breaks his theory in a scrupulously delineated 'political interest.'"[38]

Benita Parry has, in a recent survey of current theories of colonial discourse, objected to Spivak's view of the subaltern as that which is necessarily silenced by "the epistemic violence of imperialism." Parry argues for a positive vision of "the native as historical subject and combatant, possessor of an-other knowledge and producer of alternative traditions." For instance, it should be possible, she argues, "to locate traces and testimony of women's voice on those sites where women inscribed themselves as healers, ascetics, singers of sacred songs, artizans and artists, and by this to modify Spivak's model of the silent subaltern."[39] But it is certainly a rather gross misinterpretation to suggest that Spivak denies the existence of these traces and this testimony, for they are the very signature of the subaltern's silence: only as trace does this "voice" appear to us, only as that which has been produced and then, as it were, tra-duced into the present do these "alternative traditions" come to light. Hence the need for "care" in approaching them: a careful consideration, and a careful assertion, of what must remain at an insuperable distance from us.

In my own argument, this emphasis on a founding catachresis by which alone we may speak of other worlds and other voices gains a temporal (nostalgic) dimension that Spivak would quite probably criticize. What my approach shares with hers is, however, an insistence on reading the "indeterminacy of the global text," on considering this text with a vigilance that, as she herself says in response to Parry, would "have us look to the negotiation of the double bind rather than celebrate a desire not to be bound."[40] For Sangari and Parry such "vigilance" is, clearly, not enough because the ground of its possibility is an admission of complicity with a reprehensible world. An attenuated complicity, Parry notes near the end of her survey, is perhaps all that can be expected from *some* people. For instance, Kipling and Conrad, "those old favourites of Literature and Empire criticism," are interesting, she remarks, because at the same time that their texts are indubitably "discourses of imperialism" they also demand to be read as "the location of an internal interrogation," one that puts into question without displacing the very discourse they embody. In other words, not all bad, but not all good either. Only once all ties with the "inside" are broken can this ambivalent response give way to a fully positive one: "The labour of producing a counter-discourse displacing imperialism's dominative system of knowledge," she goes on to claim, "rests with those engaged in developing a critique from outside its cultural hegemony" (p. 55).

That a critic like Parry should make this transparent appeal to the "outside"—that bastion of authenticity of which nineteenth-century exoticism dreamed—is no small irony, but only in this way is she able to ground her adamantine distinction between an impure "discourse of imperialism" and a pure, unsullied counter-discourse. For writers like Conrad and Segalen, on the other hand, to produce a counter-discourse is also always to produce a "discourse of imperialism." This is the insight that allows them to *intervene* in the present, to negotiate between it and an irrecuperable but valued past—thereby creating that double space, the space of duplicity, which is their literary and political dwelling place. Theirs is a world without "inside" or "outside," with neither Same nor Other; or rather, it is a world where such categories have been disempowered, vacated of their original force, and stand revealed as no more than constructions, beautiful (or ugly) fictions.

Insisting on the fundamental "weakness" of our own position when it comes to authenticity or liberation may seem a facile and politically dangerous exercise. As one critic of Vattimo and *pensiero debole* puts it, "In a world still full of manifest disparities in social and economic power, and of political oppression, there is even more reason to continue to employ a 'strong' ontology to justify human freedom."[41] But the chance that Vattimo sees in this admission of "weakness," and the chance that he is willing to take, is, I would argue, indeed "revolutionary"—in the original circular, as opposed to linear, sense of this word. The challenge of (post)modernity has become one of learning to live with our exotic memories, with the ruins of everything that came before us and that once, once upon a time, seemed to offer us a fullness and a "strength" that is no longer really ours to be had. Perhaps, as Vattimo puts it, it is our "piety for these ruins that is the only real motive for revolution, more than any project otherwise legitimated in the name of some natural right or some necessary historical progress."[42] What we have lost we cannot, and must not, help recalling, though it remains to us only in the guise of its absence. Even as we are parted from it—and because none of us are so innocent as to be merely the passive victims of terror, ourselves incessantly depart from it—our vision of another world returns to us, as trace, as testimony. When the thought of all that can no longer have a place in our world takes its (unreal) place in this world, the "dying fall" of modernity deviates, "ever so slightly," as Lucretius might have said. In this slight deviance, this declining of our decline, resides the idea of "human freedom" that, in all its "weakness," underwrites the following pages.

Chapter 2

THE HOLLOW MEN

DESPOTIC INDIVIDUALS AND THE FICTION OF IMPERIALISM

- *"Mistah Kurtz he dead": Conrad and the Imperial Figure*

  Do you see him? Do you see the story? Do you see anything? It
  seems to me I am trying to tell you a dream.
  —————J. Conrad, *Heart of Darkness*

The late 1890's have often been referred to as witnessing the "climax of
imperialism." A rather pedantic objection to the word "imperialism"
does, however, immediately spring to mind. How can one speak of an
empire without an emperor at its head? The question is, of course, in
many ways a spurious one, but in raising it, we immediately encounter
the founding contradiction of any *modern* imperialism: the imperial
idea would seem to be incompatible with the process of democratization that took hold of most of Europe during the nineteenth century.
How is it possible to combine the imperatives of a society (ostensibly)
moving toward egalitarianism and those of an imperial system in
which, by definition, one group autocratically exercises power over another—a power embodied by the sovereign figure of an emperor? To
speak of modern imperialism is, from the outset, to speak in oxymorons. This improbable overlap of the modern and the imperial, one of
the enabling conditions of nineteenth-century exoticism, is what I will
be charting in the following discussion of Conrad's *Heart of Darkness*
and, subsequently, Verne's *Michel Strogoff*.

A major dispute in eighteenth-century political theory revolved around the applicability of the word "despotism" to the governance of European nations. The founder of the Physiocrats, François Quesnay, when meditating on the best method of government, spoke approvingly of a "despotisme légal." Rousseau's response to Quesnay was immediate and virulent: the first term, he affirmed, killed the second; they were "two contradictory words that, brought together, signify nothing."[1] Here we have a stark opposition between two Enlightenment ideologies: one tending toward despotism and empire; the other toward liberalism and democracy. The fundamental intervention of the French Revolution in many ways tipped the scale for Rousseau's exorcism of the despotic from the realm of legality. The modern European State would be founded upon liberal principles; liberalism and despotism were no longer engaged in a dialogic struggle for mastery (as with Rousseau and Quesnay) but definitively opposed to each other as legality to illegality. Enlightenment was henceforth to be judged only according to the standards of democracy; despotism, as a positive political alternative, was banished from much of the Continent. However, although the liberal position achieved dominance within Europe, the idea of a "legal" or "enlightened" despotism maintained a certain validity in the realm of "unenlightenment," that is to say, abroad. During the first half of the nineteenth century, the legal despotism favored by Quesnay still seemed, to most politicians, an appropriate way for metropolitan Europe to administer its peripheral territories.

In a parliamentary speech of 10 July 1833, the future Lord Macaulay, then-secretary of the East India Company's Board of Control, gave a succinct formulation of the difference between British rule at home and British rule abroad when he affirmed that India was governed as an "enlightened and paternal despotism."[2] From the standpoint of a Rousseau, Macaulay's simultaneous appeal to both enlightenment and despotism could only appear politically regressive; and yet, as long as enough spatial distance obtained between center and periphery, it was a regression that could be tolerated. Early- and mid-nineteenth-century colonialism—or what we can conveniently, if somewhat misleadingly, refer to as the Old Imperialism—incorporates the possibility of a despotic as opposed to a liberal power in its formal or informal dealings with peripheral states. As John Stuart Mill put it later in the century, in an article entitled "A Few Words on Non-intervention" (1859), "The sacred duties which civilized nations owe to the independence and nationality of each other are not binding towards those to whom nationality and independence are a certain evil, or at best, a questionable good."[3] For Mill, an imperial system remained the most suitable means of governing those peoples who had not yet learned to represent themselves abstractly as members of a democratic nation-state. At some point, however, as Macaulay himself made clear in his speech, native peoples would indeed arrive at this point: he goes on to affirm, in the name of an eventually self-governing India, that "we are free, we are civilised, to little purpose, if we grudge to any portion of the human race an equal measure of freedom and civilisation" (p. 141).

At the time of this speech, a year after the first Reform Bill, liberal democracy in England was still in its initial phases: even on the domestic front constitutionalism was as yet conceivable, as it were, only in the form of an "enlightened paternalism." In Macaulay's call for an "enlightened and paternal despotism," the word "paternal" mediates between the modernity of enlightenment and the antiquatedness of despotism, enforcing a familial image that both softens the imperial connotations of despotism and guards against a too liberal enlightenment; it would continue to fill this mediatory role in England, even though the third term of Macaulay's formula, "despotism," had dropped out of sight. But as the century drew on and as the process of enfranchisement and of democratization expanded, paternalism itself came to seem an unsatisfactory way of describing how a truly modern State functions. Suggesting as it does an imbalance of power in what should—one person, one vote—be a situation of equality, paternalistic authority itself falls victim to the increasingly democratic imperatives of twentieth-century Europe (resurfacing, to be sure, as part of reactionary political salvage projects like fascism). The modern State must be represented as neither despotic nor paternal, but merely enlightened. What effect, we might ask, would such a shift have on a turn-of-the-century Macaulay's portrayal of colonial rule?

Following through on our logical progression—that is to say, on the logic of Progress—we can imagine this hypothetical turn-of-the-century politician speaking, from the standpoint of a new, unqualified enlightenment, about an India well on the path to democracy: an India ruled according to the dictates of an enlightened paternalism from which the archaic figure of the despot has definitively disappeared. By this logic, the founding contradiction of the Old Imperialism—the twofold postulate of democracy at home and despotism abroad—had to give way, or at the very least be represented as giving way, to a more "civilized" relationship between metropolitan and peripheral territories. This change in the ground rules for portraying European power in the age of the New Imperialism did not, of course, necessarily correspond to a real democratization of colonial rule—in fact, the opposite is most often the case. As Phillip Darby has pointed out, for instance, "increasingly, towards the end of the nineteenth century, there was a tendency for British rule in India to become more authoritarian," not less.[4] The ideal of self-government, which Macaulay (despite, or precisely because of, his despotic perspective) held out to Indians, slips, as Darby puts it, "into the distant, unforeseeable future" (p. 43). Regardless of this real backsliding, though, the despotic sobriquet itself could no longer adequately fill the representational needs of a political power committed to figuring itself as benignly paternalistic in its treatment of "those to whom nationality and independence are a certain evil, or at best, a questionable good."

The new planetary nature of colonialism at the turn of the century involved a lessening of the distance that had in part enabled the contradictory balancing of different political systems typical of the Old Imperialism. In 1876, at the midpoint of a transitional decade in which the "inner-directed era of European nation building gave way to the outer-directed age of global conflict,"[5] the opposition between new and old modes of figuring imperialism surfaced very emphatically in the parliamentary debates leading to the proclamation of the Royal Titles Act. If Victoria's controversial adoption of the title "Empress of India" symbolically confirmed the tendency of mid-nineteenth-century imperialism (enlightenment at home, despotism abroad), the intense opposition that many parliamentarians mounted against the passage of this act was a signal that the old-style imperialism favored by Disraeli was proving less and less palatable to "enlightened" minds. Throughout the course of these debates, the battle line is strongly drawn between a despotic and a liberal interpretation of the imperial idea. Out of the extensive amount of material generated therein, we can cite a typical instance of each position.[6]

First, the despotic interpretation: "We stand in the relation of the paramount Power towards them [the Indian principalities] as what may be called, roughly, feudatory and subordinate States and . . . we occupy towards them that position which is most accurately described—of all the titles that I am aware of—by that of Emperor" (Sir S. H. Northcote, chancellor of the exchequer, 228: 91). In its most extreme version, the position was ably summarized by Sir George Campbell, who asserted that it was time for Victoria to assume in name as well as in effect "the position hitherto occupied by the Great Mogul in India"—albeit not as absolute sovereign but as "Representative" of the British nation.

Those who supported the new title inevitably stressed that it was meant not to signify an individual but only to mark the fact of having an empire. If this were, however, truly the case, those taking up the liberal position countered, then what need was there of such a factious term? As Robert Lowe, one of the few MPs who thought it conceivable that Britain might someday lose India, pointed out, "The Emperors of Hindostan were Mahomedan conquerors. Would it be wise or prudent in us to confound in name our wise and beneficent government with that of the Rulers who preceded us?" (227: 414) Here Lowe is appealing to standards of wisdom and beneficence compatible with, if in some ways different from, the enlightened values supposedly at work in the governance of most European nations. The battleground, then, is clearly marked out: Percy Wyndham asserts without qualms that "the Government of India is essentially a despotic Government as administered by us, although it includes more than one individual" (227: 1736); Gladstone replies that this is indeed the case but adds that such despotism should be lamented as "our weakness and our calamity."

Victoria had her way; "Empress of India" entered Britain's political vocabulary, and to "the substance of ancient greatness" was added "the glitter of modern names," as one parliamentary commentator derisively put it (228: 106). But, ironically, even as it achieved this nominal confirmation, the Old Imperialism of a Disraeli was on the point of giving way to its New Imperialist successor. Lord Rosebery's gradual conversion to the imperialist cause is a key gauge of the change in official colonial policy that marked the last decades of the nineteenth century: "In Disraeli's time Rosebery had been opposed to the way the Government then used the word Empire, a word about which he felt 'a gloomy foreboding.' It then lacked liberty and smacked of oriental despotism. It was too closely associated with India.'" By 1895, however, he had established himself as one of the leading voices of Liberal Imperialism, in which the despotic idea, if not the imperial name, was to be excised from the story of territorial acquisition and rule. Ridding the Empire of its imperial vestiges is the paradoxical imperative of the New Imperialism, as it engages in and is engaged by a process of rationalization that must (in theory, to be sure) lead to the transformation of an enlightened despotism into an even more luminous paternalism, one better suited to the global pretensions of colonial power in the age of the

New Imperialism. And it is here, on the point of this transformation, that we can begin to tell Conrad's story as it unfolds in *Heart of Darkness*. Before doing so, however, we must take one further look at the fundamental turning between the eighteenth and nineteenth centuries that is the point of departure in this section.

What is *modern* about the enlightened State is that the locus of power has shifted from the despotic body of a sovereign figure to an abstract entity representing the people. Roberta Maccagnani has pointed this out in an excellent discussion of the Marquis de Sade's relation to the exoticist project:

> The sort of sovereignty of the subject laid claim to by Sade is that of the ancient despot, the absolute monarch of the *Anciens Régimes*, who based his power on his dominion over bodies and his capacity for their total subjection. With the fall of these regimes and the advent of modern egalitarian democracies, the subject loses the idea of sovereignty, for it has been completely absorbed into the body of the State, which posits itself as the only, and abstract, holder of all forms of power.   (Maccagnani, p. 68)

With the coming of modern egalitarian democracies, the sovereignty of the ancien régime subject (figured most dramatically by the absolute monarch) disappears from the immediate political horizon. Sade's post-revolutionary protagonists both model themselves after this archaic subject and yet find themselves at an insuperable distance from their model. Figures of and in crisis, they are the embodiment of an entirely new sort of subject who can never be what he models himself after: namely, the individual, forever conditioned by a modern state of affairs that denies his sovereignty.

But, as I stated in the introductory chapter, the individual's essentially posthumous nature was not immediately evident to him. Hence the attraction of a project like exoticism, which appeared to offer the individual the possibility of self-realization: where better to escape the ills of mass society than in those "unenlightened" locales in which, as we have just seen, the archaic model of subjectivity still persisted as a political system? Exoticism arose as a (doomed) reaction against the absorption of the individual into the abstract unity of the modern European State: it was motivated in part by a desire to renew the lost privileges of the ancien régime subject in territories that were not yet under the total dominion of enlightenment. As long as an openly despotic relationship between Europe and its periphery was in force, as it was during the greater part of the nineteenth century, this desire for renewal might continue to appear feasible abroad. However, with the coming of the New Imperialism, and the translation of liberal politics into *Weltpolitik*, the exoticist project confronts its own impossibility: the imperial can now be figured only as an archaic system to which any real return is precluded. The sort of allegorical interrogation that I am studying in this book raises, impossibly, the imperial figure from its grave, bringing to light a sovereignty no longer tenable within the logic of "enlightened" colonialism.

The imperial system acted as a buffer between the two very distinct realms of "civilization" and "savagery"; situated between the two, it served to differentiate the one from the other and thereby confirmed the existence of both. By the turn of the century, though, liberal democracy could no longer have recourse to this mediatory system; confronting the contradiction of equal rights at home and inequality abroad became imperative. Those who had formerly been subject to the rule of an "enlightened and paternal despotism" had now to be represented anew, according to the discursive criteria of what I termed "enlightened paternalism": savagery, and its difference, was to be brought more into line with the now-global pretensions of European democracy. This discursive position was adopted by at least one participant in the Royal Titles debate who asserted that "there were many educated Natives who recognized and appreciated our institutions, and was this title of Empress to be sent to them as a message of peace and goodwill? Was the house to stamp that despotic title upon them in perpetuity?" (Mr. Anderson, 228: 140) The liberal directives underlying this parliamentarian's speech are at work in much of the literature written about the colonies during the age of the New Imperialism. For the most part, turn-of-the-century colonial literature can be read as an attempt at coming to terms with the challenge of speaking paternalistically rather than despotically about the subjects of imperial rule. As Martin Steins has remarked, it sets out to make this familial image "prevail over the resentments and phobias that public opinion had inherited from the nineteenth century."[8]

In contrast to this assimilating and "enlightened" approach, a work like Conrad's *Heart of Darkness* (first published in 1899 in *Blackwood's Magazine*, and then collected in *Youth—A Narrative: And Two Other Stories* [1902]) continues to put into play apparently phobic representations of natives as "savages." As I will argue, Conrad's decision to portray natives in this way is a corollary of his Romantic belief in the individual's sovereignty—a belief that was ever more at odds with the

New Imperialist world in which he found himself writing. From this disjunction between personal ideology and historical development arises the basic ambiguity of Conrad's position on European expansion, which Terry Eagleton has summed up quite nicely: "Conrad neither believes in the cultural superiority of the colonialist nations, nor rejects imperialism outright."[9] We must now consider a little more closely the reasons behind this ambiguous attitude.

Following Avrom Fleishman's classic interpretation, we can say that Conradian ideology is traceable to the "organicist doctrine of self-realization through identification with the community."[10] Organicism affirms the unity of the individual and his society, positing at the head of this community a charismatic figure who embodies the positive qualities of all its members. In Conrad, the exemplary instance of this social relationship is the hierarchy established between a ship's captain and his crew. Marlow's description in *Chance* (1913) is typical and illuminating: the captain is "a remote, inaccessible creature, something like a prince of a fairy-tale, alone of his kind, depending on nobody, not to be called to account except by powers practically invisible and so distant, that they might well be looked upon as supernatural for all that the rest of the crew knows of them, as a rule."[11]

But, we must ask ourselves, has this unity of the individual and his community ever been a present possibility; have the conditions for its realization not "always-already" come and gone; is it not the nostalgic construction par excellence? The organicist doctrine is, and cannot help being, a belated ideology. The individualistic project of "self-realization," of being rescued from the ills of an atomized society, could itself never have become an issue until *after* the dissolution of that traditional community in which the "untimely" individual places his empty hope. For all its desirability, the community envisioned by Romantic organicism is no less accessible to modernity than the archaic subject upon whom the post-revolutionary individual has modeled himself.

Returning to Eagleton's remark, then, we can say that for Conrad the "colonialist nation" could never be a manifestation of cultural superiority because it was so obviously the antithesis of an organic community; it was a modern State, founded upon abstract principles and "material interests." However, imperialism, at least a certain imperialism, held out a slim hope for Conrad's organicist imagination: where an enlightened despotism held sway, modernity might yet be averted. But if the project of (re)instituting an authentic community, and thereby (re)creating the conditions for the individual's self-realization, was still conceivable in the despotic world of the Old Imperialism—the world of Conrad's youth (and of his ideology)—the unrealizable nature of this project had become all too evident by the end of the century. Conrad the writer thus finds himself torn between the appeal of an imperial system that seemed to offer the individual a chance (but the individual has no real chance) and the necessity of registering its, for him, repelling successor.

We can bring out the complexity of Conrad's position by referring to a double-barreled distinction established early in *Heart of Darkness* between, on the one hand, "efficiency" and "inefficiency" and, on the other, "conquerors" and "colonists." Marlow makes this distinction in the course of his evocation of the Romans' encounter with the "utter savagery" of darkest Britain: they would have felt, he asserts, the "fascination of the abomination" (p. 50). This "fascination" is clearly the same as the "horror" that Kurtz, as a result of what we will see to be his sovereign solitude, has been able to sense and express, and that Marlow, enfolded within the colonial enterprise, has lost all direct contact with (though he will be able to record its traces in the language and the gestures of that "remarkable man"). Marlow admits as much: none of "us," he assures his listeners aboard the *Nellie*, would have felt this fascination, saved as we are by our efficiency, "the devotion to efficiency." Now, Conrad, in a letter of 31 December 1898 to his publisher William Blackwood, had charged those tackling "the civilizing work in Africa" with "the criminality of inefficiency";[12] but a careful reading reveals that, in the sense defined by the text itself, both Marlow and the Company are "efficient." Both, that is, are blind to the horror that Kurtz and the Romans feel—blind to "savagery" as a force that must still be reckoned with. Kurtz's ability to feel the horror, then, is a sign of his "inefficiency" within the economy of late-nineteenth-century colonialism.

The word "efficiency" obviously has a positive valence for Marlow: it was, as Ian Watt has pointed out, the watchword of the Liberal Imperialists;[13] it was also the motivating force behind Benjamin Kidd's immensely popular *Social Evolution* (1894). Efficiency justifies the British effort. But at the same time, as their shared blindness to the horror shows, it is impossible to make a distinction on the basis of mere efficiency between the "real work" being done in British colonies and the reprehensible work of the Company; efficiency is a necessary but not sufficient condition for licit territorial expansion. Hence, Marlow has-

tens to add another distinction that would draw a definitive line between the two: the opposition between efficiency and inefficiency is
supplemented by one between conquerors and colonists.

Not only were the Romans inefficient, they were conquerors to boot;
their administration was little more than a "squeeze." They were not,
Marlow sums up, "colonists." Conquest is not just the affair of the Romans, however, but a present concern—even if, as in the case of the
Company, it has become an "efficient conquest": "The conquest of the
earth, which mostly means the taking it away from those who have a
different complexion or slightly flatter noses than ourselves, is not a
pretty thing when you look into it too much. What redeems it is the
idea only. An idea at the back of it; not a sentimental pretence but an
idea and an unselfish belief in the idea—something you can set up, and
bow down before, and offer a sacrifice to" (pp. 50–51). The colonist, as
opposed to the conqueror, is redeemed by the "idea"; it forms the necessary complement of "efficiency."

Again, idealism was a common battle cry of the day, as we can see
from the following passage in John Seeley's *Expansion of England* (a famous series of lectures originally given in the early 1880's): "The material basis of a Greater Britain might indeed be laid, that is, vast territories might be occupied, and rival nations expelled from them. In
this material sense Greater Britain was created in the seventeenth and
eighteenth centuries. But the idea that could shape the material mass
was still wanting" (p. 72). However, everything depends on who or
what would embody this "idea"; for Seeley, here showing himself in
accord with the spirit of his age, "individuals are important in history
in proportion not to their intrinsic merit, but to their relation to the
State" (p. 7). Conrad's position is, at heart, quite the opposite.

Once we begin to think Marlow's two sets of opposing terms together, though, the unviability of his position becomes clear. Combin-
ing these terms, we are faced with four logical possibilities, two of
which are patently unsatisfactory: the inefficient and efficient conquests undertaken by the Romans and the Company, respectively.[14]
What possibilities remain? The ideal resolution, clearly, would be an
"efficient colonization"—and yet the novelty of Conrad's approach will
lie in simultaneously affirming the necessity of this efficient colonization and showing it to be the one thing missing from the text and, by
extension, from political life. And here is where our discussion of Conrad's ideological starting point—namely, a Romantic valorization of
the individual's place in society—becomes especially relevant. For

Conrad, the individual and not the State must be the repository of "ideas": hence the absolute necessity of finding (or inventing) a figure like Kurtz—a man possessed of "ideas" who exists at a more or less complete distance from the efficient world of New Imperialist conquest that, at least in the first half of the story, occupies the entire horizon of Marlow's experience. For Marlow, Kurtz will end up being rather more than just another Company agent: as Renato Oliva has pointed out, "Marlow throws Kurtz the life-preserver of the *idea* and from *conqueror* raises his status to that of *colonist*, albeit a corrupted one; he gives him a soul and, at the same time, the possibility of personal salvation."[15] Because Conrad is unable to credit fully the demands of his own ideology, however, Kurtz's sovereign difference, his capacity for operating outside the (global) boundaries of civilization, proves in the final analysis no more than a "deficient" fiction.

Conrad thus turns Kurtz into the embodiment of an inefficient colonist (the fourth term of our *combinatoire*), one who still feels the horror of "utter savagery" and, indeed, has himself reverted to it. But despite his inefficiency, this "hollow sham" of a man provides a disconcerting counterbalance to the efficient yet reprehensible conquest of the Company in all its technocratic anonymity. He conjures up—if only for an instant, an instant that has, from the beginning, passed away—the figure of that efficient colonist who is necessarily missing from the text. The slot of the efficient colonist is revealed as an empty one. Any attempt to think this "imperialist" future can only lead back to the past—to a time, that is, when one could still believe in what has become unbelievable: namely, the sovereign individual and the exotic "outside" in which he was to have acted. Unable to follow the lead of much turn-of-the-century literature about the colonies, which subscribes to the assimilatory language of paternalism and subordinates the authority of the individual to that of the State, Conrad is forced, through the chiasmus of efficient conquerors and an inefficient colonist, to represent the incompatibility of efficiency and the saving idea. The efficient colonist can be figured only through his disfigurement—a rendering hollow of the heroic individual who should, ideally, be the vehicle of a redeemed imperialism.

Intimately connected to the individual's hollow presence in *Heart of Darkness* is the portrayal of natives as "savages." I have said that with the shift to a paternalistic mode of discourse a word like "savage" ceased to fill the same political and representational needs that it did earlier in the century; once the colonial nations have apportioned the

entirety of the earth's surface, "savagery" is necessarily *ex*cluded from
the world as a real alternative and *in*cluded, under another name, as a
(lesser) part of a newly global civilization. Inadequate to the discursive
needs of the New Imperialism, savagery nonetheless remained a central trope in turn-of-the-century popular culture. Indeed, a jingoistic
insistence on savagery and the civilizing mission becomes, if anything,
aggravated outside governmental circles at this time: "Late in the century, a change quite clearly comes over the popular literature of all
kinds: it becomes aggressively, and defensively, imperialist."[16] Conrad's conservation of "savagery," a natural corollary of his attachment
to the exoticist project, thus leads to a curious overlap between his own
writing and the pulp literature of his day in which, among other
things, the figure of the hero retained a positive consistency that "serious" writers had long since put into question: the hero of adventure
stories and romances unproblematically communicates with alternative worlds of fantasy and savagery, a mediating role that Kurtz himself
plays. But, and here is the critical difference, with Conrad the opposition of savage and civilized worlds no longer holds true: it is itself as
hollow as the individual who at once keeps these worlds apart and
joins them together.

The immense distance between these two worlds is dramatized in
Heart of Darkness by two very different ways of occupying territory, of
"filling the earth." On the one hand, we have the abstract method of
territorialization practiced by the State: Marlow points out near the beginning of the novella that the "many blank spaces on the *earth* had got
filled since my boyhood with rivers and lakes and names" (p. 52; my
italics). The blank spaces of mystery that the exotic subject could conceive, as it were, of coloring in on his own have been covered over by
an abstract informational network that controls and orders the globe.
The earth has been partitioned into various national domains, marked
in Britain's case by "a vast amount of red." This graphic moment is in
direct contrast to a later incident that occurs as Kurtz is being taken
away from the Inner Station. A "savage" spectacle breaks out; the natives, Marlow asserts, "*filled* the clearing, covered the slope with a mass
of naked, breathing, quivering, bronze bodies." They are led by three
men "plastered with bright *red earth* from head to foot" (p. 145; my italics). The opposition between an immanent earth and the earth as a
graphic abstraction given a transcendent unity by the colonialist nations could not be more striking. Marlow, as an envoy of civilization,

already a part of the colonial machine, is at a complete remove from this savagery: it has ceased to exist for him. The natives, he says, are incomprehensible, shouting out "strings of amazing words that resembled no sounds of human language" (pp. 145–46).

With the coming of the New Imperialism, savagery drops out of sight, recedes into the inhuman. Or, rather, as the "savages" disappear back in time and beyond the pale of humanity, they are recoded according to the dictates of a more contemporary discourse, as objects of a benign paternalism (or, alternatively, as exploited members of a capitalist work force). The reality of the "savage" can be grasped only through the despotic mediation of a Kurtz: Marlow, appalled by the deep murmurs of "that wild mob" and the shouts of the helmeted woman, must have recourse to the "atrocious phantom" of the sovereign subject if he is to make any sense of this archaic experience. "'Do you understand this?' . . . 'Do I not?'" Kurtz replies, "gasping, as if the words had been torn out of him by a supernatural power" (p. 146). Kurtz alone is able to come between Marlow and this primitive world; he demarcates a (textual) space in which they can still be thought together. Two worlds meet in this one figure to whom the native chiefs offer up "unspeakable rites" and the civilized, efficient Marlow comes to attach himself with almost filial piety.[17]

Kurtz maintains the lines of contact with a world that no longer has a place in our own. Marlow, in turn, mediates between "us" and this "atrocious phantom," making us see (and think) the ghost of that sovereign individual who would otherwise be forever relegated to the darkness of the past. Marlow thus participates in two stories: he shuttles back and forth between a non-heroic New Imperialist narrative in which the range of his actions is contingent upon the orders handed down to him by the Company and another, eroticized tale of fascination for a hero of sorts. He is both the successor to the Dane Fresleven in a story of efficient conquest and an initiate into Kurtz's archaic, inefficient colonization—doubly incriminated by the valueless contract he has signed with an impersonal overseer and by the damning allegiance that he feels toward a disgraced and (reversing the biological norm) illegitimate father. In his duplicity, Marlow is, ultimately, a figure of the author himself, uneasily situated between what he can no longer believe in and what defies belief—between, as Conrad would put it in one of his *Last Essays*, "Geography and Some Explorers" (1924), "the single-minded explorers of the nineteenth century, the late fathers of militant geography whose only object was the search for truth" and "the vilest scramble for loot that ever disfigured the history of human conscience and geographical exploration" (pp. 10, 17).

As Fredric Jameson remarks in *The Political Unconscious*, Conrad's historical moment is one of "peculiar heterogeneity," a transitional period in which the passions and values of the individual subject reveal themselves as essentially dependent upon trans-individual institutions (pp. 279–80). Conrad registered this shift, and yet he was unwilling either to place his trust in the pluralist State or to project himself beyond his historical moment in a utopic vision of some more "genuine" collective. As I have only begun to suggest here, Conrad's response to this historical moment, the moment of the fin de siècle, was to follow up on the shadowy traces of a past that could no longer display itself in any terms other than those of "deficiency" or "hollowness." I will give a more detailed account of this strategic response in the discussion of *Lord Jim* in Chapter 5. For now, however, we must turn back the clock a few decades and examine the work of a writer for whom the contradictions put into play in this section have yet to take on their full, and tragic, significance. Jules Verne, as we will now see, comes before—that is, both precedes and finds himself already in the presence of—the moment that Conrad inhabits, the moment of a crossing between an obsolete subjectivity and collective values that are as inconceivable now as they were in the days of the New Imperialism.

Imperial Fictions and the Boundary of Colonialism: Jules Verne's 'Michel Strogoff'

> In Europe we were Asiatics, whereas in Asia we, too, are
> Europeans. Our civilizing mission in Asia will bribe our spirit
> and drive us thither. It is only necessary that the movement
> should start. Build only two railroads: begin with the one to
> Siberia, and then—to Central Asia,—and at once you will see
> the consequences.   —Feodor Dostoyevsky, *Diary of a Writer* (1881)

The debate leading to the proclamation of the Royal Titles Act took place from February to May 1876. On 16 March of that year, it was announced in Parliament that Imperial Russia had absorbed the Central Asian khanate of Kokand "and added that territory to the wide-stretching dominions of the Czar" (Sir William Fraser, 228: 111). This bit of information was used as a further justification for Victoria's as-

sumption of the title "Empress": turning India into an officially imperial territory would, it was argued, show Britain's determination to
hold fast to its Asian possessions in the face of Russian expansionism.
As the chancellor of the exchequer, Sir S. H. Northcote, had put it earlier in the debate, when making his pitch for the new honorific: "Is it
well that to the Emperor of Russia should be given in those countries
[of Central Asia] a title which appears to the people there to be much
higher and greater than the title borne by the Queen?" (227: 1751)
Those who disliked the idea of having an empress took exactly the opposite tack: the title, they argued, was inappropriate for a British sovereign since it was "associated with conquerors like Napoleon, and
despots like the Russian emperors" (228: 852).

The annexation of Kokand was part of a Russian drive into Central
Asia in the decades immediately following the Crimean War. Conquering Kokand and the neighboring khanates of Bokhara and Khiva
had, indeed, long been a goal of Imperial Russia. As the doyen of Central Asian studies, Arminius Vámbéry, put it in 1865, "The three khan-
ats are the only members now wanting to that immense Tartar kingdom that Ivan Vasilyevitch (1462–1505) imagined, and which he began
actually to incorporate with his Russian dominions, and which, since
the time of Peter the Great, has been the earnest though silent object
of his successors."[18]

The incorporation of these Central Asian territories within the
boundaries of the Russian Empire would, however, become feasible
only toward the middle of the nineteenth century, when Russia's
techno-military capacity so far surpassed that of its once-formidable
adversaries that any Russian offensive was almost certain of success.
Such an offensive seemed even more imperative, given the rapid expansion of British power in the Indian subcontinent. What is more, it
could be readily justified, even in a country ruled by "despots like the
Russian emperors," as the most effective means of furthering the cause
of civilization at the expense of barbarism. As one Russian general
claimed in 1875, toward the end of the offensive: "The introduction of
Russian authority into Central Asia has done great service to the development of ideas common to all mankind. Arbitrariness, anarchy,
and despotism, which reigned in these lands we now occupy, no
longer exist. Slavery has disappeared. . . . Our Central Asian wars
have always brought with them the triumph of justice and truth since
civilization has conducted and is conducting a struggle against barbarism and ignorance."[19] Liberal appeals to the virtues of civilization,

definitive military supremacy as a consequence of industrialization, rivalry with another colonial power—features such as these clearly mark the conquest as "a product of nineteenth century, rather than earlier, Russian expansion."[20]

Until the arrival of the Russians, Central Asia had remained, as far as the rest of the world was concerned, one of the least known regions of the globe. As for accessibility, it could still be claimed in 1840 that "Central Asia, off-limits to the inquiring traveler even to this day, is in the same conditions as the interior of Africa."[21] Some thirty years later—in a classic evocation of the "torn-veil" trope that is such a predictable element of nineteenth-century exploration literature—the Central Asian specialist Frederick von Hellwald describes a radically different situation:

In the trace of the Russian warrior science strides forward with rapid pace, yet ceaselessly spying, observing, and minutely examining all that meets its onward course. That which only twenty years ago was a mystery shrouded in obscurity, doubtfully hinted at by the educated and cautiously mentioned by the learned, at this day stands bared to view and manifest to all. Now is the veil torn asunder, the barriers are thrown down, and whatever is still unexplored must in a few years reveal its hidden secrets to the Russian soldiery.

(Hellwald, p. 1)

Such predictions would be amply fulfilled. In the decade following the occupation of Khiva in 1873, the Imperial Russian Geographic Society ascertained the formerly vague boundaries of Central Asia with scientific accuracy, while the czar's bureaucrats set about the task of organizing and administering the Empire's new territories.

We should hardly be surprised that Jules Verne (1828–1905), chronicler of nineteenth-century science's march across the globe in the sixty-odd novels that constitute his *Voyages extraordinaires*, took an interest in Russia's Central Asian enterprise. What may be more surprising, however, is that when, in the early 1870's, Verne turned his novelistic attention to the exotic but timely subject of Russo–Central Asian relations he chose not to represent the triumph of a rapidly modernizing nation over its "backward" neighbors. Instead of constructing his story around the fall of the khanates, Verne wrote the novel *Michel Strogoff* (1876),[22] which takes as its starting point an entirely fictional invasion of the Russian Empire by these very same khanates. The rather startling manipulation of history effected in this novel is by no means just the innocent by-product of a fertile imagination; in fact, an abusive use of history is one of the enabling conditions, not only of what we will come to identify as Verne's liberal brand of "imperialist exoticism" but also of the exoticist project itself.

From what I have already said about the belatedness of this project, it should not be difficult to guess at the reasons behind this antagonism between history and exoticism: if the individual is to preserve his (fictional) autonomy in the face of an encroaching modernity, then the imminence of this threat must be downplayed. We find a similar process at work in Conrad's *Heart of Darkness*: the Stanley Falls that Conrad himself had known was a much less "savage" place than Marlow's Inner Station. It was, in fact, "quite a large settlement, which was beginning to acquire many of the trappings of civilisation; by 1893, at least, they included a hospital, a police barracks, and a jail."[23] Nonetheless, Conrad chose to figure Kurtz as supremely isolated. It is only because of this sovereign solitude that Kurtz can be thought to possess a supplement of knowledge that differentiates him from the world of the New Imperialism. Thus, near the end of *Heart of Darkness*, a representative of the Company approaches Marlow and, citing Kurtz's "knowledge of unexplored regions," insists that the Company is entitled to "every bit of information about its 'territories'" (p. 153). Only once the State has gained a monopoly of such information will the sovereignty of Kurtz be fully ruled out. By transforming a growing Stanley Falls into the desolate Inner Station and by limiting the number of geographically identifiable points of reference (indeed, the word "Africa" is never mentioned in the text),[24] Conrad apparently grounds the existence of Kurtz in an exotic "elsewhere," thereby deferring the State's total mastery of the earth.

Of course, as we saw, Kurtz is very much an impossible subject, one whose hollowness leaps out at the reader; if Conrad wants to draw attention to the figure of the individual, he also recognizes that this cannot be done without a complementary negation of that same figure. In the world of *Michel Strogoff*, by contrast, such negation is unthinkable; sharing the heroic convictions of nineteenth-century exoticism, Verne portrays both the imperial figure and the realm of the Other as potentially compatible with his own day and age. However, the troubled monologue with history that Verne must hold fast to if he is to tell this heroic story—one that I will, as it were, be rewriting in the form of a dialogue—signals the novel as a text in transit, situated on the boundary between an Old Imperialism that it condones and a thoroughly modern colonialism that it emphatically rejects. Described first from a structuralist and then from a New Historicist perspective, this borderline situation, and the double vision to which it gives rise, is the subject of the remainder of this chapter.

The Double Voyage and the Voyage of Doubles

The plot of *Michel Strogoff*, that breviary of heroism which, as he tells us in *Les mots*, the young Sartre found so affecting, centers around a massive attack on Russian Siberia by hordes of Tartars, Kazakhs, Turkomans, and Uzbeks—in short, "a general invasion of the Russian Empire in Asia." The attack is led by the despotic Emir of Bokhara and abetted by the treachery of the Russian rebel Ivan Ogareff. As the novel begins, the telegraph lines between Moscow and Irkutsk, capital of Eastern Siberia, where the Czar's brother is stationed, have been cut. In order to inform his brother both of the seriousness of the Tartar attack and of a plot against his life by Ogareff, the Czar assigns one of his couriers, Michel Strogoff, the mission of carrying a letter to the Grand Duke. After many misadventures, the most memorable of which is doubtless his apparent blinding at the hands of one of the Emir's headsmen, Strogoff reaches Irkutsk, and the invaders are quickly put to flight.

One of the most enthusiastic, and perceptive, readers of Verne in recent years has been Michel Serres. His structuralist approach emphasizes the archetypal motifs that underlie Verne's work: in *Michel Strogoff*, for instance, he identifies the resurgence of an Oedipus story that has been overdetermined by other tales from Greek myth and the Bible. To be sure, this approach is, despite its brilliance, open to the criticism of more or less ignoring the historical and political context in which Verne wrote.[25] Still, of all Verne's novels, *Michel Strogoff* would seem one of the most suitable for the sort of reading that Serres proposes. As Pierre Macherey has pointed out, it is a work in which "the myth of science is . . . replaced by a purely novelistic myth."[26] Serres himself remarks in his *Jouvences sur Jules Verne* that there is little trace in this novel of Verne's usual preoccupations with the contemporary world: we find in it "no science, or so little, a segment of the steppes, a limited historical episode" (p. 37). Science, and the world of Progress it signals, seems to have given way to a purely mythopoeic narrative of heroism that begs to be read in archetypal terms. As I will show in the next section, however, this narrative—whose few "scientific" elements, according to Serres, are geographical (the Siberian steppes) and historical (the Tartar invasion of Russia)—can unfold only in the absence of that very real episode to which, if only at the level of a "political unconscious," it anxiously responds: namely, the ongoing Russian conquest of Central Asia. Before reinstating the problem of history, though, I will pursue a rather more structuralist account of *Michel Strogoff*, in order to identify in greater detail the central protagonists of nineteenth-century exoticism: the ostensibly full-bodied predecessors of Kurtz and Marlow.

A distinction that Serres makes in the introduction to his book on Verne can serve here as our point of departure: it is possible, he asserts, to read all voyages according to three codes. The first two, the *geographical* and *scientific*, form a cycle: every displacement in geographical space may also be the occasion for a scientific inquiry "sweeping slowly across the encyclopedic *cursus*" (p. 22). Verne himself anticipated this connection in the very first of the *Voyages extraordinaires—Cinq semaines en ballon* (1863)—when he had its hero Samuel Ferguson state that "it's not enough to cross Africa, one must see it" (p. 78). *Traverser et voir*, to explore and to turn what is explored into an object of knowledge: let us call this doublet of geographical displacement and objective knowledge the "literal" level of the exotic text. *Michel Strogoff*, however, consistently occupies Serres's third level, which he identifies as the domain of the novelist proper: what is at stake here is an "initiatic, religious, mythic pilgrimage in search of a lost figure, that of God, of the father . . . or of some more enigmatic secret" (p. 23). Strogoff's passage from Moscow to Irkutsk is one such voyage of initiation: leaving behind the realm of the father (the Czar), he passes through an archaic world in which the barbaric Other appears to hold sway, eventually to find himself once again in the presence of what had been temporarily lost (the paternal figure, this time in the person of the Grand Duke).

Serres suggests that we can identify this mythical dimension of the text, which I will call its "allegorical" level, in every properly literary work. In the particular case of *Michel Strogoff*, this dimension is unthinkable without recourse to the exotic. The hero's initiation centers around the encounter with a world that, in its barbarism, is radically different from his own; were there no exotic realm, there could be no heroic voyage as such. The possibility of this voyage depends upon the possibility of the exotic. If the "exotic" were some timeless category, such a contingency would hardly be cause for concern, but the exoticist project is, as I have insisted, fraught with temporality, always at odds with a modernity that threatens to disempower it. In order for the exotic to function in Verne's text, then, its real existence must be verified at the literal level of the text: the author needs to establish an unproblematical correspondence between the geographical-scientific "facts" (the *vraisemblable*) and his imperial, initiatic story.

In other words, Verne must ground the allegorical in the literal; that this grounding is supremely deceptive will become apparent in the following section when we juxtapose Verne's story and its absent historical context. Here, however, we need emphasize only that Verne himself allows us to read the literal and allegorical levels as potentially incompatible. The voyage of Michel Strogoff, it turns out, is doubled by another: that of the French and English journalists Alcide Jolivet and Harry Blount, who re-present Strogoff's heroic itinerary in more down-to-earth terms. These "distinguished products of modern civilization" stand for, and on, the literal ground that must be present if Strogoff's own imperial story is to be read as something more than a mere flight of fancy. Going over the same territory as the hero and reporting back to their respective employers on the Tartar invasion of Russia, the journalists appear to act as guarantors of the allegorical voyage. Ultimately, though, this guarantee can be no more than a partial one since the journalists are markedly modern protagonists and indeed must be so if they are to fill their authenticating role. As such, they cannot help but signal the colonial present whose absence from the text is absolutely essential for the smooth unfolding of Verne's imperial story.

The double voyage is, then, in potential contradiction with itself from the outset: instead of grounding the allegorical tale, the parallel story of the journalists may well serve only as a "modernizing" disruption. This double-bind is not, obviously, something that the author himself can probe in any depth without definitively problematizing the exoticist project in which he is engaged; its presence does, however, make itself felt in the many "surface" distinctions that Verne himself draws between the two worlds, or what we can term the two actantial universes,* of Strogoff and the journalists. These explicit distinctions all point toward, without acknowledging, the basic incompatibility of what Verne must nonetheless continually posit as being at bottom compatible.

First and foremost, Strogoff's voyage takes place in a world of au-

---

*A.-J. Greimas, following Vladimir Propp, distinguishes between "actors" and "actants": between, that is, the potentially limitless number of "surface" characters in any given story and the limited set of functions (Subject, Object, Sender, Receiver, Helper, Opponent) to which these correspond at the "deep" level of narrative syntax. In this section, I have based myself, very loosely, on his functional analysis of narrative. See Greimas, *Structural Semantics*, esp. chap. 10. For an interesting commentary on this aspect of Greimas's work, see Jameson, *Political Unconscious*, pp. 119–29.

thority. This authority is represented by the *lettre impériale* that the Czar (or, in actantial terms, the Sender) has written to the Grand Duke (the Receiver) and entrusted to Strogoff (the Subject). These imperial characters owe their clearly defined identities to the existence of this authoritative document (the Object): the Czar creates, Strogoff transmits, and the Grand Duke receives it. Not only the Russians but also their Tartar foes inhabit this world of authority: hence, Strogoff is warned, they will have every interest in intercepting the Czar's letter. The authority of both imperial powers is grounded in, and justified by, a written document—be it secular (the Czar's letter) or sacred (the Emir's Koran). The cost of any unauthorized reading of these documents is indeed high. Although Ogareff does intercept the letter, he is able to read it only after he has been severely maimed by the hero. Strogoff, in turn, finds himself in a position to read this same letter only after he has been (apparently) blinded according to the torture prescribed in the Koran.

The journalists also possess letters, of a sort; however, the "letters accrediting [them] in Russia with the English and French chancelleries" (p. 264) conjure up the image of a vastly different sort of authority. These letters, which are the handiwork of anonymous bureaucrats, allow Jolivet and Blount to pursue their journalistic project in relative peace—at a significant distance from the imperial struggle that is to form the object of their reportage. From the first scene of the novel, at a reception thrown by the Czar for a large group of dignitaries, the journalists stand out in an imperial world because of their lack of a clear identity: they are "two guests, distinguished by no uniform, no decoration." Yet this lack of identity notwithstanding, they have still managed to gain access to "fairly precise information" about the invasion of Siberia (p. 14). The source of their unauthorized information is obscure, contingent upon chance, and yet mysteriously efficacious; ultimately, the success of their enterprise can be traced to the fact that "their journals were not sparing with them when it came to money." The voyage of the journalists is, it turns out, not so much authorized as "accredited," *financed*.

Money, Verne asserts, is "the surest, the most rapid, the most perfect element of information known to this day" (p. 17). For the journalists, currency and information can be reduced to one and the same (groundless) thing; they inhabit a world that is uncannily similar to that of the Balzacian novel, in which "bodies, minds, identities are treated as goods, installed in a circuit of exchange of which money is the universal measure of value."[27] But if in Balzac the rupture with ancien régime tradition has already occurred, Verne still holds out the possibility—"elsewhere"—of an alternative relation to value. In the imperial world of *Michel Strogoff*, the power of money is at once contained by and grounded in another and greater authority: significantly enough, Strogoff keeps not just money but the imperial letter in his purse. The letter acts as a guarantor of what would otherwise be a degraded, and foundationless, means of communication. Authoritative documents such as the Czar's letter or the Emir's Koran are proof against a modernity that Verne nonetheless wants to admit into his text in a supporting role.

This negative vision of a world ordered, or disordered, according to the dictates of what we might call "money/information" is a commonplace feature of the post-revolutionary critique of modernity. We need not insist on it here, except to note that with Verne this critique will, only a few years later, become more explicit and more exasperated in his *Les cinq cents millions de la bégum* (1879), a novel that marks "a fundamental turning point in the work of Jules Verne."[28] In *Michel Strogoff* the world of money/information appears to be neither the only nor the most important world, but the ability of Jolivet and Blount to move at will through the supposedly autonomous realm of a non-modern locale and to carry out effectively the very same job of information retrieval and distribution that they perform at home anticipates a world in which the problem of modernity knows no bounds. "True jockeys of this steeplechase, this hunt after information" (p. 17), the journalists are subject to, and subjects of, the same sort of all-encompassing "dromo-logic" (to use a word coined by Paul Virilio)[29] that will characterize that other steeplechase, the New Imperialism.

This modern *chasse* is on the point of supplanting traditional forms of the hunt (significantly, Michel Strogoff's biological father was a *chasseur*). With the journalists, primary nature has given way to "this habit, become a second nature to them, of living on and by information" (p. 14). The sort of individual identity required for the transmission of the imperial letter has been obliterated from this second nature: the journalists are practically indistinguishable from one another (or, to put it another way, they fill indifferently the same actantial function). As such, they anticipate the degraded, plural subject that Verne will come to associate with mass society—the sort of subject exemplified, for instance, by the lucre-loyal Americans Craig and Fry in *Les tribulations d'un Chinois en Chine* (1879), "who formed no more than one being in two persons" (p. 68). This new plural subject forms the ideal audience for Jolivet and Blount. The press and mass society develop in step with each other: indeed, as the sociologist Serge Moscovici has maintained, "with mass society, the press becomes the foremost source, the origin of opinions that spread instantaneously and without intermediary to the four corners of the country, indeed to the world as a whole."[30] As we have seen, this global diffusion is more or less defused in *Michel Strogoff*; Jolivet and Blount gain entry into the world of the novel, but throughout remain the comic subordinates of an imperial story to which their own must run parallel. As the novel draws to a close, however, the paths of Strogoff and the two reporters part, and in this divergence we can read an end to the double voyage and the beginning of another, eminently modern journey.

After the Grand Duke has finally received the imperial letter, Michel Strogoff, now married to his faithful companion Nadia, retraces his steps, returning whence he came. The journalists, by contrast, choose to continue on into China since "there is talk of difficulties that are going to arise between London and Peking" (p. 444). What is perhaps most significant about this next stage of their journey is that it will double the modern line of communication that, at the outset of their invasion, the Tartar hordes had severed: the telegraph line. As we were told at the beginning of the novel, the line proceeds from Irkutsk to the Mongolian frontier, "and from there, for thirty kopecks a word, the post delivers the dispatches to Peking in a fortnight" (p. 24). Jolivet and Blount follow this soon-to-be restored line and, indeed, anticipate its further extension; no longer rivals as they were at the beginning, they are now committed to working in tandem, joined in a sort of discursive wedlock that comically replicates the marriage of Michel and Nadia. But where the joining of hero and heroine marks a return to order and the closing of a circle, Jolivet and Blount's "honeymoon" will take them into a disturbingly aligned future, one that we barely glimpse here and away from which the author directs our gaze. In Verne's imperial world, the heroic individual has taken center stage, and we can know nothing of what is waiting in the wings. For the reader, Irkutsk is truly the end of the line.

Strogoff and the journalists, as we have seen, come from two different, if apparently compatible, worlds. Envoys of the press (and by extension, the European nation-states), mouthpieces of mass society, the journalists circulate in a world of money/information that is anything but exotic. They are only witnesses of the imperial story and have no relation to what we might call the actantial core of nineteenth-century exoticism, which is what we must now examine. The exotic text (both imperialist and exoticizing, though each in different ways, as we will see in the following chapter) revolves around what I call the *imperial family*. In its most nuclear form, this family contains two members: a figure of authority and a hero to whom this imperial figure delegates his authority. Or, in Greimassian terms, a Sender and a Subject. We should also note the presence of a third, but in the case of *Michel Strogoff* rather peripheral, member of this family: a female companion who aids the hero and whom he ultimately marries (a Helper/Object).

A later text like Conrad's *Heart of Darkness* will unceasingly invoke this paradigmatic structure but without being able to reconstitute it fully; a "tangled hierarchy" of the imperial family is what must result from the merging of *Heart of Darkness*'s two conflicting stories. In the first story, Kurtz was to have taken on the dimensions of the imperial figure; in the second, he is merely a disempowered bureaucrat whom the Company (the new Sender) orders Marlow to retrieve in the name of an efficient civilization. The Subject's role is, in turn, equally problematical, given his duplicitous allegiance to the authority of both Kurtz and the Company. Caught in a double-bind between modernity and what comes (or came) before it, the only "heroic" gesture of which Marlow proves capable is the act of storytelling itself—which, at least within the terms of his story, is no act at all. One sign of this inaction is Marlow's strange celibacy: there are no female companions (and no future) in this world of his. Kurtz's forever Intended, and the despot's imperial mistress, "treading the earth proudly, with a slight jingle and flash of barbarous ornaments," at once "savage and superb" (p. 135): Marlow is midway to both and capable of touching neither—if not with a lie.

Such complications and ambiguities are far from the surface of Verne's novel, in which the imperial family is present in the unproblematical form of the Czar, Michel Strogoff, and Nadia. What is more, this family is doubly present in the text. Whatever negative qualities the three family members might be thought to possess have been shunted off, in a manichean process of doubling, to an extremely unpleasant triad of characters: the Emir, Ivan Ogareff, and Ogareff's gypsy lover, Sangarre. These three figures, who taken together can be identified with the three-headed beast of myth,[31] fill the structural role of Opponent (or, even more precisely, of anti-Sender, anti-Subject, and anti-Helper/Object, respectively). But for all that these two imperial families are stark opposites, the differences between them are by no means as essential as those separating Strogoff from the journalists. The two families belong to the same imperial world, although the one is "enlightened" and the Other "barbaric"; for this reason, they are able to inter-act with each other. Let us consider each of them in closer detail, starting with the Czar, "one of those rare sovereigns whom almost an entire world has gotten used to obeying, even in their thoughts" (p. 12).

The Czar provides a sovereign role model for his subjects (Napoleon fills a similar function for the Romantic individual in many a nineteenth-century novel, those of Stendhal, for example). One striking feature of this imperial power is the Czar's "pre-narrative" status in *Michel Strogoff*: he makes only one appearance, at the beginning of the novel during a fête thrown at the New Palace. The sovereign's proper place is the banquet, a gathering oblivious to those "parasitical" relations, as Serres would put it, that are the precondition of narrative. The fête is at the origin of the story, but its static time must be interrupted if this story is ever to begin. The Tartar invasion comprises just such an interruption. This break in a closed system is necessary if a second feature of imperial power, its dynastic quality, is to emerge: the Czar's sovereignty must repeat that of his predecessors. The Tartar invasion thus recalls an earlier one. In 1812, Jolivet notes, "in the middle of a fête given in his honor, the emperor Alexander was informed that Napoleon had just crossed the Niemen with the French vanguard" (p. 20). Although the Czar must remain where he is, his authority is such that he can delegate his powers of execution to a lieutenant, who, venturing forth from the static world of the banquet, will free the imperial system of its parasites and thereby return it to a state of equilibrium.

These parasites, of course, have their own imperial system, similar in form—if not in content—to that of the Russians. "Undisputed sovereign, having at his disposal the life and fortune of his subjects, and whose power is without limits" (p. 260), the present Emir of Bokhara, Féofar-Khan, is himself part of a dynasty. He is, we are told, a "modern Ghengis Khan" (p. 35), who by invading Russia is doing no more than following "in the footsteps of his predecessors." Like the Czar, he too inhabits a pre- (or, in this case, perhaps we should say anti-) narrative space that is best described as spectacular. The "dazzling" spectacle of the Russian fête will be doubled later in the novel by a *fête tartare* that is, in its own way, as aesthetically *éblouissant* (to use a word that recurs in the descriptions of both imperial spectacles) as the Czar's. But whereas the power of the Russian sovereign is controlled, tacit, benign, the Emir's authority continues to exhibit itself as unenlightened cruelty; indeed, the Tartar fête culminates with the atrocious blinding of Michel Strogoff. The territory that extends between these two unmoving poles, between the "civilized" and the "barbaric," is the proper domain of the second member of the imperial family, the hero.

One look at Michel Strogoff suffices for the Czar: "What the Czar easily recognized was that he was 'an enforcer of orders' [*un exécuteur d'ordres*]" (p. 38). The sovereign figure's powers of execution can safely be delegated to such a man; with imperial authorization, Strogoff leaves the static and dynastically ordered world of the fête for the expansive domains of the Czar. He becomes, in short, the protagonist of an adventure narrative, a "mobile persona" whose task is to cross one or more boundaries (and, if the adventure is successful, to return across them).[32] In this particular case, the primary boundary—there are countless secondary ones—is the Ural Mountains, "the frontier which Michel Strogoff must cross to pass from Russia into Siberia" (p. 126). The ultimate purpose of all this border crossing is to consolidate the Czar's imperium, to make the boundary between Russia and Siberia disappear; Strogoff's mission completed, Asian Russia will no longer be a "land of exile" but an integral part of the Czar's "new reign."

The success of the Subject's performance depends, of course, upon his competence, which Greimas defines as "the wanting and/or being able and/or knowing-how-to-do of the subject."[33] Strogoff's competence to be an imperial hero is never in doubt, given the Czar's immediate recognition of him as an *exécuteur d'ordres*. Several qualities especially fit him for his task: a willingness to subordinate his own desires, a capacity for disguise, an appropriate cultural background, and a genetic pedigree. In order to cross the relevant boundaries, the hero of an adventure narrative must lose his own identity and adopt a disguise. Strogoff, the imperial courier, becomes Nicolas Korpanoff, a simple merchant; his ultimate disguise, of course, is that of a blind man. The hero must also have certain cultural aptitudes: chief among Strogoff's special talents is his knowledge of languages. As with Kipling's Kim, it is immense; he knows "almost all the idioms in use from Tartary to the Sea of Ice" (p. 71). And, again like Kim, he has the right (racial) stuff: "His powerful head showed off the handsome features of the Caucasian race" (p. 37). Powerful, handsome, and Caucasian, Strogoff has entirely identified himself with the Czar's will; his own desire does not, with one significant exception, enter into the story.

In the preceding two paragraphs, I have sketched the ideal hero of an adventure narrative. More specifically, I have described the main actant in Verne's imperialist exoticism. As I explain more fully at the beginning of the next chapter, imperialist exoticism is about transmission, not transgression. Strogoff is the bearer, or transmitter, of a message the Czar wants to arrive at Irkutsk; in order to carry out the Czar's will, our hero sublimates his own desire. But the hero of such a novel cannot be a mere automaton; the success of Michel's mission depends in large part upon the strength of his own character. At some point, therefore, he must assert himself, in an act of limited transgression, by disobeying the imperial orders and thereby giving evidence of his own sovereign power. This lapse occurs when Strogoff reveals his identity to the Tartars in order to save his mother from the knout (a prominent instrument of torture in the novel).

Strogoff's transgression leaves him briefly in the power of his sinister double, Ivan Ogareff. Ogareff, the anti-Subject, has all of Strogoff's qualities but in a distorted form. The primary distortion in Ogareff's character is clearly racial: "Having in him a little Mongol blood through his mother, who was of Asian origin, he liked trickery. . . . Deceitful by nature, he gladly had recourse to the basest disguises, on occasions turning himself into a beggar, excelling at taking on all manner of forms and comportments. Moreover, he was cruel, and would act as a torturer if needs be" (p. 186). With Ogareff, disguise is a permanent state of affairs: appearing as a gypsy, a Tartar lieutenant, or in the uniform of a Russian soldier, he has no true identity to which he can return. But the knowledge gained in his years as a Russian military officer is just what is needed to organize the Tartar invasion; he will be its *âme* just as Féofar is its *tête*. His resemblance to a hero is such that he will, near the end of the novel, be able to impersonate Strogoff ("he had taken the name and position of the man he thought reduced to powerlessness"; p. 414) and gain the trust of the Grand Duke—although, needless to say, in the manichean world of *Michel Strogoff* this confusion between hero and villain, between Subject and anti-Subject, is not destined to last long.

Unlike his self-restrained double Strogoff, Ogareff is incontinent when it comes to his own desires. He indulges freely in them—a fact that accounts for the erotic nature of his rapport with the female companion. The gypsy Sangarre, "sans patrie, sans famille," has given herself "corps et âme" to Ogareff. Not only is she his faithful Helper ("whatever order he gave her, Sangarre would execute it"; p. 258), she also functions as his sexual Object. Verne, as one might expect, does not emphasize this point: Sangarre thus remains first and foremost the deceitful abettor of Ogareff's treacherous plans. Her genteelly eroticized status is nonetheless worth noting because it appears to be a natural corollary of the fact that she is the novel's most exoticized character. Verne reserves his most properly exoticist descriptions for Sangarre: "She was a savage [*c'était une sauvage*] worthy of sharing the wigwam of an Apache or the hut of an Andaman"—a woman who, given the opportunity, would torture Michel's mother "with all the refinement of a Red Indian" (p. 258). And so on. In the person of Sangarre, "that savage spy, damned soul of Ivan Ogareff" (p. 256), a complicity between the erotic and the exotic makes itself felt. It will prove a central feature of Pierre Loti's exoticizing exoticism in which the third member of the imperial family is more or less completely transformed from a Helper into an Object of desire.

Although it raises the prospect of this transformation, Verne's imperialist exoticism just as quickly suppresses it. The Subject's desire is not what counts here; or, rather, it is what can be realized only at the end of the novel, once the imperial mission has been accomplished. After the defeat of the Tartars, Strogoff's faithful Helper, Nadia, will indeed be given to him in marriage. This symbolic exchange of vows between Michel the Siberian and Nadia the Lithuanian both joins together the two extremities of the Czar's realm and lays the biological foundations for the perpetuation of a political order that, as actors in an imperial story, the hero and heroine have helped restore. The imperial and biological families unproblematically merge into one another. If, as Edward Said has argued, "the history of the nineteenth-century novel documents the increasing awareness of a gap between the representations of fictional narrative and the fruitful, generative principle of human life,"[34] then it is obvious that Verne's novel stands to the (out)side of mainstream European narrative (Said's "nineteenth-century novel"). Verne not only closes off this gap between the principles of narrative and those of biology (or, indeed, between the political and the personal) when he has Strogoff and Nadia marry; he appears oblivious to the very existence of any such gap. The increasingly difficult encounter with modernity that preoccupies the "nineteenth-century novel" and that results in a breakdown in the lines of communication between literature and life seems entirely absent from *Michel Strogoff*.

Well, not quite. And it is this "not quite" that we will pursue in the following pages. To lead into those remarks, I pose one last question:

Having identified the imperial family and its negative double in *Michel Strogoff*, who or what have we left out? Most notably, perhaps, the various indigenous peoples of Central Asia that make up the opposing camp of Féofar-Khan. This "cosmopolitan crowd," which forms the ethnographic backdrop to Verne's imperial story, is often described in less than flattering terms: "The Tartar horsemen were pullulating, and at times it seemed as if they were coming out of the earth, like harmful insects that a thunderstorm brings swarming to the surface of the ground" (p. 278). In degrading the human to the status of the animal ("les insectes nuisibles"), this simile is typical of much "Western" literature in the way it goes about "othering" indigenous peoples. But what is perhaps most interesting about this image of insects swarming out of the ground is that it seems to raise, almost despite itself, the problem of autochthony. What Verne's simile evokes is the fact that the Tartars, like the Russians whose territory they are invading, exist in a primary relation to the earth. They come from somewhere. And here, I would argue, we have one of the few signs in *Michel Strogoff* of a historical event that is never openly mentioned in the novel but without which it is entirely unthinkable: namely, the Russian conquest of Central Asia. It is to the doubling of history and fiction, of real and imaginary conquests, that we must now turn.

Into Darkest Asia: Colonialism in 'Michel Strogoff'

A first reading of *Michel Strogoff* reveals very few direct historical references: the Russian Czar, for instance, is not named—a fact attributable to political discretion on both Verne's and his editor Hetzel's part as well as to the novel's overtly mythopoeic character. Nevertheless, he is obviously an idealized version of Alexander II, ruler of Russia from 1855 to 1881 and perhaps most famous for freeing the serfs and initiating a regime that was, at least in contrast to that of his predecessor, Nicholas I, relatively liberal and modernizing. Verne's Czar is frequently credited with "a new way of governing": pursuing a benign internal politics, he pardons political exiles and shows great restraint in enforcing imperial ukases. The enlightened despotism with which Voltaire and Diderot credited certain absolute monarchs in the eighteenth century would seem, in the person of this clement sovereign, to be alive and well and harnessed to rather more progressive ideals.

We do not have to go far, then, to find a contemporary model for Verne's Czar.[35] His ferocious alter ego, the Emir of Bokhara, however, is not so readily identifiable, with good reason. The state of affairs prevailing in Central Asia for the first twenty years of Alexander II's reign was, in fact, exactly the opposite of what Verne portrayed in *Michel Strogoff*. The khanates—feudal, semi-organized nations that, along with Afghanistan, formed the buffer zone between the Asian empires of Britain and Russia—were in complete disarray; far from presenting any threat to the Russian Empire, they were "in a state of almost continuous war with one another"[36] and in the process of becoming the luckless victims of Russian territorial expansion. Unable to organize themselves around any one charismatic figure and lacking the armaments to wage a modern war, they were, like many of the African territories soon to be seized during the Scramble for Africa, in no position to oppose the march of European conquest. For the Russians, "the risks involved were small. Russian casualties were extremely light, native ones crushingly heavy and often vitiated by wholesale massacres after battles."[37] Although the Czar's army suffered occasional defeats in its Central Asian campaigns during the 1860's and 1870's and local resistance continued well into the twentieth century, techno-military superiority practically assured a Russian victory.

Verne's fiction completely occludes this colonial process. Indeed, the single mention of the word "colonies" in the text establishes colonialism as a primarily defensive position. The word crops up early in the novel as part of the narrator's description of Omsk, the center of Western Siberia's military network, which was meant to keep the Kazakh populations at bay:

Here, then, are the limits that these nomads, not completely subdued, have more than once attacked and, at the War Ministry, there was every reason to think that Omsk was already greatly menaced. The line of military settlements [*colonies militaires*], that is to say, those Cossack posts stationed at intervals from Omsk to Semipalatinsk, must have been broken at several points.   (p. 32)

The "colonial" line to which Verne is referring is the Irtysh line, part of a series of fortifications that for a century separated Russian Siberia from the steppes of the nomadic Kazakhs, who were themselves a buffer between Russia and the Central Asian khanates of Bokhara, Khiva, and Kokand.

Much of what Verne has to say about the Kazakhs, who had for the most part been under the nominal control of Russia since the 1740's, is traceable to Alexis de Levchine's *Description des hordes et des steppes des Kirghiz-Kazaks* (1832; translated from Russian into French in 1840). Based on information gathered mostly in the early 1820's, Levchine's book was obsolete in one important respect. The Irtysh line, and the other fortifications built in the eighteenth century during "a period in which Russian troops actually found themselves in a defensive attitude before the Kazakhs,"[38] were no longer, as this passage would lead us to believe, Russia's primary frontier: "Between 1824 and 1854 Russian troops effectively occupied the Kazakh Steppe, placing the entire steppe for the first time in history under the rule of a sedentary society."[39] By the time of Alexander II's ascension in 1855, a new line of fortifications had been established much further to the southwest and southeast, along the Syr-Dar'ya and Ili rivers. These lines would be joined in 1864 when the rapid subjection of the khanates began.

Verne, to be sure, also used more contemporary sources, and his account of the Russian fortifications is at points inconsistent, as when he describes those of the Ishim line (which extended the Irtysh line west toward Orenburg) as having been abandoned "once the Muscovite government believed these hordes reduced to absolute submission" (p. 176). The important point, though, is not whether these "colonies" are being kept up but that, as the fact of the invasion makes clear, they are still necessary. What is more, Verne never puts the independence of the khanates themselves in question, despite the momentous events of the decade preceding the publication of *Michel Strogoff*. By 1868 the major cities of Tashkent and Samarkand had been taken and the Governate-General of Turkestan established; a rapid succession of campaigns against the three khanates, culminating in the full-scale attack on Khiva in 1873, led to the complete vassalage of Bokhara and Khiva and to the formal annexation of Kokand in 1876.

Jean Jules-Verne, in his recent biography of Verne, though affirming that these events inspired the novel, sees little basis in Turgenev's complaint that the Tartar invasion was inconceivable. "To imagine," Jean Jules-Verne contends against Turgenev, "that the Uzbeks of Khiva might have thought to ward off Russian ambitions on their capital by invading Siberia was not unreasonable."[40] But this is inadequate reasoning on two points: first, the Uzbeks of Khiva were in no position to defend themselves, much less launch an attack on distant Siberia; second, there is absolutely no mention of a threat to the Central Asian khanates in the novel. The Tartar invasion is not a defensive reaction or a preemptive strike; it is a completely offensive, indeed gratuitous, attack on Russia, "a formidable invasion threatening to detach the Siberian provinces from Russian autonomy" (p. 22). Verne's scenario is thoroughly *déraisonnable*, and we must ask ourselves why this should be the case.

Although Verne's views on colonialism are by no means simple, one would expect him to look with favor on the changes going on in Central Asia. As Simone Vierne has said, he considered "colonization" to be "the progress that needed to be brought to backward peoples,"[41] and one could hardly (at the time, certainly!) have argued that the Russians were not bringing "progress" to the "backward" khanates. Perhaps in the past Russia had been open to the accusation of being as barbaric as its neighbors, but it was now quite clearly a modern colonial power on a par with England or France. As far as the penetration into Turkestan goes, even Frederick von Hellwald, by no means an apologist for the Russians, argues that they "no longer comport themselves like wild and devastating conquerors, but act like true pioneers of civilization [by promoting industry and trade]."[42] Quelling the barbaric khanates would seem a crowning effort of so-called Western civilization. And yet Verne chose to ignore this effort and to transform "the seat of cowardice and effeminacy" (Vámbéry) into a powerful war machine bound together by the charismatic figure of a "modern Ghengis Khan."

Jean Delabroy has provided the beginnings of an answer as to why this should be so. What is at stake in *Michel Strogoff*, he says, is "the positive evolution [*le devenir positif*] of an issue that is after all global, like the liberal politics of modern States."[43] Delabroy maintains that this coming-into-its-own of a liberal politics, the sort of politics that Verne himself valorized, is effected in the novel through a dialectical encounter between the Same and the Other, Europe and Asia. Expanding on Delabroy's insight, we can say that the text's encounter with the spectacle of the Other serves to confirm the positive evolution of the Same: both the power and the desirability of the liberal State become apparent through this confrontation with a prior form of the State that is at once genealogically connected to and essentially different from its enlightened successor. This barbaric Other will have a double status: it is both that which is doomed to disappear in the progressive light of a liberalizing modernity and that which must be represented as having not yet been surpassed. This dialectical revelation of the liberal State thus simultaneously anticipates and forestalls the Other's complete disappearance.

The opposition between Imperial Russia and its exotic Other is, as Delabroy shows (p. 153), most vividly exemplified in the contrast between the Czar's fête, which opens the novel, and Féofar-Khan's *fête tartare*, which provides its memorable centerpiece. *Michel Strogoff*, as we saw in the previous section, begins with a moment of serene unity: "general harmony" reigns and "a national dance" is under way at the

New Palace in Moscow. This, then, is the realm of the Same, but one whose necessity has not, as yet, been dialectically affirmed through a confrontation with what is Other than it. News of the Tartar invasion interrupts this harmonious gathering; the spectacle of civilization is suspended, and a heroic narrative commences that will eventually lead its hero into the sight of an atrocious anti-spectacle "composed of all the indigenous elements of Central Asia" (p. 295). This *fête tartare* poses the (empty) threat of a barbaric end to the ongoing story of civilization.

Notwithstanding the danger it apparently presents, this Other spectacle possesses a certain picturesque charm that can be unproblematically drawn into the realm of the Same. Hence Verne singles out two very distinct moments in his extended description of the *fête tartare*: a harmless and pleasing decorative prelude, and a barbaric climax. We first witness the peoples of Central Asia performing some of the cultural activities—"songs, dances and *fantasias*"—that are peculiar to their region. This initial moment, one of what we might call aesthetic execution ("These ballerinas," we are told, "executed with much grace a variety of dances"; p. 306), has nothing menacing about it. Indeed, civilization, in the person(s) of Jolivet and Blount, finds this folkloric display absolutely charming: it should provide the reporters with "a hundred lines of copy" (p. 298). Here, the Other is envisioned within the boundaries of the Same—recorded and recoded in the spirit of an attentive tourist or a conscientious ethnographer. This cultural shell is all that will survive of barbarism once its political power has been definitively quelled.

But this apparently innocuous scene of aesthetic execution quickly gives way to an "exécution à la mode tartare"—a scene of torture that provides ample evidence of both the Other's power and its savagery: "The spectators, remaining in the area around the square, as well as Féofar-Khan's staff, for all of whom this torture was simply an added attraction, waited for the execution to be carried out. Then, its curiosity appeased, this savage horde would go throw itself into a state of intoxication" (p. 312). In having Michel Strogoff tortured, the Emir displays an imperial sovereignty that is at once necessary (for it confirms, by way of negative example, both the existence and the desirability of the enlightened Same) and necessarily incomplete: the hero is not really blinded, although he will have to feign blindness for the last third of the novel. The political economy of liberalism demands both that the illiberal power of despotism be on exhibit and that it prove, ultimately, impotent in the face of civilization's triumphant march.

But if we agree that this is the dialectical process by which the consolidation of "the liberal politics of modern States" is effected in *Michel Strogoff*, we must still pose one critical question: Why should Russia, whose autocratic ways Verne had criticized only a few years before in a work like *Vingt mille lieues sous les mers* (1870), be the "hero" of this modern story? Why, in other words, should an attenuated form of the despotic Other end up filling the role of the enlightened Same?

I would suggest that an answer might well lie in the problematical conjuncture of two seemingly incompatible ideological projects in Verne: exoticism and mid-nineteenth-century liberalism. As we have seen, in *Michel Strogoff* the dialectical encounter between Same and Other, which is central to the exoticist project,[44] is effected in the service of a liberal politics that to a certain extent valorizes the world of modernity. And yet, as I have stressed, exoticism is an essentially antimodern project, more properly consonant with a tradition-oriented ideology like Conrad's Romantic organicism. Verne's marriage of modern and anti-modern ideologies is, then, an unlikely one, to say the least; what makes it at all possible, however, is the fact that both are grounded in the (groundless) figure of the individual.

In both the English utilitarian strain of mid-nineteenth-century liberalism (Mill) and its French utopian counterpart (Saint-Simon), the individual is given the same central role that he plays in exoticism. But whereas the exotic subject is engaged in a struggle to assert himself against the modernity that is at once his precondition and the sign of his impossibility, the liberal subject goes to work on behalf of that modernity, in the (untenable) belief that he is not thereby acting to the detriment of his own sovereign authority. The inventors, explorers, and technocrats of Verne's early novels embody the idea of an individual who maintains his authority and yet at the same time pledges allegiance to the forces of Progress. Authority is vested in the individual, but this individual (with a few significant exceptions, such as Captain Nemo) goes on to invest himself in a society dedicated to pluralism.

But for how long can this delicate balance of individual sovereignty and a plural society be thought of as holding true? Not long, if we are to judge by the fate of one of Verne's favorite characters, the explorer. Ideally, the explorer is at once a heroic individual and the representative of an enlightened society that is in the process of extending its power to the far reaches of the globe, thereby bringing "progress" to "backward" cultures and widening the domain of a benevolent civilization. For this reason, as Marc Soriano notes, all Verne's explorers have a good conscience in the early novels: "they represent Civilization and Progress, facing the barbarity of inferior races."[45] But once civilization has gained a definitive purchase on barbarism and savagery, the built-in obsolescence of this heroic individual becomes evident: the explorer is, and cannot help being, an intermediate, transitional figure—one whose apparent centrality is destined not to last.

Verne's later novels bear this out: after 1879, as Marie-Hélène Huet has argued, the figure of the explorer disappears from the *Voyages extraordinaires*. As she also suggests, this absence is symptomatic of a political situation gone badly awry: "The great powers have not been able to play the role that was assigned them, and the explorers have made way for merchants or armies."[46] Inevitable as the disappearance of this particular figure might seem to us, for Verne it will be only one sign among many of liberalism's failure to live up to its individualistic promise: no longer a central player in the story of civilization, the individual has been absorbed into the body of the State, "which posits itself as the only, and abstract, holder of all the forms of power" (to recall Maccagnani's argument). That the individual and modernity could be at one was the dream of Verne's heroic liberalism—a dream intimately connected, as we have seen, to the continued existence of an archaic Other. For Verne, this delicate equilibrium eventually gives way (but, we must ask, when has it not already given way?) to a modern state of affairs in which neither the sovereign individual nor the exotic Other has any real place in the world.

The explorer becomes a bureaucratic cog in the colonial wheel; a heroic reporter like Gédéon Spilett in *L'île mystérieuse* (1874–75), "a real hero of curiosity, of information, of the unknown, of the impossible" (p. 16), will be reincarnated in the pluralized body of Jolivet and Blount. Such examples of the individual's degradation point to a growing pessimism in Verne, a gradual loss of faith in his own liberal ideology. Far from creating a situation conducive to the individual's growth, the forward march of Progress leads us beyond this figure to an entirely modern and yet, at least from Verne's perspective, undesirable place. As Jean Chesneaux has pointed out, "As one enters the age of imperialism, starting from about 1880–90, the Vernian dream of dominating nature through science and work becomes debased by its contact with the violence of State machinery and the power of money."[47] In the last quarter of the century, Verne's early optimism breaks down in the face of a modernity whose anti-individualistic foundations are becoming ever more apparent to him. He bears witness to an ineluctable process of decline that no less a liberal than John Stuart Mill had already analyzed earlier in the century, in a piece entitled "Civilization" (1836), with a curious mixture of resignation and foreboding: "By the natural growth of civilization, power passes from individuals to masses, and the weight and importance of an individual, as compared with the mass, sink into greater and greater insignificance."[48]

But for Mill civilization is not yet a global problem: "There is," for instance, "no danger of the prevalence of democracy in Syria or Timbuctoo" (p. 173). Or, he might well have added, Czarist Russia. And here we can return to the problem of *Michel Strogoff*, and the question of where this novel stands in relation to Verne's growing disillusionment with the direction of liberal politics. If the individual and the modern European State were incompatible, and this was becoming all too obvious to Verne, might there not still be places in the world where the sort of heroic liberalism in which he believed could, at some point in the future, flourish? Or, in other words, might not the "prevalence of democracy" in a place like Russia be figured in terms of a future "hope" rather than of an extremely unlikely "danger"?

In turning to a country that was organized autocratically, one in which democratic pluralism had yet to triumph, Verne could still posit a future for that liberalism whose promise had, in Europe and America, already been broken. The Czar's clement authority and Michel Strogoff's heroic performance embody the dream of individual sovereignty that was a foundation stone of mid-nineteenth-century liberalism. The positive imperial power of Verne's Russia *prefigures* the sort of truly liberal society that is to come, one in which the individual's authority will not be subordinated to the overbearing forces of a pluralism gone out of control, and in which the technocratic dream of dominating nature will not have been degraded by the "violence of the State and the power of money."

Verne's imperial system, as we saw in the previous section, directs our gaze away from the negative future that Jolivet and Blount embody. This system is not, however, as static as one might at first suspect; it has its own dynamism (of which Strogoff's long and arduous voyage is, indeed, the very emblem), one that ultimately points us toward a very different, positive vision of the future. An attenuated version of the despotic Other plays the role of the enlightened Same: in this way the strategy of prefiguring a truly heroic liberalism is achieved. Autocratic Russia, liberalizing but not yet pluralist, opens itself up, at some point in the not so distant future, to the sort of political system that Verne saw to be rapidly slipping away into Europe's past. But, and here is the critical complication that my entire discussion has been leading up to, as the prefiguration of an authentically liberal regime to come, Verne's Russia cannot (yet) be figured as a modern colonial power since, according to the logic of Verne's own liberal ideology, an "enlightened" and progressive colonialism can come into being only after the triumph of liberalism.

And yet this "enlightened" colonialism did not await its logical precondition: the Central Asian khanates were being brought under the global sway of "civilization" by a colonizing power whose techno-military superiority and humanitarian pretensions already marked it off as modern to the core, notwithstanding the autocratic presence at its head of "despots like the Russian emperors." In theory, to be sure, Verne could have no objection to Russia's "civilizing mission"; it would certainly appear to represent (recalling Simone Vierne's formula) "the progress that needed to be brought to backward peoples." But in practice—the prefiguring practice of *Michel Strogoff*—to have told the story of Russia's Central Asian enterprise would have been to reveal this attenuated Other as indistinguishable from that Same whose redeemed presence this Other at once conjures up and defers to the proximate future. The conquest of Central Asia is a sign of the modernity that has to be absent(ed) from the text if Russia is to maintain its necessary difference from the realm of the Same. Without an abusive use of history, however, this pre-colonial condition could not be met: "civilization" had already penetrated the heart of "darkest Asia."

In order to represent a time before both liberalism and colonialism, Verne needed to invoke a geopolitical situation that had long since been surpassed. In order to salvage his ideological project from a modernity that it both looked forward to and viewed with growing consternation, he turned back, and could not help turning back, to a time when the eighteenth-century Irtysh line was still the proper point of reference in matters "colonial." In this anachronistic world, the barbaric power of the Tartars was still a real threat: it could be repulsed but not eliminated. That the forces of "civilization" will eventually subdue this power is the tacit assumption of Verne's novel, just as the despotic figures of the Czar and his heroic lieutenant look forward to the exercise of individual authority under a truly liberal regime. This positive colonialism and the regime that will enable it have yet to come: they remain, and must remain, upon the horizon of *Michel Strogoff*. But the peculiarly nostalgic nature of this horizon should by now be evident. The colonial line of the Irtysh had already been crossed; the prospects it offered were entirely fictional.

Chapter 3

THE DREAM AND THE FETISH

SOVEREIGN OTHERS AND THE ABSENCE OF MODERNITY

- *Gauguin and the End of the Line*

  Whither is fled the visionary gleam?
  Where is it now, the glory and the dream?
  —W. Wordsworth, "Intimations of Immortality"

As he tells his wife in a letter of March 1892, Paul Gauguin came to
Tahiti with hopes of royal patronage: "On my arrival I had much to
hope from the King." Pomare V, the last ruler of Tahiti, had no effective
control over his own kingdom; even so, for a Gauguin just arrived from
France, this sovereign figure doubtless appeared the very embodiment
of the exotic land upon which he had resolutely set his artistic hopes.
However, Pomare died on the very morning of Gauguin's appointment
with him; "him dead," Gauguin continues, "15 days after my arrival,
it was like the cracking up of Tahiti and for me especially."[1] The death
of this figurehead not only marks the end of Gauguin's own hopes but
the end of the line for Tahitian culture and the definitive entrenchment
of colonial power: with Pomare's demise, "Tahitian soil is becoming altogether French, and little by little the old state of affairs is going to
disappear."[2] The symbolic import of this event so impressed itself on
Gauguin that he would begin *Noa Noa* (1900), the published account of
his first stay in Tahiti, with a description of the king's funeral: "There

was one king less and with him were disappearing the last vestiges of
Maori customs. It was well and truly over: nothing left but the Civilized
[C'était bien fini: rien que des Civilisés]."³ The passing away of this sovereign figure and the consequent triumph of "civilization" signal the
end of Gauguin's exotic dream, a dream whose end thus precedes its
beginning.

A dozen years later, a young naval officer by the name of Victor Segalen will find himself in a remarkably similar position of belatedness
with respect to the by-now-legendary French painter. In one of his first
published works, a 1904 article written for Le Mercure de France, Segalen
recounts a recent pilgrimage to the Marquesas Islands, Gauguin's last
place of residence in Polynesia. "Gauguin dans son dernier décor" is
not an account of a meeting between these two men, but of a lamentable absence—the controversial artist had died only a few months before Segalen's arrival from Tahiti, where he had been stationed for the
past half-year. After paying an extended homage to the hors-la-loi
whose genius had flourished in these remote islands of the Pacific, the
young officer concludes his article with a melancholic portrait of the
Marquesan people rapidly dying off from an assortment of diseases.
He then goes on to ask, "But what are these if not the varied forms of
that other scourge: the contact with 'civilized man' [le contact des 'civili-
sés']. In twenty years, they will have ceased to be 'savage.' They will,
at the same time, forever have ceased to be."⁴ The imminent eradica-
tion of savagery, the ongoing and contaminatory expansion of a so-
called civilization—as with Gauguin's own reflections upon the death
of Pomare, Segalen's account is firmly grounded in both the ideological
dichotomies of nineteenth-century exoticism and the fatidic pessimism
that, by the turn of the century, had become the prescribed way of
speaking about matters exotic.

Segalen's relation to this disappearing Other is, however, different
from Gauguin's in one important respect: whereas Gauguin had
dreamed of a direct contact with the Tahitian sovereign, Segalen's
dream of the Other is at a double remove from what it envisions, necessarily mediated by the heroic figure who preceded and predeceased
him. A coming to terms with this doubled (and duplicitous) distance
from the exotic characterizes Segalen's work as a novelist, as we will
see in the following chapter. However, at this early point in his career,
Segalen, ringing out the knells of a still-extant savagery, has yet to take
(full) notice of the secondary, mediated nature of his relationship to the
exotic. Direct contact with the Other of the sort envisioned by earlier

exotic writers is still very much a part of his discursive project, for all
that he can realize this contact only in the entropic terms of nineteenth-
century exoticism's second, pessimistic phase.

Another twelve years pass, and Segalen, nearing the end of his life,
once again takes up the subject of Gauguin in an extended biographical
portrait written as a preface to the artist's correspondence with
Georges-Daniel de Monfreid.[5] Strange to say, "Hommage à Gauguin"
(1916) is an entirely more sanguine work than "Gauguin dans son dernier décor." As he tells the story of "this proud savage," mixing in some
of his own impressions of Polynesian life, Segalen displays none of the
anxiety over the eventual fate of "savagery" that marks his earlier article. Rather, he indulges freely and without regrets in an unproblematically heroic tale: the exotic subject and his alternative society,
whose double requiem Segalen had sung at the beginning of his career,
come to life again—this time gilded with the splendid and ahistorical
trappings of myth.

According to Segalen's account, Gauguin superbly realized the
transgressive desire that he had repeatedly and obstinately expressed
before his embarkation for Tahiti: "*Je veux aller chez les sauvages*." Having
abandoned Europe, the artist crossed over into a world of pure difference where his only companion would henceforth be "the native of old
regained" ("l'antique indigène retrouvé"; p. 97). Gauguin "did not ex-
ert himself in returning to the Maoris of times past: he found himself
in them, very close to them, and unaffectedly painted the man of days
gone by" (p. 104). His genius allowed him to rediscover the native population as it once was—and apparently still is, to judge from the idyllic
description Segalen himself gives of the Maoris: "The Maori man cannot be forgotten once one has *seen* him, nor can the woman cease to be
loved once one loves her. Paul Gauguin knew how to love over there
[*là-bas*], and to see more powerfully than anybody, with two large
round eyes, these living beings, amber and naked, who, if they are to
be painted, must not be compared to any other human species" (p. 98).
The Maori nose, their lips and eyes, the "discreet and naturally an-
drogynous" hips of the female: Segalen re-presents their corporeal features to himself, recalling one by one the captivating parts that make
up the whole of these incomparable, naked human beings. The *antique
indigène retrouvé* here rises up free of civilization's sartorial constraints,
inhabiting a *là-bas* where it is certain that "the sun's reign . . . is not
marked by the same hours that compartmentalize us" (p. 102).

The "savages" who, just twelve years before, were on the point of disappearing forever, have apparently emerged unscathed from their encounter with a noxious civilization; "vivants ambrés et nus," they have reassumed their rightful place alongside the exotic subject, Gauguin, who lives and loves beyond the pale of European society. This heroic myth, however, exacts a high price: in order to tell it, Segalen must forget the years that have intervened between then and now, disregarding the exacerbation of a historical process that he had earlier lamented. Segalen's idyllic rendering of Gauguin's dream is separated from its exotic original by a New Imperialist gulf that he must pass over in silence if his myth is to salvage the integrity it envisions. This nostalgic revival of the exotic past, which has its analogue in the later works of Joseph Conrad (see the first section of Chapter 5), is related to, but ultimately quite different from, the nostalgic perspective that I have termed decadentist. Whereas the former necessarily cuts itself off from the world of colonialism, the latter forgets neither this world nor the world that colonialism has (irreparably) covered over. As I will argue in subsequent chapters, this is the position that characterizes the Conrad of *Lord Jim* and the Segalen of *René Leys*. In these middle-period works, which are situated, as it were, between Segalen's two Gauguin articles, between the failure of the exoticist project and its revival as myth, the exotic past can be remembered only athwart a degraded colonial present that denies its very possibility.

The pellucid myth of "Hommage à Gauguin" attempts, then, to regain the original dream of exoticism—or, rather, a certain mode of exoticism: namely, what I have referred to, against the imperialist exoticism of *Michel Strogoff*, as exoticizing exoticism. The transmissive project that generates Strogoff's passage through Siberia ultimately leads him back into the realm of the Same; his voyage takes place under the watchful eye of the Czar, whose paternal authority the hero does not wish to transgress. The exotic functions here as the antithetical component in a dialectical process that serves the task of political integration: in his recourse to the Other, Verne is concerned with furthering the progressive aims of a heroic liberalism. The imperial family of *Michel Strogoff*—the benevolent figure of the Czar, his heroic lieutenant Michel Strogoff, and Strogoff's female companion Nadia—embodies a (relatively) civilized way of life that contrasts favorably with the brutally archaic ways of its exotic double, that unholy trinity of anti-sovereign, anti-hero, and anti-heroine.

Significantly, though, Strogoff's exotic double Ivan Ogareff, a little Mongol blood notwithstanding, is himself Russian, although through his treachery he has made himself irredeemably Other. In abandoning all allegiance to the Czar, Ogareff transgresses the world of his own beginnings; he will permanently assume the mantle of the exotic subject that for Strogoff can be no more than a temporary, if necessary, disguise. Viewed in terms of *Michel Strogoff*'s imperialist exoticism, Ogareff's dream is a nightmare, a negative impulse within the otherwise ordered economy of the text. However, viewed in terms of another, excessive economy, Ogareff is no villain but, rather, the very model of a hero inasmuch as he has passed from the realm of the Same into that of the Other, with no intention of effecting the dialectical return that imperialist exoticism requires. He succeeds in establishing a personal contact with the *antique indigène retrouvé*; indeed, he plays an essential part in what we might now refer to in more positive terms as the *exotic family*.

Centered around the powerful man who heads it (the Emir) and a woman who, in all her "savagery," is the very personification of alterity (Sangarre), this exotic family would be incomplete without the addition of a third member: the transgressing subject (Ogareff) who has come to live among them, who both sees, sees powerfully, and loves (to recall Segalen's description of Gauguin). His primarily erotic investment in the exotic will be directed toward the two other family members. He identifies with the native ruler, whose despotic sovereignty he can both model himself after and possibly benefit from, and he effects a liaison with a woman who, unlike the pristine Nadia, is as much sexual Object as faithful Helper. In turning to the Other without thought of returning, this exotic subject will attempt to (re)gain the power that he could not exercise, on his own terms, in the realm of the Same. By these transgressive means he fashions himself as a true individual, in opposition to his own increasingly civilized, modern, and gregarious society.*

Having looked at imperialist exoticism in the previous chapter, I will in the following pages consider its transgressive double, as we find it articulated in the early novels of Pierre Loti. As with Verne, Loti's work

---

*Whereas the manichean atmosphere of a novel like *Michel Strogoff* promotes this simple opposition between a transmissive and a transgressive mode of exoticism, other nineteenth-century writers will encourage, at least up to a certain point, a rather more murky ideological perspective that succeeds in focalizing both modes around a single character. I am thinking here, for instance, of Walter Scott's historical romance *Waverley* (1814), whose hero appears to waver in his allegiance between "primitive" Scotland and "civilized" England—although there is never much doubt as to the eventual fate of this halfhearted Jacobite.

can be read as (more or less unconsciously) registering a break in the exoticist project, away from a positive assertion of the sovereign individual and toward a growing resignation about his eventual fate in the world of the New Imperialism. Verne was able to maintain the coherence of his exotic-liberal dream only by sundering the imperial fiction of *Michel Strogoff* from the "forward" march of events, occluding the latter in favor of the former. Likewise, in order to pursue his erotic and supremely Romantic adventures, Loti must continually avert his gaze from a disturbing colonial presence that would appear to confirm the absence of what he desires. Loti will repeatedly conjure up the figures of a native ruler and an indigenous paramour, but to little or no effect. The male sovereigns with whom he would identify himself turn out to be no more than the luckless victims of historical change; the women in whom he seeks an exotic, and erotic, fullness wind up offering him only a partial satisfaction, since in their eyes and their bodies he can already read the story of an encroaching civilization. What Loti encounters in the place of the Other is, ultimately, nothing more than a series of signs that point toward that Other's absence; however, in order to ground himself as an exotic subject and maintain the possibility of his transgression, he must continually (mis)take these signs as betokening the Other's presence.

I think we can usefully, if perhaps only by analogy, consider this taking-for-present of what is absent, this attempt at figuring as real what has become patently unreal, as having more than a little in common with *fetishism*. For Freud, as Giorgio Agamben reminds us,[6] the original scene that structures the experience of fetishism occurs between the (male) infant and the mother: the infant bears witness to an absence—namely, that of the mother's penis. Perceiving this absence as a menace to himself (a sign of possible castration), the infant endeavors to deny it by seeking out its presence in surrogate objects. The fetishist, averting his eyes from a painful absence, tragically repeats this infantile operation—tragically, because the object he seeks can never be found as it originally was (or, more exactly, as it originally "never-was"). The only way that the fetishist can maintain the presence of the object that he desires is to invest in its absence—that is, in some object that recalls, without ever being, the ineluctably absent maternal penis. "Symbol of something and, at the same time, of its negation," the fetish-object is always insufficient, since its presence signals the absence of the object that ought to be present—a fact that the fetishist himself cannot but be obscurely aware of and that explains his tendency "to collect and multiply his fetishes." The fetishist collects, to use Agamben's nice phrase, "a harem of objects" that provide him with only a momentary satisfaction; to come to rest in any one of these objects would be to face up to the absence that inhabits it and that the fetishist is intent upon denying.

A thoroughly critical awareness of fetishism, such as Freud's, exposes the process by which the fetishist maintains his impossible dream; in thus taking an objective (scientific) distance from this process, the critic denies his own involvement in it. Such a denial is precisely what Conrad and Segalen will deny themselves; although they reveal the inadequacy of the exoticist project that a writer like Loti attempts to enact, they nevertheless choose to repeat this gesture—to continue reaching out to what has clearly become, and what they affirm as being, unattainable. Theirs is what we might call a "conscious fetishism" (or, if you will, an "affirmative deconstruction"). Loti's "innocent" (strong) attempts at establishing contact with the Other give way to a "guilty" (weak) re-enactment of this same dream, one whose precondition is the absence of what (never) was. Vitally aware that the "outside" they so desire has been fully inscribed within the global network of colonialism, these exemplars of the fin de siècle imagination persevere in search of it. In at once negating and affirming the exoticist project, Conrad and Segalen engage in a double game that enables them to inhabit a space between the patently unreal and the apparently all too real—an intervening space, space of rhetorical intervention, that defers a colonial world it cannot differ from. This space, where different/differing meanings concur, is the (im)proper domain of allegory.

Gauguin himself, to return to our point of departure, soon came to register the impossibility of his original desire to be "chez les sauvages." It can be argued, however, that during his first stay in Polynesia, in the early 1890's, he produced works primarily grounded in a belief that, despite the intrusive presence of colonialism on the islands, the native of old whose companionship he so desired could still be directly encountered and recorded on canvas. This Gauguin dreams of realizing the exoticist project that he outlines in *Noa Noa*: "Will I succeed in regaining a trace of this so distant and mysterious past? I didn't fancy the present. To regain the old hearth, to revive a fire in the midst of all those ashes. And to do all that alone, without any support" (pp. 19–20). But by the time Gauguin returns for his second, and final, sojourn in the Pacific, the desire to physically and artistically re(dis)cover the old familiar hearth of the exotic has become inseparable from the "worthless" present ("le présent ne me disait rien qui vaille") that he had originally hoped to leave behind. It is his exotic future ("arriverai-je . . . ?") that lies behind him now, no more real than those traces of the past scattered like unseen embers upon his (lack of a) way. The dream has ended, and all that remains for him is sadly to dream it again, upon awakening. At least this is what I would like to suggest in briefly comparing a painting from Gauguin's first years on the island with a later re-version of, and reversion to, that "naively" exotic work.

As Wayne Andersen has pointed out, *Manao Tupapau* ("The spirit of the dead watches"; 1892) and *Nevermore* (originally titled in English; 1897) share a similar construction.[7] In the foreground of each painting is a nude female, reclined across the canvas. The background of the earlier painting is an indeterminate wash of deep violet; in the later work arched windows, separating off the room in which the woman is resting from the world outside, open out onto a sky filled with mysterious colors. In both paintings, this native woman is being watched from behind. As its title makes clear, the unobtrusive figure dressed in black who dominates the top left corner of the earlier work comes from the spirit world, but it has assumed a familiar form that the native woman would have no difficulty in recognizing. "I make the ghost simply a little old woman," Gauguin writes to his wife in a letter of 8 December 1892, "because the young girl, knowing nothing about the theatricals of the French spiritualists, necessarily sees the spirit of death attached to a dead person, that's to say someone like her."[8] The theatrical "spirit" that for Gauguin can be only a source of irony is entirely absent from the familiar, and yet superbly exotic, scene that he has chosen to depict in *Manao Tupapau*. In the second painting, however, the native spirit has been replaced by a somber-colored bird perched on the window sill—a bird that, given the work's title, cannot fail to conjure up Edgar Allan Poe's Raven. Beyond the wall, in the center background of the painting, two natives, etched out against the indefinite horizon, are bent over each other in discussion of some dark and eternally unknown matter.

This later work reads, I would argue, like a commentary upon Gauguin's original desire, the desire for exotic origins that finds expression in the seamless unity of *Manao Tupapau* and its familiar vision of death. *Nevermore* portrays, as Poe would have said, "the dream of a dream"— at once displacing and resuming the dream it dreams. Between the native woman and her world, a figure from Western literature has been inserted—a figure of the artist himself, who is gazing, not only at the woman, but at the unseen person painting her: the exotic subject who sees, sees powerfully, and loves. Inserted into the text, allegorized, this disturbing authorial figure signals a new destiny that has taken the place of the traditional "spirit of the dead." Gauguin once said of this second spirit that it was not actually "Poe's crow on the watch, but the bird of the devil";[9] the devil of colonialism, I think we can say, has divided up the world into an inside it controls and an outside that can be "nevermore." Between these two worlds perches *l'oiseau du diable*: no longer looking out upon exotic horizons but inward upon the painter and the painted, the dreamer and his vanished dream.

Nevermore: The Exotic Beginnings of Pierre Loti

An altogether singular beginning, when you think about it,
this beginning of our story! —Pierre Loti, *Aziyadé*

As Peter Hulme has recently emphasized in his book *Colonial Encounters*, the discourse of colonialism always hesitates over the beginning moment, a moment bursting with "legal and ideological implications" (p. 193). When does colonialism begin, and who began it? In answering these foundational questions and thereby beginning its own story, colonialist discourse necessarily glosses over all Other beginnings, ruling out the time before the time when colonialism began. Nothing has truly begun before the beginning of colonialism: just as colonialism physically disposes of indigenous peoples, its discourse disposes them, rhetorically, as the "savage," "barbaric," or "prehistoric"—as that which, in other words, has yet to begin and, indeed, could never have begun on its own. This, as Hulme argues in his discussion of Shakespeare's *Tempest*, is Prospero's position with regard to Caliban: the former's authoritative account of his arrival on what he states to have been an "uninhabited" island effectively nullifies the latter's "claim to original sovereignty" over this island. And yet, as Hulme stresses, Prospero is nonetheless greatly troubled by his servant's claim—one to which Shakespeare himself alerts his audience, despite the historical veil that Prospero casts over it: "We are made aware that Caliban has his own story and that it does not begin where Prospero's begins. A space is opened, as it were, behind Prospero's narrative, a gap that allows us to see that Prospero's narrative is not simply history, not simply the way things were, but a particular *version*" (p. 124).

But what are we to make of this version and the alternative story,

story of alternatives, that issues forth from behind Prospero's totalizing
narrative? The answer to that question, of course, must depend upon
the degree to which we remain subject to, and subjects of, the power
embedded in this secondary discourse. Might not the gap that Shakespeare opens up clear the way for the real emergence of that Other beginning and an end to colonial subjection? Although this is probably
the conclusion Hulme would like us to draw, I believe that to confront
the power of colonialism and its second beginning is to begin to see not
the possibility of an Other beginning but its real impossibility for us.
If colonialism has already begun—if, indeed, in the form of a global
political power it is the beginning that has everywhere begun—then
the "claim to original sovereignty" can amount to nothing more than
an effect, a rhetorical effect, of the very cause that has supplanted it.
To situate oneself squarely within "the colonial age, the age of world
economy and global power in which we live,"[10] is to acknowledge the
purely rhetorical nature of all such claims; far from innocent, they are
themselves produced by the power whose beginning they at once contest and consolidate. However much we might desire it, the space that
Shakespeare opens up is entirely fictional; only by considering what is
behind us as such can we begin to think, not the end of colonialism,
but the ending that is colonialism, and with it the *unreality* of any exotic
solution to the problem of modernity. To then persevere from this position of weakness in voicing these (im)memorial claims is to take up
the (allegorical) burden of a language that troubles the power to which
it nonetheless remains subject.

The literary beginnings of the French naval officer Julien Viaud, better known as the *académicien* Pierre Loti (1850–1923), are indissociable
from both the transgressive dream of nineteenth-century exoticism
and a dawning awareness of the global power that at once produces
and thwarts this belated dream. As his biographer Lesley Blanch has
remarked, Loti "is generally dubbed an exotic writer. In his earlier
books, certainly. Yet the exoticism of the first three was never to be repeated. Travels in exotic lands continued to produce some of his finest
writing, but in a detached rather than romantic vein."[11] Loti's beginning intention as a writer is to salvage the Romantic figure of the individual by positing him in an exotic land beyond the boundaries of
modernity. But what his early work, quite despite itself, never fails to
come up against is the impossibility of his project, a point that I will be
arguing here twice: first, through a close reading of the opening para-

graphs of his literary debut, *Aziyadé* (1879); and, subsequently, through
a more macroscopic analysis in which I briefly map the decline of the
exotic family and the shifting fortunes of the word "colonialism" in his
initial triptych of books.[12] Loti's exotic story, as we will see, begins, and
can only begin, after its ending—in the wake of a colonial story that
has already begun (it). It is this singular imbrication of *histoires* that I
propose to account for in the remainder of this chapter.

AN UNFAMILIAR SPECTACLE: 'AZIYADÉ' AND THE INTERRUPTION OF HISTORY

Russia's annexation of Kokand was not the major diplomatic event
of 1876; Europe's attentions were directed mostly to the Balkans, where
the ever-vexing Eastern Question was taking another precipitous turn.
An insurrection in Bosnia-Herzegovina against the crumbling Ottoman Empire sets off a chain reaction of events that will lead Britain and
Russia to the brink of war. Revolt spreads to Bulgaria, where it is brutally crushed by bands of Turkish irregulars; these "Bulgarian Horrors"
provoke an almost unprecedented outcry among the British public.
War between Serbo-Montenegrin forces and the Turks brings Russia
into the fray; opposed to any development that may enhance the Czar's
ability to threaten British primacy in India, Disraeli is forced to intervene in favor of the Turks. Hostilities between the two powers are,
however, narrowly averted. An international congress meeting in Berlin in 1878 to decide the fate of the Ottoman Empire clearly establishes
"the close connection between the traditional Eastern Question and
the emerging colonial question."[13] Russia gains new influence in the
Balkans, Britain is compensated with Cyprus, and France is given a
free hand in Tunisia (which, by 1881, will become a French protecto-
rate). Six years later the second Berlin Congress (1884–85), devoted in
great part to the problem of partitioning Africa, consecrates imperialism as "the recognised *Zeitgeist* and an approved European policy."[14]

A month before the Turkish atrocities, another bloody incident occurs that further fuels the fires of this burgeoning crisis: the French and
German consuls in Salonica are murdered by a Muslim mob, an event
that leads to the rapid convergence of European gunboats on Salonica
and the Straits. Eager to placate the wrath of the Great Powers, Turkish
authorities promptly have the guilty parties executed. It is at this precise moment in history that Pierre Loti's novel *Aziyadé*—or, to be more
precise, the journal of an English naval officer by the name of *Loti*—

begins.* Here, in its entirety, in the original French, is the novel's first
chapter, or, if you will, the journal's first entry:

16 mai 1876
. . . Une belle journée de mai, un beau soleil, un ciel pur . . . Quand les
canots étrangers arrivèrent, les bourreaux, sur les quais, mettaient la dernière
main à leur oeuvre: six pendus exécutaient en présence de la foule l'horrible
contorsion finale . . . Les fenêtres, les toits étaient encombrés de spectateurs;
sur un balcon voisin, les autorités turques souriaient à ce spectacle familier.
  Le gouvernement du sultan avait fait peu de frais pour l'appareil du supplice; les potences étaient si basses que les pieds nus des condamnés tou-
chaient la terre. Leurs ongles crispées grinçaient sur le sable.

(p. 289; ellipses in original)

(. . . A beautiful day in May, a beautiful sun, a clear sky . . . When the foreign boats arrived, the executioners, dockside, were putting the final touches
on their work: six hanged men were performing their horrible final contortion
in the presence of the crowd . . . The windows, the rooftops, were thick with
spectators; on a neighboring balcony, the Turkish authorities were smiling at
this familiar spectacle.
  The sultan's government had gone to little expense for the torture apparatus; the gallows were so low that the bare feet of the condemned men were
touching the ground. Their contracted nails were grinding on the sand.)

Aziyadé thus opens out onto the "familiar spectacle" of a public execution—familiar, we might add, not only to the Turkish authorities but
also to nineteenth-century European readers, for whom such scenes of
torture (and here one thinks, for instance, of *Michel Strogoff*) served to
identify the barbaric Other in all its exotic difference from the realm of
civilization.

  Michel Foucault has argued in *Discipline and Punish* that the rapid
disappearance of the scene of torture from Western society is one of
the more flamboyant signs of our modernity. The decades immediately
preceding and succeeding the turn of the nineteenth century see the
rapid effacement of the punitive spectacle from juridical and public life
and its replacement by a new post-Enlightenment technology of discipline and punishment whose purported aim is not torturing the body
but reforming the soul of the criminal. The continued presence of this
spectacle—and of the figure of the sovereign around whom, as Foucault also argues, pre-Enlightenment legal practice revolved (pp. 53–

*For the sake of both convenience and theoretical clarity, I distinguish throughout
between the author Pierre Loti and the Romantic hero of his first novels, *Loti*. The same
distinction will be made in the following chapter between Victor Segalen and *Segalen*,
the narrator of *René Leys*.

54)—can henceforth betoken only the absence of civilization. In its individualistic polemic with an increasingly bureaucratic and impersonal society, the exoticist project is attracted to this absence; the scene of torture exemplifies an Other way of life that has yet to be brought under the panoptic gaze of modernity. The superbly exotic scene with which *Aziyadé* begins, however, will soon be situated in the harsh light of global politics: as we find out a few pages on, it was the European powers who forced this "familiar spectacle" upon the Turks. Moreover, this hegemonic relation between the exotic Other and the colonial Same has already been inscribed in the temporal construction of the book's initial chapter.[15]

The first two sentences put into play three different but related temporal situations, which together delineate the historical dilemma of Loti's early novels.

Time$_1$ Une belle journée de mai, un beau soleil, un ciel pur . . .

Time$_2$ Quand les canots étrangers *arrivèrent*

Time$_3$ Les bourreaux, sur les quais, *mettaient* la dernière main à leur oeuvre: six pendus *exécutaient* en présence de la foule l'horrible contorsion finale . . .

For now, let us bracket out the first situation, merely pausing to note that it is unmarked by any verb and exclusively built around aesthetic-descriptive categories ("belle," "beau," "pur"). The second and third, by contrast, are clearly located in time and syntactically connected to each other. On the one hand, we have a single event, enacted by the "canots étrangers" and recorded in the past historic (aorist) tense, or what Emile Benveniste once referred to as "the tense of the event outside the person of a narrator";[16] on the other hand, an ongoing scene of torture registered in the imperfect.

The relation between time$_2$ and time$_3$ is one of both grammatical and political subordination. The spectacle of the Other becomes visible to the reader only after the arrival of the foreign (European) boats; this inaugural event preempts the exoticist project, which would give precedence to the Other and establish its autonomy from the realm of the Same. The intrusion of these unfamiliar spectators de-familiarizes the spectacle of exoticism, providing it with a new, colonial direction ("arrivèrent," significantly, is the only verb of motion in this opening section). The primacy here of the *passé simple* confirms a view of the Turks that Gladstone, using a powerful ocular metaphor, would put forward at the time of the crisis: "The conduct of the race has gradually been brought more under the eye of an Europe, which it has lost its power to resist or to defy."[17] Colonial discourse disempowers the "familiar spectacle" of a despotic tradition, drawing it within the scope of an ostensibly more "enlightened" vision.

The brief chapter following this incipit reinforces the grammatical subordination of the Other scene to the forward motion of the "canots étrangers." The actors in this ongoing spectacle had initially retained an "imperfect" identity that distinguished them from the forces to which they were nonetheless subordinated. However, this identity itself dissolves, as both torturers and tortured are now brought, indifferently, into the sphere of the past historic tense:

L'exécution *terminée*, les soldats *se retirèrent* et les morts *restèrent* jusqu'à la tombée du jour *exposés* aux yeux du peuple. Les six cadavres, debout sur leurs pieds, *firent*, jusqu'au soir, la hideuse grimace de la mort au beau soleil de Turquie, au milieu de promeneurs indifférents et de groupes silencieux de jeunes femmes.   (my italics)

(The execution at an end, the soldiers withdrew and the dead men remained exposed to the public eye until the close of the day. Standing right on their feet, the six corpses looked up until evening, with the hideous grimace of death, at the beautiful sun of Turkey, in the midst of indifferent strollers and silent groups of young women.)

In this second chapter, the chief protagonists in the scene of torture have been entirely converted to the time of history ("se retirèrent, "restèrent") or, alternatively, reduced to the definitive stasis of past participles ("terminée," "exposés"). The indigenous, habitual time of the Other is no longer present as anything more than a memory of its initial, and already "imperfect," appearance in the opening chapter; the past historic tense seems to have taken full control of the narrative.

However, the temporal dimension of *Aziyadé*'s beginning moment is not completely taken up by these two hierarchically disposed times. Here we must begin to interrogate what I earlier identified as the work's first temporal situation (time$_1$), thereby also opening up the question of the subject through whose eyes we are witnessing this historic scene (and through whose memory that Other, dissolving imperial spectacle is being filtered). Although the writer has yet to identify himself—has yet, as it were, to differentiate his own *discours* from the colonial/exotic *histoire* that he is recording[18]—he has in fact already been identified in the heading to the first chapter: "Journal de Loti" (and also, to be sure, in the work's preface—a point to which I will return). The opening sentence of *Aziyadé* is clearly a part of this journal,

La population de Salonique conservait encore envers nous une attitude contrainte et hostile; aussi l'autorité nous obligeait-elle à traîner par les rues un sabre et tout un appareil de guerre. De loin en loin, quelques personnages à turban passaient en longeant les murs, et aucune tête de femme ne se montrait derrière les grillages discrets des *haremlikes*; on eût dit une ville morte.

(The population of Salonica still maintained a constrained and hostile attitude toward us; so those in authority required us to drag our swords and a whole apparatus of war through the streets. Here and there a few figures with turbans would pass by, keeping close to the walls, and no woman's head showed itself from behind the unobtrusive latticework of the *haremliks*; one would have thought it a dead city.)

Structuring this passage is a manichean distinction between *nous* and the local population; the "appareil de guerre" assigned to "us" by the *autorité* is in a clear relation of dominance to the "appareil de supplice" constructed by the *autorités turques* for the reparatory executions. As part of the *nous*, the subject is closed off from the native population; the absence of any woman's head marks the impossibility for him of coming into contact with the exotic world and thereby distancing himself from the colonial one of which he is a part. The space of the Other is moribund, covered by a funereal veil that Pierre Loti, in his later works, will offer no hope of lifting.

   In his first novel, however, which adheres—though it can do so only partially—to the transgressive project of nineteenth-century exoticism, a head full of potential significance will make its appearance on this deathlike stage: "I imagined myself to be so completely alone that I felt strangely touched [*j'éprouvai une étrange impression*] upon glimpsing close by me, behind thick bars of iron, the top part of a human head, a pair of large green eyes fixed upon mine." Only once he is alone, or at least believes himself to be alone, can the subject receive the right sort of "impression"—one that will, by virtue of its exotic unfamiliarity, open up the possibility of an alternative to the colonial story in which he has been (con)scripted. This initial encounter with Aziyadé's captivating eyes will, indeed, allow for a temporary reprieve from his political identity. Returning to the quai that day, *Loti* finds he has missed the *canots* that were to have taken the soldiers back to their corvette. Thus stranded, he can begin to establish his first practical links with the "outside" world. That the colonial boat cannot, ultimately, be missed is what the rest of *Aziyadé*, though, repeatedly confirms. *Loti* will never be truly alone: doubled, and, by extension, duplicitous—a colonial subject wearing an exotic mask, to recall Roberta Maccagnani's nice phrase—his every "impression" of the Other will be falsified, his every contact with it no more than a project(ion) that has, from the beginning, been canceled out of his sight.

Nineteenth-century exoticism is grounded in a binary opposition between the world of the Same and that of the Other, between modernity and what is not (yet) modern. Its project is to begin again, not here but there; to go from the inside to what is outside, from one sort of (present) time to another. Now, whether the realm of the exotic was ever free from the sort of impurity that modernity (and, by extension, colonialism) represents for the exoticist imagination is, of course, a moot point. What needs to be emphasized here, rather, is that for most of the nineteenth century the sort of uncontaminated cultural wholes figured in Enlightenment thought and then adapted by the Romantic generation for quite different, individualistic ends were able to fulfill their rhetorical task of persuading both others and oneself that alternatives to modernity still existed. As David Simpson remarks, in an argument that applies even more strikingly to non-European locales, Wordsworth's glorified rural societies "function discursively, however true to life they may or may not have been, *as* alternatives, and however fast he saw them to be disappearing."[20] By the end of the century, however, this oppositional discursive strategy no longer functions in an uncomplicated manner: for a significant number of fin de siècle writers, the global presence of colonialism has put an end to the possibility of any such exotic alternatives.

The ternary situation at the beginning of *Aziyadé* marks a moment of transition away from exoticist dualism to the homogeneity of a New Imperialist world. The binary opposition of Same and Other has been irreparably weakened: no longer functioning as a real alternative, the realm of the exotic has been at once pushed back into an irrecuperable past and brought under the dominion of an all too possible and overbearing colonial present. Between these two poles (between which there is no longer any real choice) is the place of the subject and the journal he writes, tending toward the one world that he cannot escape and the Other that he can never(more) inhabit. In its own right, as we have seen, the writing (or *écriture*) of the journal appears to offer the possibility of remaining outside, or to the side, of this political doublebind; for Barthes, the journal-"text" belongs "to no determination, to no teleology" (p. 121). But if the beginning of *Aziyadé* tells us anything, it is (however unintentionally) that writing is never in its own right: the journal and its inter-mediate space is constituted by the very state of tension that it would seem to elude.

In a sense, of course, nothing could be simpler than resolving this state of tension: either by granting the exotic Other a renewed autonomy and denying the hegemony of the colonial Same; or, more drastically yet, by entirely doing away with this oppositional—and, after all, merely ideological—way of thinking. But perhaps, and it is in anticipation of this "perhaps" that I have been writing, our own fin de siècle requires something more, or less, of us than such simple resolutions. I suggest, in closing here, that what opens up in the intolerable closure of the incipit of *Aziyadé* is the possibility of a politics that takes this state of tension as its beginning, rather than its end: a politics of the impossible, duplicitously (re)figuring alternatives that have, from the beginning, been effaced by the particular version of history to which we are subject. I have asked, What is it to begin in the wake of a beginning that has ruled out all Other beginnings? I would now like to (prepare to) answer: it is to know that we have come to the end of the beginning and, with a sense of this ending, to begin if not anew then again. It is to begin to recall what is no more, and no less, than an exotic memory—no longer present but absent, no longer real but unreal: an original sovereignty, an origin that is at once behind and before us, at once necessary and impossible. It is to begin to think this beginning and its end together.

Hors d'oeuvre: Reading Colonialism in Loti's Early Novels

Loti, we are told in the opening lines of *Le mariage de Loti*, "was baptised [*fut baptisé*] 25 January 1872, at the age of twenty-two years and eleven days," in the gardens of the late queen of Tahiti (p. 59). After all that has been said about the significance of the aorist tense in *Aziyadé*, the essentially funereal nature of this exotic christening may be surmised. That *Loti's* new identity does not coincide with an authentic rebirth but points instead to some rather less categorical beginning is borne out at the level of plot by the fact that *Loti's* old self, Harry Grant, officer in the English navy, has by no means disappeared from sight with the emergence of this second self; his name is conserved "in both the public records and the muster rolls [*rôles*] of the Royal Navy." *Loti's* new identification with the realm of the exotic ultimately amounts to nothing more than the adoption of a theatrical role. The christening is, in fact, only a *scène* that has been enacted within the limits of the world whose very limits it apparently marks—although an awareness of this theatrical condition is precisely what *Loti* must avoid if he is ever to believe in (the fiction of) his exotic identity.

This intra-diegetic split between Harry Grant and *Loti* stands as a *mise en abyme* of that real-life one between the colonial subject Julien Viaud, lieutenant in the French navy, and the exotic subject who authored, in the name of *Loti*, *Aziyadé* and the *Mariage*. It is essential to remember that these two works were first published anonymously. Their anonymity establishes a tenuous distance between two otherwise incompatible subjects, Viaud and *Loti*: at the same time that it provides a necessary bridge between the colonial reality of the one and the exotic fiction of the other, it also fails to reveal, to reveal by naming, the latter's dependency upon the former. Only for as long as the authorship of these books has not been ascribed to the military officer Viaud can the Romantic persona *Loti* be figured as real. In his third novel, *Le roman d'un spahi*, Viaud takes as his own the name of *Loti*, or rather that of Pierre Loti. With this *pseudonymity* (Viaud equals Loti) the distance between his two selves disappears, but so, too, does the possibility of a genuine exoticism, for there can no longer be any doubt which side of the geopolitical fence the author inhabits. Once the mask of anonymity has been dropped, *Loti* and the *récit sauvage* of which he was (to have been) the hero vanish from sight; the exotic dream, which would seem to have barely begun with *Aziyadé* and the *Mariage*, comes to its abrupt and colonial end with *Le roman d'un spahi*. The name *Loti* will survive only as a memory-trace in the author's, Viaud's, chosen nom de plume. It is the precipitate fall of this name from exotic grace into the public domain that I will be charting in the following account of his initial triptych of books.[21]

Aziyadé is, of course, primarily a love story; however, the hero's daring romance with the harem girl Aziyadé takes place—and, given the ultimately political nature of the exoticist project, this is certainly not a matter of chance—against the potentially spectacular historical backdrop of dynasties in transition and empires at war. *Loti*'s arrival in Istanbul, which prepares the way for a new and more serious phase in his relationship with Aziyadé after their early days in Salonica ("it's an entirely fresh start, a new way of life, in a new country, with new faces, and for who knows how long"; p. 317), coincides with a possible renovation of Turkish imperial rule: the deposition of the mentally unstable sultan Murad V and the coronation of his successor, Abdul-Hamid II, in whom the exotic subject will initially place a slim hope for the continued autonomy of the locale in which he finds himself. "It could be," *Loti* remarks, "that his accession will open a new era for Islam and provide Turkey with a little glory yet and one last gleam of brilliance"

(p. 334). If *Loti*'s own project of fashioning himself as an individual is ever to be realized, it is precisely this "new/old" era that will have to be inaugurated—one that would confirm the Ottoman Empire's glorious past and bypass, or at least defer, the undistinguished presence of modernity, "the egalitarian wind, reeking of coal smoke, that blows out of the West" (p. 445).

Notwithstanding both the frequent deprecations against this new sultan sprinkled throughout the rest of *Aziyadé*, many of them having to do with his proclamation of a resolutely modern constitution, and *Loti*'s at times intensely ironic, but necessarily fleeting, awareness that his own efforts at escaping the world of his beginnings may well be no more than an extended bit of playacting, *Aziyadé* represents Pierre Loti's most concerted effort at figuring the reality of a world in which colonialism has yet to begin—a world beyond the end of the colonial line. He achieves this in large part by downplaying the European presence, military or otherwise, in Turkey. The few usages of the word *colonie*, for instance, describe a "colonial" situation that is strictly curtailed and, furthermore, potentially transient. When *Loti* speaks of the "colonie de Péra" (p. 393), he is referring not to a political territory but only to those Europeans who live in the modernized (European) part of Istanbul, far from the authentically Muslim (Asian) quarter in which, under the pseudonym Arif, he is living out his affair with Aziyadé and "nothing from the West has yet arrived" (p. 381). By dividing the Turkish metropolis into two halves—a colonial part that is no more than a repetition of the European city, and an exotic one that is as yet unsullied by the influence of modernity—he apparently conserves a space in which the hero can still operate free from "the customs of the West."*

*The cosmopolitan, as opposed to pastoral, nature of the exotic locale in *Aziyadé* is worth emphasizing. Istanbul is, we are told, "the true desert of men, of which Paris was once the classic example, an assemblage of several large towns where everyone lives as he pleases and without being monitored" (p. 362). His exotic city thus harkens back to a more authentic, if supplanted, version of the European metropolis. It is this same positive vision that we find in a writer like Montesquieu, for whom, as David Simpson reminds us in his *Fetishism and Imagination*, the city encouraged "a libertarian environment dissolving social ranks and increasing the urge for toleration and self-expression" (p. 46). For early critics of modernity like Rousseau and Wordsworth, by contrast, the city is a "place of alienation and repression" that is best avoided. Although their ensuing valorization of "rustic" country life influences most nineteenth-century visions of the exotic, in his first novel Loti will invoke a pre-colonial, ancien régime metropolis that instead takes its genealogical bearings from Montesquieu. (That the very idea of a native quarter is, in fact, an effect of colonialism rather than a real alternative to it is what Timothy Mitchell shows in his analysis of nineteenth-century Cairo in *Colonising Egypt*; pp. 161–71.)

The one other mention of the world *colonie*, following almost immediately upon the first, expands logically on the limited nature of the European presence in Turkey: if it can be thus limited, then it is also quite possibly not permanent. Returning to the native quarter from Pera, *Loti* crosses paths with the coupé of the Russian ambassador Ignatiev, who is on his way back from a session of the international conference (December 1876–January 1877) in which the European powers were attempting to settle the issues raised by the "Bulgarian Horrors" and the ongoing war with Serbia. The Turkish government has been presented with a joint European demand for severe restrictions on its sovereignty in the predominantly Christian territories of Bosnia and Bulgaria; these proposals, invoking as they did foreign supervision, were clearly, as one contemporary onlooker put it, "incompatible with the claim of independence."[22] A refusal on the part of the Turks to comply with these measures, *Loti* hypothesizes, could only lead to a catastrophic war between the Porte and Alexander's Russia: "All the ambassadors would clear off at the same time, with a cry of 'Run for your life!' to the European colony. One would then see terrible things, great confusion, and a lot of blood" (p. 393). The enactment of this hypothetical scenario in which Turkish sovereignty (re)asserts itself will necessarily result in the dissolution of that "colonie d'Europe" of which *Loti* is an unwilling member and against which he is attempting to define himself. But if the Russo-Turkish war that ensues from the Porte's refusal of European demands puts an end to this colonialism, it would also appear to clear the way for an even more drastic form of that same power: what must follow upon the Turks' seemingly inevitable defeat is the definitive dismemberment of the Ottoman Empire and the establishment of the sort of unlimited, permanent colonial presence that was, indeed, eventually agreed upon by the Allies in their secret First World War treaties (and averted only through the collapse of the Russian Empire).

The possibility of a resolution to the duplicitous situation (unwilling colonial subject, would-be exotic subject) that *Loti* at once finds himself in and yet cannot fully acknowledge—for to do so would be to undermine, once and for all, his transgressive project—depends upon the prolongation of this state of "limited colonialism." Under these circumstances, if the crossing from one world to the other is constantly interrupted and ironized, it nonetheless still appears as a potentially feasible project. By contrast, the dramatic hypothesis of decolonization that *Loti* envisions, while clearing the way for the categorical transfer of allegiances that alone can make of him a truly exotic subject, would not open out onto an inhabitable future since this renewal of Turkish sovereignty could lead only to a catastrophic defeat at the hands of the Russians. Definitively freed of his colonial blinders, the exotic subject will have to confront a vision not of (a new) life but of death and ending.

The no-win situation that would emerge once the exotic wheat is finally separated from the colonial chaff is nicely captured in the double ending of *Aziyadé*: when the holy war does break out, *Loti* first leaves Turkey along with the rest of the "limited colony" and then returns to fight, and die, on the side of the Turks. *Loti* departs, returning to England (just as Viaud would leave for Paris): colonialism vacates the scene of exoticism. Unlike Viaud, however, *Loti* will return to Istanbul in the novel's entirely imaginary coda, thus completely sundering himself from his erstwhile colonial identity. For the first, and only, time he has acted in a *non*-incidental manner (to use Barthes's term); for the first, and only, time the *journal de Loti* will not fall short of the heroic story that it invokes. Yet this gesture of exotic *engagement* comes too late—as far as both his own love story and history are concerned. *Loti* goes back, but only to discover in Istanbul a heightened version of the "ville morte" that he had encountered in and from the beginning: "I crossed over this pile of ruins and ashes that had once been affluent Phanar; it was nothing more now than one great scene of destruction, a long series of funereal streets, thick with charred and blackened debris" (p. 517). Istanbul is in ruins, and Aziyadé, the exotic heroine, dead and departed. Nothing remains for him but to hark despondently to "the final mort of Islam and the East" (p. 521).

Loti will thus experience the exotic locale non-duplicitously only at the moment of its complete disappearance; his emergence as a heroic individual, fully distinct from the colonial *nous*, can be achieved in no other way. We should not, however, let ourselves be taken in entirely by this desperate affirmation of the Romantic individual and a doomed alternative culture. The ruins of Istanbul that he conjures up here serve a definite ideological purpose: this vision of the Other's apocalyptic destruction is but another, though perhaps the last, resort of the exoticist project, which here takes the drastic step of trying to prove the reality of its object precisely by annihilating it.

Whether one finds this final episode successful in achieving its end(s), however, this dramatic ending depends upon an abusive use of history—not because it leaves unfigured the "full colonialism" that would have resulted from this holy war, but because such a war was never, contrary to what we are led to believe, fought to the death. Viaud himself left Turkey in 1877, but the European *colonie* remained; indeed, "limited colonialism" would be a permanent feature of Turkish politics for the next forty years. Rather than allow the Turks to commit political suicide, the British defended the sultan, the chief advantage of whose survival "was simply that it allowed Britain to construct an unofficial empire, still apparently under Turkish rule, and to keep out other powers, where her strategic interests were most closely involved."[23] The Ottoman Empire lingers on; its ruins will henceforth signal not a recently destroyed glory but an all too present attachment to the modern world of colonial power. Nor does the exotic subject die the sort of heroic death that would confirm, if only on the point of its ending, his potential as an individual; he will survive himself, entering into a new relationship with history—one in which the transgressive dreams of *Aziyadé* have turned into the cornerstones of memory.

Loti's second novel, *Le mariage de Loti*, deals with a period in his career earlier than the events depicted in *Aziyadé*, as if the political tensions revealed in the first might be eased by a return to less immediate circumstances. In recounting his experiences in the Tahiti of the early 1870's, Loti at once registers an advance in the progress of colonialism and endeavors to secure an even more radical distance from it. Tahiti, unlike Turkey, is the scene of a "full colonialism" that has dissolved the island's indigenous way of life; as he bitterly laments, "civilization has made too many inroads here . . . , our ridiculous colonial civilization, all our conventions, all our habits, all our vices, and the savage poetry is passing away, with the customs and the traditions of the past" ("la civilisation y est trop venue . . . , notre sotte civilisation coloniale, toutes nos conventions, toutes nos habitudes, tous nos vices, et la sauvage poésie s'en va, avec les coutumes et les traditions du passé"; pp. 63–64). More or less voided by its immersion in this "ridiculous colonial civilization," Tahitian culture has for this reason ceased to offer the exotic subject what previous wayfarers, such as his older brother, had apparently been able to grasp: "that exotic life, calm and filled with sunshine, Tahitian life as it had once been lived by my brother Rouéri" (p. 147).

In one of the few critical discussions of the *Mariage*, Alec Hargreaves has identified two contradictory stories at work in the novel: one in which European colonialism plays the role of villain, and another in which traditional Tahitian culture is blamed for not fulfilling Loti's dream-image of it.[24] This contradiction is undoubtedly present in the *Mariage*, and we would do well to pursue its significance a little further. The contradiction stems, I would argue, from *Loti*'s duplicitous status as both an exotic and a colonial subject. As an exotic subject in search of the Other, he cannot fail to be anti-colonialist; as an exotic subject who finds himself in a situation of "full colonialism," however, he is inevitably disappointed by the indigenous culture since it can no longer furnish the geopolitical alternative that his ideological project requires and that the *Loti* of *Aziyadé* could still envisage because of the apparently limited nature of colonialism in Turkey. The only standpoint from which *Loti* can possibly judge Tahitian culture is that of the ridiculous civilization which, via colonialism, has unfortunately displaced what he would have liked to valorize.

The sovereign figure, whose singular person should (according to the discursive logic of nineteenth-century exoticism) stand for the whole of the exotic world that he rules over and with whom the exotic subject is to identify himself, crops up in the *Mariage* but in an even less impressive incarnation than that of *Aziyadé*'s constitutional sultan. Tamatoa, son of the old queen Pomare, who on the very first page is significantly introduced as "the late queen Pomare," is hopelessly demented, although physically splendid. His insanity, clearly, symbolizes his own culture's lack of a political future: "Of prodigious height and herculean strength," he is nonetheless incapable of leading his people. The night *Loti* spends sleeping in the same room as the temporarily sedated Tamatoa will indeed provide him with an opportunity—a necessary one, as far as the exoticist project is concerned—for identifying himself with the native ruler; however, given the king's mental condition, this direct encounter with the sovereign figure of the Other will be anything but satisfactory (pp. 104–8). The true ruler of Tahiti is, in fact, the aging queen Pomare; she alone remains in touch with the cultural tradition of the old Tahiti: "Only the queen Pomare, out of respect for the traditions of her country, had learned the names of the ancient deities and conserved the strange legends of olden times in her memory" (p. 118). As a woman, however, and a defunct one at that, she can only partially fill the role of imperial figure that is such an essential part of the (predominantly masculist) exotic literary tradition. Not insignificantly, perhaps, a few pages after this respectful nod to the queen's erudition, *Loti* will treat his reader, for no obvious reason, to a brief pseudo-anthropological disquisition on her excretory habits (pp. 120–21)!

The "herculean" aspect of the king's *body*, however, is one, if perhaps the only, positive attribute that still does attach to the sovereign figure—and here we come to Loti's more radical attempt at keeping the world of colonialism at bay. Whereas the king's insanity is a clear trope for political impotence and a sign of cultural decadence, his still vigorous body remains strangely attractive, a potential source of difference upon which the exotic subject can fix his gaze—pointing as it does away from a colonizing-colonized culture and toward all that is not culture: that is to say, sheer nature. If Tahitian culture has, from the beginning, been brought within the fold of a civilization that denies it, as a purely natural phenomenon the island still seems to offer the very model of an exotic locale. It is a place where "the hours, the days, the months, fly past . . . differently from elsewhere," and where "time elapses without leaving traces, in the monotony of an eternal summer" (p. 101).

Colonialism is still, in this sense, a limited phenomenon, even though it now holds sway over the entirety of native culture. The further one gets from the capital, the more likely one is to come into contact with this inviolate nature since, despite their already devastating effect on the Tahitian way of life, the *colons européens* are still "very rare, and almost entirely confined to the town of Papeete" (p. 150). Far from Papeete, "yonder where civilization has not arrived," the one remaining charm of the island emerges in all its glory. "Listen," we are urged, "to the great calm of this nature, the monotonous and eternal murmur of the breakers against the coral reefs; look at these magnificent surroundings, these knolls of basalt, these forests suspended over dark mountains, and all this, lost in the midst of that majestic and boundless solitude: the Pacific" (p. 84). That this sublime landscape is also an uninhabited one is hardly a matter of chance: everything human has already been brought within the closed circuit of a lamentable civilization and must therefore go unsaid. The exotic remains as nature, and yet in and of itself this nature lacks any significance (that is, any narrative potential) since everybody, including the exotic subject himself, appears to have been excluded from it. Some twenty years later, another traveler in the South Seas, Victor Segalen, would point to the same dilemma: "Nature has doubtless remained intact," he admits, "but civilization has been infinitely disastrous for this handsome Maori race."[25] Whereas for Segalen such "disaster" means an abrupt end to his exotic dreams, *Loti* will attempt to resolve the dilemma by forging an erotic link with this still intact nature, in the person—or, to be more exact, the body—of the native girl Rarahu.

Loti desires this young Polynesian girl inasmuch as, and only inasmuch as, she is a synecdochal sign of that Tahitian nature which has yet to be affected by the power of colonialism. To the extent that she can be kept separate from the realm of culture, both her own and *Loti's*, she will continue to incarnate the exotic for him—although, given the equivalency of culture with everything human, her body will necessarily appear to him in a benignly *in*human form: "Rarahu had eyes of russet black, full of exotic languor, with a coaxing gentleness, like that of young cats when one strokes them" (p. 64). Her savage (and desirable) nature becomes even more apparent whenever she and *Loti* leave Papeete and its proto-urban environment. Visiting an isolated district of the island with her, he comes to the conclusion that "in this milieu which was properly hers, Rarahu was more herself, more *natural* and more charming" (p. 154; my italics). In the midst of nature's majestic solitude, he can still imagine keeping her "as I loved her, singular and savage, with all there was in her of freshness and ignorance."

This attempt at drawing a line between the "natural" and the "cultural" is a hopeless—not to say degrading—way of salvaging the exotic since, in denying Rarahu access to culture, it denies her very humanity. Rarahu is human and can thus never fully stand for the as yet unadulterated nature that *Loti* would pit against the corrosive (hi)story of colonialism. In telling his own story, *Loti* must continually overlook this irrefutable acculturation, fetishistically fixating upon a body that cannot fully embody what it ought to. His effort at exotic storytelling will never be more than partially successful; eventually, his story comes to its inevitable end, an ending identical to, if somewhat less dramatic than, that of *Aziyadé*. The only definitive way of affirming Rarahu's natural body is to have it die a civilized death: in the final corruption and demise of Rarahu, we can read, or at least are meant to read, the purity and life that had once, apparently, been her nature.

That Rarahu's body was never as it "once" was is what a detailed reading of the *Mariage* would repeatedly show. One especially clear instance of the novel's failure to ground its own exotic suppositions, when juxtaposed to the passage cited above ("Rarahu se retrouvait plus elle-même, plus naturelle et plus charmante"), is an earlier episode that effectively undermines, or deconstructs, her "natural" self. Arriving at their special bathing place under the guava trees one day, *Loti* spies "a horrible thing . . . in this place that we looked upon as belonging to us alone: an old Chinaman [*vieux Chinois*], entirely naked, bathing his ugly yellow body [*vilain corps jaune*] in our limpid water"

(p. 96). This substitution of a degenerate(d) body in the place of Rarahu's own body (and that of the exotic subject) clearly signals the presence of culture—and, more specifically, the world of commodity fetishism—in the place of a pristine nature. This Chinese merchant, it
turns out, has been trying to interest Rarahu in some of his merchan-
dise in exchange for sexual favors. Although *Loti* is adamant that "she
had given nothing in exchange for these singular presents" (p. 99), his
assurance is quite beside the point. Culture is, and has already been,
in the place of a nature that remains oblivious to its transactions: "The
cool, clear water plashed around him all the same—as *naturally* and
cheerfully [*avec autant de naturel et de gaîté*] as it could have done for us"
(p. 96; my italics). The "natural" essence that *Loti* later ascribes to Rarahu, appearing as it does in the aftermath of this re-placement of bodies,
can never again, if it ever could, be truly attached to her.

Rarahu's body and the "vilain corps jaune" of the "vieux Chinois"
are in a position of equivalency that *Loti* can only deny. To maintain
their difference, he must overlook this metonymical substitution of the
one for the Other, and persevere blindly in his affirmation of her "savage nature," just as he must pass over his own apparent interchange-
ability with this merchant, who stands for everything that he must dis-
associate himself from if his discursive project is to be realized. The
juxtaposition of these two episodes shows what *Loti* cannot fully admit
to: given this substitution, any further affirmation of Rarahu's "natural" essence is merely rhetoric. Far from being a person, she is, as he
himself says at one point (although without grasping the true irony of
his remark), no more than a figure of speech, "a touching and sorrow-
ful personification of the Polynesian race, which is dying out from contact with our civilization and our vices, and which will soon be no more
than a memory in the history of Oceania" (p. 194). Against all his exotic
intentions, the author of *Le mariage de Loti* keeps coming up against this
disconcerting insight: the Other of whom he dreams is but a memorial
figure of speech, one that can only come in the place of that which has
already been replaced. The dead end of ideology is this beginning of
rhetoric.

Loti's third work, *Le roman d'un spahi*, registers a shift away from the
desperate exoticism of the first novels and a partial coming to terms
with the presence of colonialism. The West Africa it depicts is a markedly colonized locale. The "most characteristic and worthwhile of the
works devoted to the colonial soldier at the time of the [New Imperi-

alist] expansion,"[26] the *Roman* no longer has as its primary concern the construction of a space that would be exotic to colonial society (be it an alternative culture or the alternative to culture that nature apparently offers) but, rather, the transition from an older to a new form of colonialism. The world of Saint-Louis—*la vieille colonie*, "town that already has a past, colony of days gone by that is dying" (p. 29)—is on the point of giving way to its New Imperialist successor, in which there will be absolutely no room for the exotic subject to maneuver, either in the direction of a real identification with a native ruler or a satisfactory erotic link with an indigenous female.

The novel's hero, the spahi Jean Peyral, is situated at an (almost) complete remove from the sovereign figure of the Other. Peyral is entirely engaged by the strict directionality/destinality that orders the colonial world (time$_2$); whereas *Loti*'s sojourns in Turkey and Tahiti were characterized by their indefiniteness, Peyral's West African posting is for a definite five years (a fact central to the unfolding of the plot). By contrast, the black king Boubakar-Ségou, "a myth of sorts, whose strength lay in escaping, in always hiding himself in the depths of his murderous country, and in remaining untraceable [*introuvable*]" (p. 205), operates in an exotic realm that is increasingly difficult to pinpoint. It is only by virtue of his virtual absence from the world of the *Roman* that the "mythic" Boubakar-Ségou can be thought, unlike his predecessors Abdul-Hamid and Tamatoa, still to incarnate a political force that must yet be reckoned with. That this "mythic" strength cannot stand up to the reality of colonial conquest is what the ending of the novel makes abundantly clear: Boubakar-Ségou's death in a skirmish with Peyral's regiment marks the final disappearance of what had up to this point been *introuvable*—a territory hidden from the power of colonialism and a sovereign figure free of it. When both of these (re)appear in a fin de siècle work like Conrad's *Heart of Darkness*, they will be caught up in a web of allegory that takes as its point of departure the impossibility of this open clash between exotic and colonial worlds with which the *Roman* ends.

If Boubakar-Ségou, by virtue of his well-nigh "mythic" status, is certainly the most striking embodiment of the exotic sovereign in Loti's first three books, Peyral's black mistress, Fatou-Gaye, inhabiting the same colonial world in which he himself lives, significantly lacks the positive qualities that still seemed to attach to the earlier heroines. Like Aziyadé, she is, certainly, the embodiment of another culture, but hers appears to exist only in its subordination to the European conquerors.

She is a child of nature, yes, but this nature is, unlike Rarahu's, patently caught up in a circuit of exchange and prostitution. *Loti*'s fetishistic attempt at re-membering the indigenous female is more or less abandoned here, for Peyral can see in Fatou-Gaye only the disquieting marks of her status as a colonial subject. The aesthetic appeal of her hands, for instance, is only superficial: "beautifully black outside, [they] were pink on the inside"; the *décoloration intérieure* of these exotic appendages evokes for him "something dreadfully inhuman" ("quelque chose de pas humain qui était effrayant"; p. 102).

This disquieting play of colors, along with the simian likeness it conjures up for Peyral, is, of course, primarily an aspect of the Africanist (racialist—if not, in Loti's case, racist) myth that the *Roman* helped to create,[27] but the appearance of this sort of derogatory language must also be read in terms of the descending trajectory of Loti's exoticizing project. Because he can no longer avert his gaze from the historical context that enframes it, the unwilling colonial subject comes to deny the vision of beauty and alterity that Fatou-Gaye conjures up for him: to affirm the Other would, under these circumstances, be to affirm only its absence. Unable to commit himself to this absence, indeed, appalled by it, he resorts to the stereotypical language of colonialism—in his own defense.

What we are dealing with here, I think, is a repression of difference. Homi Bhabha, in one of the most sophisticated and recondite accounts of colonial discourse, has equated fetishism and stereotyping. Like the fetish, he argues, the stereotype is founded upon a denial; the obvious fact that not all people have the same skin/race/culture—in other words, that difference exists—is denied through recourse to a "limited form of otherness," "a fixed form of difference": namely, the stereotype.[28] The stereotype is "a form of multiple and contradictory belief in its recognition of difference and disavowal of it" and forms, says Bhabha, the primary point of "subjectification" for both colonizer and colonized. We might well argue, by contrast, that exoticizing, as opposed to colonialist, stereotypes take exactly the opposite tack, attempting to deny the presence of the Same by affirming that of the Other. In the same way that the one mode of stereotyping cannot, ultimately, contain difference, exoticist affirmations of difference are broken into by the very homogeneity they would deny. Once the "reality principle" of colonialism has made itself felt in this way to the exotic subject, he may well end up producing a negative reading of whatever traces of difference he does encounter, for they can now remind him only of what he has lost. He will deny them, through stereotyping, in a defensive measure meant to palliate his own dejection at finding himself trapped within a world in which these differences can, as it were, make no real (exotic) difference to him.

But if in the *Roman d'un spahi* both Loti's story and his language anticipate the possibility of a new colonial beginning (and in the second section of the following chapter I will discuss this anything but Romantic possibility in some detail), they nonetheless do so in a remorseful way that keeps referring this new beginning back to the definitive ending of exoticism. These two moments prove indissociable: if Peyral seems the first in a new breed of colonial heroes, he is also the last avatar of the exotic subject whose fate is now so clearly sealed. Peyral's deference to home and country is matched by a desire for the exotic that, in its own degraded way, will prove just as strong as *Loti*'s, even if neither he nor his author can ever (again) hope to extricate this desire from his new colonial identity. "He loved all this more than he thought," we are told. "He loved his Arab fez, his sword, his horse—his great and damned land, his desert" (p. 172). The fez, ornament of the Other that has become part of a colonial uniform; the vast and solitary desert, now brought within the fixed boundaries of the map-makers and the military strategists: simulacra of alterity, they still exercise a peculiar fascination on Peyral, a fascination strong enough in the end for him to choose Africa over France after his five years of service are up (and all hope of marrying his childhood sweetheart Jeanne gone).

Like everything having to do with Peyral, this decision is an essentially double one: a choice of (colonial) life and (exotic) death. On the one hand, in choosing Africa, he has only begun to build upon his own colonial beginnings: prolonging his life as a spahi, Peyral is the very figure of a colonialism that has come to stay. But then again, he has also chosen the unhappy ending, the lack of a future, that must await—and that already awaits—the exotic subject in this New Imperialist world of his choice: with no place left to go but onward, on toward the end of the beginning of his colonial story, Peyral will die in the same skirmish that draws the mythic sovereignty of Boubakar-Ségou to a close. Unlike the death of *Loti* in *Aziyadé*, however, this death confirms nothing if not the absence of that which the exotic subject has died for (an absence that the fin de siècle, if not Loti himself, will begin to interrogate). Peyral has fallen, and will always fall, to one side, the wrong side, of the line that separates the exotic world of his desire from the one world of his beginning and of his end.

Peyral's double condition mirrors, in its own way, the ambivalence that we saw to lie at the heart of the pseudonymous name of Pierre Loti, which at once obliterated the distance between colonial and exotic subject—between Viaud and *Loti*—while reducing the latter to nothing more than a memory-trace. In closing, a few more words need to be said about the fate of the *Roman*'s author, who in this final novel of his youth has for the most part projected himself onto, and distanced himself from, the third-person narrative of Jean Peyral (*il*). Although the would-be subject of *Loti*'s exotic stories (*je*) has virtually disappeared from this novel, traces of him remain and point toward two rather different, if related, resolutions to his own authorial dilemma. Occasionally, he will (re)surface as part of the *nous* that, as we saw in discussing *Aziyadé*, had to be left behind if the singular adventures of *Loti* were ever to be lived/told; however, the sort of direct adhesion to the world of colonialism and its language that is explicit in such narratorial phrases as "notre pays de France" (p. 58) will never gain much momentum in the reluctantly colonial prose of Pierre Loti. Within the world that he can no longer see his way out of, Loti will tend toward as ostensibly neutral a narratorial position as possible: this second resolution to his dilemma no longer aspires to close off the story of colonialism by opening up another one but to empty the former of all or most of its unpalatable significance.

What begins to emerge in the *Mariage* and the *Roman* as a compensation for the impossibility of disengaging the subject of exoticism from its colonial mire is what we might call a "travelogic" approach to the world—a fixation upon the merely picturesque and incidental that neglects, without contesting, its own attachment to the (hi)story of colonialism. The *Roman*'s opening pages provide a good example of this discursive strategy, whose subject is, properly speaking, no one in particular: "Descending the coast of Africa, once one [*on*] has passed the southern tip of Morocco, one proceeds alongside a desolate and interminable country for entire days and nights." The present tense of the travelogue and its impersonal subject, *on*, are depoliticized versions of the colonial present and its politically charged subject, *nous*. Grounded in this colonial present, the travelogue is nonetheless predominantly silent about its own subordination to and implication in the power that rules over it. Whereas the incidental quality of *Loti*'s journal once served to defer, and thereby preserve, the possibility of a truly significant action, the travelogues of Pierre Loti embrace a world of picturesque details and events that, in their insignificance, appear to have no meaning beyond themselves.

In speaking of truly insignificant actions that disregard the (colonial) meaning that appears beyond them, I am thinking especially of a remarkable scene from the *Mariage*—remarkable, that is, by virtue of its complete irrelevance to the story being told. To put this scene in its (lack of) context, we must first recall *Loti*'s description of the "vieux Chinois" as he bathes in that special place underneath the guava trees. After hurriedly getting dressed upon Rarahu's arrival, we are told, the merchant "let down his long graying queue with a real air of coquetry"—a transparently phallic gesture. Given *Loti*'s erotic attachment to the unsullied, "natural" Rarahu, this *queue* cannot help but pose a threat to the exotic subject and his ideological project. Outside the coherent time of the narrative, however, this erotic importance can no longer be so readily attached to the same object, as an apparently unrelated incident much later in the novel attests.

Two-thirds of the way through the *Mariage*, *Loti* temporarily has to leave Tahiti, embarking with his fellow sailors on "six months of expeditions and adventures that have nothing to do with this story" (p. 217). However, one incident from this "unattached" period of time is reported, in a brief chapter entitled "Hors-d'oeuvre chinois." This episode is in no way germane to *Loti*'s story; it is, we are told, "a ludicrous souvenir, which has nothing in common with what has come before, even less with what is going to follow, and which has no more than a simple chronological link with this story, a connection of dates [*un rapport de dates*]" (pp. 215–16). Attending a play in the Chinese quarter of San Francisco, *Loti* and a friend conceive of a "satanic idea" when faced with "a line of shaven heads, adorned with priceless queues that ended in silk plaits." The idea, "the rapid execution of which was favored by the arrangement of the seats, the darkness, the [audience's] mental concentration," is to "tie up the queues two by two, and clear off." Once outside the exotic locale in which his recuperative *oeuvre* still makes sense, the subject of writing is reduced to recording events that in their banal insignificance can be justified only by the simple "rapport de dates" that orders the chronology of an anything but exotic world.

In fact, these meaningless travelogic intrusions in the early novels of Pierre Loti do not so much mark a fall as a return—a return to the

situation of Julien Viaud, the French naval officer who from 1872 to
1877 bore witness to the world's changing political dimensions in a series of articles and drawings for such journals as *Illustration* and *Monde
illustré*. Only afterwards, after these initial words, would Viaud attempt to transform his impressions into novelistic art and to forget
thereby the colonial origin of his own work. The sort of writing that
begins to take hold in the wake of his increasingly futile attempts at
realizing his own project derives from—and, indeed, is often directly
traceable to (as with the opening pages of the *Roman*)—the unexcep-
tional travel pieces that he once signed with his own name, the name
of "Julien V . . . ." The exotic subject *Loti*, alternative self to the man
who authored these insignificant articles, has, then, always come after
what he apparently precedes. In speaking of the writer's fall from exotic grace into the world of colonialism, we have done no more than
speak of the enactment of what has already been enacted; we have
done no more than call to mind what was already no more than a memory of what never was. The "Pierre Loti" who himself comes after *Loti*
thus emerges from the anonymity of the first works as a memory of a
memory of what has never been, the fetish of a fetish, if you will. More
practically, this new name will mark Viaud's definitive resumption of
his interrupted career as the chronicler of a picturesque world without
alternatives, a world without *oeuvres*.

Chapter 4

THE PROTOCOL OF (RE)WRITING

VICTOR SEGALEN AND THE PROBLEM OF COLONIALISM

> You'll have to go to China if you want to see that!
> —Jules Verne, *Les Tribulations d'un Chinois en Chine*

● In the preceding chapters, I drew a picture of Verne's and Loti's attempt to realize an ideological project, exoticism, whose exhaustion is already implicit in their work. For Victor Segalen (1878–1919) and Joseph Conrad (1857–1924), the inadequacy of this project to the age of the New Imperialism becomes a matter for explicit concern. In their earliest works, both men find themselves in a situation more or less reminiscent of the writers we have already considered; they are attached in an as yet unproblematized, though not unproblematical, manner to the tradition of nineteenth-century exoticism—Conrad's organicist imagination tending to its imperialist strain, Segalen's aristocratic individualism to its exoticizing counterpart. Before long, however, they both confront the untenability of their initial position and, in a period of intense literary experimentation, develop a number of more equivocal responses to what they now see as a disenchanted world entirely given over to the "supremacy of material interests." It is the unfolding of one such response, which I label decadentist, that will be of primary concern in the following chapters. As I pointed out in the discussion of "Hommage à Gauguin," their later work starts to edge away from this equivocal stance, turning (back) toward an idyllic, but now completely de-historicized, vision of the exotic as it supposedly once was, in all its mythic integrity—an overtly nostalgic tendency that is, we might add, more developed in Conrad than in Segalen, who died at a relatively young age.

Of course, these differing perspectives on the exotic—early, middle, and late—are by no means so easily distinguishable: they overlap, develop unevenly, recur surprisingly—in a way that biographical periodization can hardly account for. As a heuristic construct, however, the idea of a middle period does allow us to identify a body of work guided by a common ethical perspective. We can say that this perspective takes off from the insight not only that, as Segalen put it in his last poem, *Thibet* (1917–18), "the summits fall, the mire rises, a flat universe is coming about" ("les cimes tombent; la fange monte; un plat univers s'accomplit"; p. 87)—a sensitivity to cultural homogenization that is present in Segalen's and Conrad's work from beginning to end—but also that this decline away from the realm of value has actually reached its terrible and monotonous conclusion as far as the traditional geopolitical terrain of exoticism goes. Rendering the exotic absent and their enterprise an entirely posthumous one, modernity has spread to every corner of the globe, covering over the ground of cultural difference that once seemed to offer the hope of an alternative to its intolerable closure: this is the radical vision of decline that underwrites the works of Segalen's and Conrad's middle period.

In a letter of 29 March 1912 to his friend Henry Manceron, Segalen makes it very clear what this posthumous vision entails. Speaking of the present situation in China, where he had first arrived almost three years before as a student interpreter in the French navy, Segalen laments the recent fall of the Empire and the ensuing proclamation of a republic. He goes on to point out the immensity of the task facing him if he is to write about, much less experience, the exotic world of imperial China and the difference it once embodied: "You see, the task is superhuman. To learn a vast country, and when one is beginning to perceive it, to perceive oneself that this country no longer exists, and that it has to be brought back to life. . . . And to begin with, all of so-called modern, new, republican China must be deliberately suppressed."[1] The problem facing Segalen as a writer is how best to approach this country that "no longer exists." How is he to effect the process of resuscitation/suppression that he speaks of here, assuming that a real revival of this now-dead world and a real elimination of its successor are not options. (This anti-modern dream of political restoration, we might add, may have gotten the better of writers like Pound and Céline, but neither Segalen nor Conrad went beyond the occasional flirtation with it. In my discussion of Conrad's *Nigger of the 'Narcissus,'* I will have more to say about the dynamics of this historicist faith in the possibility of a real return to and of the past.)

We can identify in Segalen's writing two central and interconnected approaches to the problem of effecting this resuscitation/suppression: a "modern" and a "pre-modern" (or decadentist) tendency, which I will contrast throughout this chapter. The approach of the "modern" Segalen is to salvage the purity of the exotic by thinking it anew, apart from its traditional geopolitical content, as *écriture.* The blank page, uncharted and unchartable except in language, reveals itself as the new repository of those values that the globe's "blank spaces of delightful mystery" once sheltered. The realm of sovereignty and alterity becomes synonymous with the work of art itself—the only inhabitation now worthy of the exotic subject, one from which all traces of the ineluctably fallen realm of the political have been suppressed. This salvational turn to language is, of course, one that twentieth-century literary criticism has tended to privilege: "Segalen has perfectly understood that the function of poetic language is to abolish the stigmata of History and duration, which bring dishonor upon the utilitarian language that we use in our daily exchanges."[2] Segalen's decision to inhabit "poetic language"—to transform the work of art into the impregnable "dwelling place [*demeure*] of his soul"[3]—is a strong, and typically "modern," attempt at overcoming (or sidestepping?) the crisis of modernity, and in taking it, not coincidentally, he marches toward his place in the contemporary critical canon.

But Segalen's conversion to the autonomy of "poetic language" is never complete: finding perhaps its fullest expression in his novels, a second approach to the problem of global modernity counterbalances this dramatic valorization of the purely literary. Rather than attempt to resolve the problem through a turn away from the contemporary world and its decadence, the "pre-modern" Segalen engages in an open, if profoundly ambivalent, confrontation with its irresoluble nature; the decline away from the realm of value, which his turn to "poetic language" was intended to overcome, is here treated as final. Only once he has thus situated himself firmly within the intolerable, uninhabitable confines of the New Imperialism does Segalen revive the question of the exotic—forcing us to consider its undeniable and irremediable absence from the present, opening up another (necessarily rhetorical) space in a world whose real closure he takes for granted, and thereby establishing an agon-izing tension between an insuperable modernity and an entirely unreal past. This, at least, is the Segalen whom I will attempt to portray in my discussion of *René Leys*. Before we turn to that novel, however, several preliminary steps are in order: first, to show the "modern" Segalen at work, as he theorizes a new and purely aesthetic vision of the exotic in his never completed *Essai sur l'exotisme*; and, second, to make a brief excursion into the fin de siècle China of Pierre Loti's *Les derniers jours de Pékin*, a book that provides the atmospheric lens through which I will read *René Leys*.

A Singular Recantation: The Colonial Artist and His 'Essai sur l'exotisme'

> In the poetic and artistic order, the revelator seldom has a
> precursor. Every flowering is spontaneous, individual. . . .
> The artist is nobody's concern but his own. He promises
> nothing to the coming centuries except his own works. He
> stands guarantor for himself alone. He dies childless.
> He has been *his king, his priest, and his God.*
> —Charles Baudelaire, *Curiosités esthétiques*

As Richard Terdiman has pointed out in his provocative *Discourse/ Counter-discourse: The Theory and Practice of Symbolic Resistance in Nineteenth-Century France*, the attempt to de-contextualize the artistic process, a goal of many aesthetically inclined writers, is nonetheless always "haunted by the negative determinants of its own constitution" (p. 289). Although speaking of Mallarmé here and his efforts at creating an avant-garde discourse, Terdiman could well have been thinking of Victor Segalen's obsessive attempt in the fragmentary *Essai sur l'exotisme* at laying the foundation for an "absolute exoticism" that would dispose, once and for all, of the threat that an impure colonialism posed the exoticist project. Segalen's effort, in this series of notes jotted down over the last ten years of his life, at completely rethinking the idea of the exotic along purely "artistic" lines ran into two major difficulties: first, he had to confront the possibility that his revisionary effort was itself no more than a highly refined symptom of the very colonialism that he wanted to rule out of his new and improved exoticism; second, and most important, although an intense critic of the tradition of nineteenth-century exoticism, Segalen was unwilling to relinquish his faith in the untimely figure of the individual who lies at its heart.

As he notes in an entry in the *Essai* (24 November 1909), "Exoticism can only be *singular*, individualistic. It does not admit plurality. One can conceive of five hundred men sharing one man's sense of goodness; one cannot conceive of a plural exoticism" (p. 46). For Segalen exoticism, restored to its purity ("la notion du différent; la perception du Divers"; p. 23), ought necessarily to "complement" the individual since, as he asserts in an outline of what was projected in December 1908 as the first chapter of the *Essai*, "only those who possess a strong Individuality can feel Difference" (p. 24). This allegiance to the impossible figure of the individual, I will argue, at once ensures the ultimate failure of the *Essai* to achieve its end(s) and determines the different approach adopted in *René Leys*.

Although the *Essai* was begun in 1908, just after the publication of Segalen's first novel, *Les Immémoriaux*, it germinated out of a note written four years earlier, which serves as the published *Essai*'s first entry. The initial paragraph of this note is an excellent gauge of the distance Segalen had taken from the exotic tradition by 1908 when the trajectory of his "mature" thinking on the matter of exoticism began: "To write a book on Exoticism. Bernardin de Saint-Pierre—Chateaubriand—Marco Polo the initiator—Loti" (p. 13). Here, to write about exoticism is to take into consideration what was conventionally referred to as such. Although Segalen already seems open to the possibility of expanding exoticism's referential possibilities (he speaks, for instance, of *"l'Exotisme sexuel"*—eventually, any sensation of difference would, if judged "authentic," be classed as exotic), the traditional geopolitical content of exoticism is still presented as an epicenter of the projected book: "Exoticism is given to the 'tropical.' Coconut trees and torrid climes." By 1908, though, Segalen will have sacrificed this point of view—at the expense of a temporary overlap between his own revisionist views and those held by the theoreticians of an emerging *littérature coloniale*.[4]

A long note dated 11 December 1908 is typical of Segalen's thinking at this time. It has become clear to him that "l'Exotisme" is something not to be resumed (his project of four years ago) but to be purged of its accreted scoriae. To get at its "initial value" ("valeur première") and thereby recover "all of the primacy of that value" ("toute la primauté de cette valeur"), one must first say what exoticism is not through a critical process he frequently refers to as *dépouillement*, or "stripping away":

> To strip away all its tawdry adornments [*le dépouiller de tous ses oripeaux*]: the palm tree and the camel; the topee [*casque de colonial*]; black skins and yellow sun; and, at the same time, to get rid of all those who use them with an inane loquaciousness. We thus won't be dealing with the Bonnetains or the Ajalberts, nor with Cook's tours, nor with hurried and verbose travelers. . . .
> Then, to strip away from the word exoticism its solely tropical, solely geographical sense.   (pp. 22–23)

Exoticism has been dragged into the colonial mud, reduced to little more than a sad repository of commonplaces. No longer thinkable in terms of the individual writer ("Bernardin de Saint-Pierre—Chateaubriand—Marco-Polo l'initiateur—Loti"), it has become the preferred domain of the lesser, because plural, writer ("des Bonnetain . . . des Ajalbert"—a status that will also be retrospectively attributed to a writer like Loti; p. 34). What has been coarsely handled by "so many whorish and touristy hands" must be cleansed; only when the notion of exoticism has been stripped away of its "secondary" impurities and returned "to the state of a clear and vivid idea" can it "again take on flesh, and like a seed, this time pure, develop freely, joyously, without obstacles but not excessively loaded down" ("reprendre chair, et comme un germe, cette fois pur, se développer librement, joyeusement, sans entraves mais sans surcharges"; p. 23).

The significance to us of Segalen's revisionary move resides in the fact that he was by no means the only person intent on overhauling the idea of the exotic at this time. With the coming of the New Imperialism and the rapid growth of literature about the colonies, a great deal of critical attention was being paid, at least by its partisans, to a nascent *littérature coloniale* that would supplant the superannuated tradition of nineteenth-century exoticism. As Roland Lebel summed up in 1931, this literature, which asserted itself "especially after 1900," was "a reaction against false exoticism, against the cliché, against prejudices and ridiculous pretensions."[5] Exoticism as "a show of scenery, an enrichment of individualism and an orientalist impressionism" was, Marius and Ary Leblond assured readers in their 1926 study *Le roman colonial*, being replaced by a less artificial, more down-to-earth project that was, at least in theory, immune to the impressionistic lures of its predecessor (p. 7). Of course, the violent and erotically charged nature of Segalen's attack on "false exoticism" (for instance, those he refers to as *pseudo-Exotes* are labeled "Panders of the Sensation of Diversity"; p. 34) clearly differentiates his own position from that of the partisans of colonial literature. It also reveals, I think, his investment in at least one surpassed category of the old exoticism, individualism, that his contemporaries were willing to jettison. The proximity of the two views is nonetheless real and significant; in order to constitute his own "absolute exoticism," Segalen will soon have to actively forget this temporary rapprochement.

For his contemporaries, the link between Segalen's first novel, *Les Immémoriaux* (1907), and an emerging colonial literature was obvious. Indeed, Charles Régismanset and Louis Cario hailed Max Anély (the pseudonym under which the novel was first published) as one of the leading lights of this literature, a veritable model for future authors. His *Immémoriaux*, they claimed in 1911, in a work significantly entitled *L'exotisme: La littérature coloniale*, "is one of the most admirable pieces of work that exoticism has inspired" (pp. 238–39). As far as these critics were concerned, most recent literature centering around exotic locales was still predominantly "a belated manifestation of romanticism" (p. 284). They interpret the *Immémoriaux* as one of the first moments in a reaction against this romanticism, one of the first examples of an "exotisme *vrai*": "a masterpiece like Max Anély's *Immémoriaux* indicates that a new exoticism is ready to be born—less artificial, more vigorous, closer to life" (p. 285). The Leblonds voice a similar opinion: "This novel of the Tahitian soul bears witness to the great difference separating our generation from Loti's" (pp. 52–53). The robust proximity to life that these critics perceived was, I would argue, a result of Segalen's inclusion of colonialism in his novel. In assiduously charting the effects of European rule on Maori culture at the beginning of the nineteenth century, albeit from the unconventional perspective of a native informant, and with an unusually acute sense of their "tragic" nature,[6] Segalen was speaking a language that his contemporaries could understand. Notwithstanding the novel's explicitly mythic dimensions, its attention to (colonial) history allows for an uneasy fit between Segalen's vision and that possessed by those other writers who, in Lebel's approbatory words, no longer write "conventional exotic books, but exact works, local works, inspired by the colony and expressing this colony, works written not to divert but to instruct the public" (p. 82).

The relation between Segalen and this emerging *littérature coloniale* seems, at least during the years 1907–8, to have been at times one of mutual interest. In a letter included in the published edition of the *Essai*, dated 10 December 1908, for instance, Segalen mentions the possibility of giving Marius and Ary Leblond a Tahitian short story that, together with others by such writers as Pierre Mille, Louis Bertrand, and Robert Randau, "will form a book for [publisher] Calmann-Lévy, *Les Exotiques*, which is to draw attention—as did *Les soirées de Médan* for Naturalism—to the existence, not of a school or a group, but of a genuine and fecund exotic juncture [*un moment exotique sincère et fécond*]" (p. 22). Although *Les Exotiques* was never published as such,[7] the apparent compatibility between Segalen's work and that of the other *écrivains coloniaux* of his time needs to be kept in mind as the effaced possibility underlying what, in terms of Segalen's own emerging aesthetics, is the more predictable claim of 13 January 1909 that since neither the *Colon* nor the *Fonctionnaire colonial* "can preen themselves on aesthetic contemplation"—occupied as they are with commerce and administration, respectively—"'colonial' literature is not in our line" (p. 40).

What Segalen had done in the *Immémoriaux* was to associate his writing with a clearly identifiable socio-historical content. Admitting this colonial content into the *Immémoriaux* necessarily raised two related problems: the apparent disappearance of alternative cultures and the subsequent decline of the truly exotic subject (or what Segalen called the *Exote*). The integrity of Tahitian culture is no more than a memory, and the European individual must, as a result, be cast in the degraded role of the proto-ethnographer Auté, whose enterprise is from the outset a posthumous one. As Lina Zecchi points out in her important— and neglected—study of Segalen, since anthropology "arises from the corpse of a culture already destroyed in its infrastructures by the colonial enterprise," Auté is undoubtedly "the most disquieting narrative product of Segalen's first novel."[8] The belatedness that I have claimed constitutes the modern individual becomes transparent with him. Auté is limited to the act of retracing what colonialism has already disfigured; like the Lévi-Strauss of *Tristes tropiques*, "vainly attempting to reconstitute exoticism with the aid of fragments and debris" (p. 32), he will always be at a critical remove from the "valeur première" that he hopes to recover.

What this means, of course, is that the second step of the *Essai*, the positive step, can never really be taken. After the negative labor of *dépouillement*, the first in the series of essays that was to have developed "librement, joyeusement, sans entraves mais sans surcharges" from this purified ground was to have been devoted to *individualisme*, but in a colonial context the individual can, as with Auté, be referred to only in the register of loss. Although this loss was not traumatic for those who adopted the pluralist values of colonialism, it severely debilitated any ideological system that still held to the centrality of the individual. For Segalen it meant, in effect, that the sort of contemporary content found in the *Immémoriaux* would necessarily have to be excluded from his reconstituted exoticism.

As Zecchi has pointed out, the greater part of Segalen's work after his first novel is a cancellation, a sweeping away, of the colonial context that generated the *Immémoriaux*'s tragic outlook; this exclusion permitted him "to avoid drafting other books analogous to the *Immémoriaux*."[9] Colonialism, bearing with it the memory of a death (death of a traditional culture, death of the exotic subject), had to be forgotten: not so much openly criticized as silenced, since even to mention it was invariably to recall the *Exote*'s degradation and his lack of Other horizons. But maintaining this silence and writing the *Essai sur l'exotisme* were two essentially incompatible projects, since by virtue of its content, however critically presented, the *Essai* would necessarily give rise to the same sort of confusion between its author and the practitioners of colonial literature as had the *Immémoriaux*. Segalen himself raises this issue at one point, when speaking of the future *Essai* (6 May 1913): "Above all, we won't be dealing with either budgets or administrative services; even though the worst fate that this book has to fear is to be perpetually carved up, confused with, perhaps even praised in good faith under the rubric 'colonial,' and classified in the literature of this same name" (p. 66). The *Essai* thus remained, for deep rather than adventitious reasons, only a series of rough drafts; unfinished, fragmentary, it could never have been completed and published without undermining its own extra-colonial ambitions.

Given this necessity of excluding the matter of colonialism from his work, Segalen's move to the extreme formalism of his Chinese-inspired poetry seems an almost inevitable recantation of his initial, historically engaged position. Attempting to cut himself off from the world of colonial budgets, he will de-contextualize the matter of exoticism, displacing it from a subject to a form: "In China I'm deliberately seeking out, not ideas, not subjects, but forms that are little known, varied, and lofty."[10] Only this formal turn will allow him to retain "the feeling of Diversity that I have, and, by way of aesthetics, the exercising of this same feeling" (p. 67). Art becomes the last enclave of the individual's sovereign authority—one that can, however, keep itself afloat only by ignoring its own political (colonial) ground. Contemporary China, the very opposite of what was "little known, varied, and lofty," is for this reason of little or no interest to a Segalen intent on denying the *Exote*'s impotency. Segalen's attempt in the *Immémoriaux* at getting under the Maori skin, the Maori *peau*, is henceforth abandoned: in the world of the New Imperialism, the exotic *peau* is necessarily an *oripeau*, false in its very nature because brought under the control of a banal and colonizing modernity. To quote Zecchi again: "The Other as a people—primitive, savage, pre-logical, to which the nineteenth century so desperately gave chase . . . can subsist only as something internal to Western culture, because on the outside it is dispersed, dissolved, assimilated as a folkloric or archaic mechanism to an impassible machinery."[11] For Segalen, the geopolitical space had become the scene of monotony, inevitably subject to what he, like Pound, although with little of Pound's reactionary belief that this entropy could be reversed, will come in his later writings to identify as *Usure*.

By 1911 Segalen's palinodic operation is accomplished: thanks to the redemptive power of art, his extrication from the mire of colonial literature and the preservation of his sovereign individuality seem to have been assured. *True* exoticism, he will affirm in the *Essai*, is necessarily absent from any literary work whose primary value derives, not from its artistry, but from its attachment to a specific geopolitical content: "Exoticism is not really a matter for exotic novelists, but for *great artists*. No true exoticism in the language of Nolly, Leblond" (p. 50). A writer like Claude Farrère, he continues, does not compare to an artist like Kipling—here, to be sure, Segalen is only echoing the widespread enthusiasm in French colonial circles for a man who Segalen himself characterized as "astonishing"—and, in turn, a crucial turn, Segalen does not compare to anyone else. "I am alone of my kind [*seul de mon espèce*]," he proclaims, loudly echoing that singular definition of the artist cited at the outset of this section ("l'artiste ne relève que de lui-même")—a definition that Baudelaire gives, interestingly enough, in his account of the 1855 World Exhibition.[12]

Segalen then goes on to argue that the prose of the Rosny brothers' *Xipéhuz* (1887)—a slight story about a prehistoric African tribe—could be compared to the *Immémoriaux* were it not riddled with such banal phrases as "ce fut l'an mil des peuples enfants" ("it was the year one thousand of the children peoples"). The uniqueness of his first novel thus emerges only once it has been redefined primarily in terms of style and language rather than content. By virtue of its artistry, the *Immémoriaux* is immune to the cultural impurities it records and at a complete distance from what had, just three years before, been referred to as "un moment exotique sincère et fécond." Seen through the revisionary lens of the *grand artiste*, the novel regains the purity that it never possessed; it has become, ex post facto, "cette oeuvre pure" (p. 75). His *oeuvre* is redeemed, but only at the expense of sacrificing its actuality, of forgetting the historical content by which others had already identified it as part of an emerging reaction against the dated tradition of nineteenth-century exoticism.

Segalen's conception of the uniqueness of his own enterprise has set the agenda for recent studies of his work. Disengaging himself from the New Imperialism and its literary exponents, fashioning himself as a *grand artiste* whose proper domain is that of "poetic language": such heroic efforts have struck a nerve of fellow feeling in contemporary critics (for reasons that it would clearly be invidious to discuss here). However, the relation between Segalen and his colonial contemporaries is of a more complicated nature than one can derive from the obvious affirmation that he is a decidedly greater writer than Farrère or Randau. These ties to the colonial world are especially relevant because Segalen himself is never entirely satisfied with the dichotomy between life and art that results from his turn to language and an "absolute exoticism" (supposedly) untouched by the entropy to which he bore witness. Even in the later notes of the *Essai*, Segalen felt obliged to acknowledge that colonialism was indeed a category of the exotic despite his polemical assertions to the contrary elsewhere: "The 'colonial' is exotic, but exoticism greatly exceeds [*dépasse puissamment*] the colonial" (p. 81). If poetry seemed an effective means of inhabiting the utopia of language, it did not answer the ethico-political question of how best to live in topographical space. If the "modernist" Segalen asserted, through the autonomy of art, the individual's possible distance from the degraded conditions of life, his "pre-modern" alter ego remained painfully aware of the necessity of living, and writing, within the hegemonic boundaries of a colonial world.

The "pre-modern" Segalen recasts himself in the mold of those very exotic novelists from whom no "true exoticism" can be expected. Segalen felt the novel to be an execrable genre, modernity's literary accomplice: the novelist, he surmised from his own experience, cannot help attaching himself to a content incompatible with the emphasis on style and language that ought to distinguish the *grand artiste*. And yet Segalen nonetheless continued to write novels, a point whose significance I will explore in the final section of this chapter. We have seen that the *Immémoriaux* lent itself to being read in the context of the New Imperialism and the literature it gave rise to (and it is surely this fact that, Segalen's own ex post facto assertions of the work's "purity" notwithstanding, causes an aesthetically inclined critic like Henry Bouillier to underestimate it).[13] With his other great novel, *René Leys*, Segalen develops an exotic strategy that does not avoid and cancel out the problem of colonialism but accepts this dead end as the *Exote*'s necessary point of departure. In returning to the degraded literary genre par excellence, he will acknowledge the inevitably colonial and hence impure nature of his writerly enterprise—an impurity that his poetry must be silent about and that his theory of an "absolute exoticism" would silence. *René Leys* reverses the de-contextualizing thrust of the *Essai sur l'exotisme*, resituating the solitary artist, "seul de son espèce," in the more peopled regions of that "moment exotique sincère et fécond," the New Imperialism.

Pierre Loti's *Petit Rêve de Souverain Chinois*

> I must liberate myself from the remembrance of too many
> descriptions—from those of Marco Polo, deliciously archaic, to
> the modern and sentimental ones of Pierre Loti—in order to
> re-enter reality, to see the much-awaited object with my own
> eyes. Writing, reading: these are indeed vain exercises. A thing
> of beauty does not exist until one has set one's eyes upon it:
> Wilde's aphorism is correct. But even before knowing how to
> read, I dreamed of Benares. If I go back to the first source of
> my memory, I see the sacred city in a Napoleonic engraving,
> hanging in my nursery. And the remembrance of it is so clear
> that this far-off dream appears to me as real and the reality of
> today seems but a dream.
>
> —Guido Gozzano, "Il fiume dei roghi" (1914)

In this passage from one of his Indian prose pieces,[14] the Italian poet Guido Gozzano raises in an extremely direct manner an issue underlying much of our inquiry in this book: To what extent could fin de siècle travelers escape the overbearing influence exercised by previous accounts of the same exotic locale that they were to visit and describe? Like the young Segalen, Gozzano conjures up the familiar names of a literary tradition—Marco Polo, Loti—and inquires whether these prior descriptions have not critically affected his own ability to see and write about the exotic. At first glance, it would appear that the poet is invoking this tradition only in order to separate himself more decisively from it—to redeem the "vanity" of writing through a liberatory act of seeing, or, as Edward Said might put it, to replace a "textual attitude" by "direct encounters with the human."[15] But, as we might guess from the reference to Wilde, Gozzano's project is a much more nuanced one than the simple plunge into reality that he seems to be preparing for here.

Gozzano was the leading voice of the "twilight poets" (*crepuscolari*), who flourished in Italy during the first decade of the twentieth century. The most characteristic feature of his poetry is its ironic compliance with Italian poetic tradition. The past, from Dante to the fin de siècle dithyrambs of Gabriele D'Annunzio, was for Gozzano a burden that he could neither wholeheartedly adopt nor decisively junk: on the one hand, this tradition seemed inescapable; on the other hand, it was, in a modern world organized around mercantile rather than artistic considerations, clearly untenable—a thing more ridiculous than sublime. "Ashamed to be a poet," he was not interested in arguing, as would Marinetti and the futurists or the formalist-oriented poets associated with the literary journal *La voce* (*vociani*), that poetry could be "made new," substantially freed of its past. Gozzano's discursive strategy, rather, consisted in repeating the outmoded language of the poetic tradition—a repetition that, given the abysmal distance between the modern world and what preceded it, could not help but be ironical. With this "overturned continuity,"[16] by which he at once preserved and undermined "Poetry," copied and defaced it, Gozzano came to terms with the vexing problem of originality; constructed upon and out of the language of others, his poetry can differ only in its very renunciation of originality.

Despite their claim of re-entering reality, Gozzano's travel writings prove no exception to the rule established in his poetry. Although he asserted the necessity of escaping from the discursive influence of a writer like Loti, of disentangling the real Benares from its most familiar literary portrayal, his actual practice was very different. Originally published for the most part in the newspaper *La stampa*, many of his descriptions of India (all written after the fact of his brief trip there for health reasons in 1912) were of places such as Benares that he had never visited; in presenting his "firsthand" vision of the Indian subcontinent he relied heavily—often to the point of plagiarism—on both the empirical observations and formal devices of other travel books, especially Loti's *L'Inde (sans les Anglais)* (1903).[17] To re-enter reality, he seems to be saying, it is not enough to merely open one's eyes. Open, one's eyes are nonetheless subject to a terrible form of closure: the oppressive but irreducible influence of a dominant discourse. Only by adopting a stance that acknowledges this closure as a fait accompli might one begin to grapple with it, overcoming "weakly" (*Verwindung*) what one can no longer truly hope to overcome (*Überwindung*). Gozzano thus refers us to a condition in which the eyes must be closed for any vision to take place—the state of dream, a dream that, significantly enough, originates out of his memory of a Napoleonic engraving.

Although the crepuscular exoticism of Gozzano merits a chapter to itself in this book, from the little said here a few signal notions can be gathered: the massive influence of Pierre Loti on the spiritual geography of an entire generation; the central role of vision in registering the exotic, or, better, the exotic topos; and the emergence of a rhetorical position that knowingly adopts the perspective of a writer like Loti instead of openly refuting it as Segalen was attempting in his *Essai*. My purpose in this section is not to enumerate the specific crimes against "Art" of which Loti stands accused in Segalen's eyes; nor, conversely, is it to claim that Segalen used Loti in the way Gozzano did. Rather, in giving an account of Loti's China as we find it in the pages of *Les derniers jours de Pékin* (1901), I want to establish a framework for my subsequent argument about *René Leys*—most notably, by emphasizing the extent to which Peking and the Imperial Palace had lost their exotic appeal as a result of the "work of the abominable conquest" that Segalen's predecessor describes in the *Derniers jours*.[18]

In a letter to his wife written on 8 November 1909, Segalen makes it clear that he has read Loti's book on China and is thankful that it in no way restricts his scope as a writer: "I have this good fortune that the vast milieu of China is intact as far as French Letters goes (for Loti did so little with it [*l'a si peu touchée*] in *Les derniers jours de Pékin*)."[19] Segalen's concern with intactness, however, seems a sure sign of anxiety on his part: to pose the question of influence, however parenthetically, is to acknowledge it as a problem. As any reader of Segalen knows, the fact that something has been touched only a little can, *dans un monde sonore*, be of critical importance—even more so, no doubt, when what has been, in Loti's words, "penetrated" ("percé à jour") is the hitherto inviolable capital of this "vast milieu": the Imperial Palace, "the center, the heart, and the mystery of China, veritable lair of the Sons of Heaven" (p. 159).

The European invasion chronicled in *Derniers jours* differs in many ways from the colonial conquests under way in Africa and the Pacific: a reaction to the Boxer uprising against the foreign presence in China, the invasion was undertaken with the limited goal of rescuing the foreigners under siege at the Peking legations and safeguarding the economic carte blanche enjoyed by Europe, Japan, and the United States. That China was an altogether different, and more estimable, place than the "uncivilized" territories then being absorbed into the various colonial empires was generally acknowledged at the time. The famous traveler Isabella Bird spoke for the majority when she remarked in 1899 that "it is essential for us to see quite clearly that our Western ideas find themselves confronted, not with barbarism or with debased theories of morals, but with an elaborate and antique civilisation, which yet is not decayed, and which, though imperfect, has many claims to our respect and even admiration."[20] In a like vein, Gilbert de Voisins, Segalen's intermittent traveling companion, emphasizes the great gap between China, seat of an ancient civilization, and the tropical colonies: "In this country, I can get a sense of living in a world of men, of fellow men, and not, as I did in negro country [*en pays nègre*], in the cage for monkeys at the zoo. An antique civilization has given them time to think. If we cannot share this thought, someday at least it might be the case that we learn to understand and admire it [*à la voir et à l'admirer*]."[21] This readily identifiable "human" quality, of course, so inspires one writer of the next generation, André Malraux, that he will learn to "see" China as the likely site of a new revolutionary culture capable of reversing the inhuman condition of modernity.

China's immensity, and its highly codified dynastic organization, necessitated a more indirect form of political control than the policies of divide and conquer most often associated with the New Imperialism. Even at the height of Western expansion, the "informal imperialism" that typified European relations with the Ottoman Empire and the South American republics remained the method of territorial control considered best suited for the economic exploitation of China: "Were China to be officially partitioned as Africa had been, it would spoil every prospect for profit. Business could never be conducted where the balance of power had been broken, in conditions similar to the English Wars of the Roses or the German Thirty Years War."[22] Nonetheless, the last years of the nineteenth century saw an intensification of European, as well as American and Japanese, interest in China that would result in an "undignified scramble for concessions" (as Bird called it); European control of the seaboard region of China was as-

sured through the parceling-out of "spheres of influence." Given the
New Imperialist vision of an "absolute ascendency in the world to-day
of the Western peoples and of Western civilisation,"[23] this control was
deemed essential for the efficient disposal of China's vast economic re-
sources. As one commentator on Far East affairs put it in 1900 in describing this new enthusiasm for territorial concessions, Europeans
had during the last four years ceased "devoting themselves purely and
simply to commerce, in order to undertake a real colonization through
the application of Western methods to the exploitation [*mise en valeur*]
of China's wealth."[24] This "véritable colonisation" was one of the primary causes of the Boxer Rebellion, the nationalist uprising that gave
rise to the joint Euro-Japanese invasion recorded in Loti's book.

As a result of this invasion, the emperor and his cortege abandon
the capital city, and, by the time Loti arrives in the Yellow Sea aboard
the *Redoutable*, Peking has been taken and the once-sacrosanct imperial
residence, "one of the last refuges on earth of the unknown and the
marvelous," established as the temporary headquarters of the occupying forces. For several weeks, Loti will find himself an inhabitant of
this *locus sanctus*—until then strictly off-limits to Europeans. He often
remarks in *Derniers jours* on this improbable turn of events, and the
following instance, in which he and a fellow military officer pass a
night of opium-induced revery in their palatial *demeure*, is typical: "We
congratulate ourselves on having come to inhabit the 'yellow City' at
a unique moment in the history of China, at a moment when everything is open and when we are still almost entirely alone, free to in-
dulge our whims and our curiosity" (p. 240). The sort of "opening" that
was to have been created in *Aziyadé* is, of course, not in question here:
the solitude that there served to guarantee the hero's enjoyment of the
exotic scene must now be figured wholly in terms of the very *nous* that
the youthful *Loti* had to avoid if he were to pursue his exoticizing project. In occupied China no such distance from one's colonial role is possible: the subject's identity is determined primarily by the national military force that enables his presence in the exotic locale. This dependency severely curtails whatever satisfaction might once have been
gained from that locale. Just before smoking some opium with one of
his fellow officers, Loti reflects: "Alas! How our solitude in this palace
would have seemed magic to us, without the assistance of any [drug-
induced] alteration, a few years earlier!" (p. 235) Colonialism has vacated the scene of exoticism: the Imperial Palace no longer contains a
sovereign figure with whom one can "magically" identify, and, not sur-

prisingly, the erotic investment in an indigenous female that was such an essential feature of the early novels is absent from this book.

The possibility of evasion that motivated Loti's original exoticism is no longer present; the only story left for him to tell is a colonial one, of invasion and its aftermath. Subservient to the ongoing military occupation, the writing of the *Derniers jours* can be no more than a pendant to it. Loti's status as an officer, the readers of *Figaro* are told (the book was first published there as a series of articles that ran from late December 1900 to the end of the following year), forbids him to correspond on military or political events; however, *Figaro*'s introductory blurb continues, he has consented to produce "a few of those marvelous *tableaux* in which he excels, but which will have nothing to do with France's military action" (29 December 1900). This open subordination of the picturesque tableau to military reality (precisely what the later Loti tends to pass over in silence, as I suggested in the previous chapter) is signaled in the book version of the *Derniers jours* by its dedication to Vice-admiral Pottier, commander in chief of France's Far East squadron and the man whom Loti served as aide-de-camp during the Chinese expedition.

This explicit circumscription of the book's content, in turn, affects its form.* In *Aziyadé* Loti had recourse to the fragmentary form of the journal as a means of preserving the otherwise untenable work of art from the threat posed by the superimposition of a colonial narrative. In the dedication to the *Derniers jours*, however, writing, in its subordination to history, reveals itself as the very antithesis of an *oeuvre*. The book is without form, in the sense that it has barely been worked upon: "The notes that I have sent from China to *Figaro* are going to be collected in a volume to be published in Paris before my return, without it being possible for me to revise them [*sans qu'il me soit possible d'y revoir*]" (p. i). Without a *re-vision* on the writer's part, no transformation of these newspaper pieces into a more elevated, artistic body of work will be possible. The volume of the *Derniers jours* is itself no guarantee of a book's existence—a fact that Loti acknowledges when he speaks at one

*The *Journal intime* upon which the *Derniers jours* was based, although equally immersed in a colonial story, is often markedly freer in its portrayal of European activities than the book. The following description of T'ung-chou (17 Oct. 1900) is a particularly good example of this relative candor: "In one of the courtyards, a mangy dog wears itself out tugging, tugging something from under a pile of broken glass: the corpse of a child whose head was smashed by the butt of a rifle (the Russians have killed hundreds of them in this manner). And the dog begins to eat [the child's] arms" (*Cahiers Pierre Loti* 13 [1955]: 6).

point of "the story of my voyage to Peking—if I should ever find the time to write it" (p. 262). The time that would be necessary to write this exotic *récit* cannot be found; it has been doubled over by another time in which the act of writing has, from the moment of its beginning, been dedicated to other, less literary ends—a point reinforced by the various renderings of this act in the *Derniers jours*. Describing one of the empress's palaces, Loti notes that it "belongs to us" and adds that it is the building which he has been "authorized to turn into [his] study for a few days, in the midst of a contemplative stillness" (p. 153). The writer's own signature can be given only under the strictures of an authoritative-authorizing military writing: his own work would not be possible without the "permis signés et contresignés" (p. 165) or the "permission dûment signée" (p. 279) that creates and enables his presence in the p(a)lace of writing, "au milieu du recueillement et du silence."

The colonial limitations of Loti's writing drastically restrict the visual impressionism that, as the introduction makes clear, will be a preferred mode of registering his exotic topic: "I have limited myself to noting the things that took place directly under my eyes in the course of the assignments that you [Vice-admiral Pottier] gave me and of a voyage that you permitted me to make in a certain China hitherto more or less unknown" (p. ii). Loti's writing will obsessively assert the primacy of (his) vision, its "direct" access to the scene being recorded. The following description of one of the Imperial Palace's many curiosity-stocked rooms is characteristic in its privileging of the seen (and also in its displacement of the act of seeing onto the impersonal subject *on*): "Without having seen it, one can't imagine [*on n'imagine pas, sans l'avoir vu*] the number of oddities, absurdities, and marvels that there are to be found in the curio-filled storerooms of a Chinese empress!" (p. 151) The intimate connection between "visualism," colonialism, and the *récit de voyage* has been remarked upon at length in recent years and requires no further comment from me.[25] The centrality of this nexus for Loti is, however, obvious: China is "a corner of the world whose name remained a matter of indifference even yesterday, but toward which the eyes of Europe are presently turned" (p. 4). Loti's eyes are, from the outset, turned in the same direction as those of the colonial powers that, in the form of an international naval squadron, appear to occupy "an infinite space": "All sides of the horizon seem thick with warships" (p. 9). This all-encompassing horizon binds together the one and the many—the writer, his reader, and the colonial machine; it is the all too apparent precondition of Loti's degraded vision of the exotic.

A unanimity of vision was the point from which *Michel Strogoff* began (the Czar's banquet) and at which it ended (the marriage of Strogoff and Nadia). In its own lackluster way, the *Derniers jours* is also structured according to the logic of this festive circularity. The sight of the naval squadron at the beginning—"one gets the impression of some celebration [*fête*] of universal coalescence, of universal concord"—is matched at the end by a "big party [*fête*] for the staff of the allied armies" organized by the infamous Colonel Marchand, chief protagonist of Fashoda (p. 432). However, this affirmation of the Same is not, as it were, dialectically "earned": the time intervening between the two fêtes does not, as in *Michel Strogoff*, fill any narrative task; between these two poles we will meet with nothing more than what was there from the beginning. No spectacle of indigenous power opposes that of the invading forces; instead of a counter-fête, we witness only one sign after another of the Other's impotence. "Everything is in ruins and teeming with corpses," Loti notes when he reaches the Chinese mainland (p. 19)—a totalizing vision that he will not cease repeating.

Having become the scene/seen of colonialism, China appears to Loti only in a truncated form, with barely a trace of what must have been its former glory; it is a country "where I can expect to encounter only ruins and corpses" (p. 43). He is in no position to offer any sustained vision of the Other and its power (although the occasional deferent nod to "the old yellow Colossus . . . still capable of sowing terror" [p. 420] does surface, calling to mind the "yellow peril" literature that was such a common element of racist diatribes against Asian peoples at the time). A monotonous litany of severed members is almost all that Loti's encounter with China produces: journeying toward Peking, he is treated to one long funereal spectacle of "severed heads with long queues, everywhere strewn about on the paving stones" (p. 82), "refuse of all sorts, carcasses with swollen stomachs, human corpses, animal corpses" (p. 35).

These obsessive visions of dismemberment that Loti records on his approach to Peking pave the way for his doleful sojourn in the imperial city itself—"this place of mystery that I will soon see, and into which, before him [General Frey, later in charge of France's colonial army], no European had ever penetrated" (p. 44). His vision of this once-mysterious place, the center and heart of China, has been made possible by a European military officer's inaugural penetration of it; an official vision will henceforth always precede the individual's. For this reason, the tropes of primacy and enchantment that ought to have functioned as the signs of exotic privilege are (unintentionally, no doubt) demoted to the status of an "as if," as when Loti reaches "the gate of the 'Imperial City' proper, the gate of the territory that had never been entered—and it's as if [*comme si*] one were laying bare to me the gate of enchantment and mystery" (pp. 134–35).

This simulated exoticism recurs when Loti and his companions visit the once-forbidden Temple of Heaven. Walking up the imperial ramp ("sentier impérial"), he notes: "It's a domineering place, constructed long ago at great cost for sovereigns to contemplate from, and we linger there, gazing out like Sons of Heaven" (p. 125). Such a likeness to the imperial figure is, however, entirely derisory: the original term of comparison is absent, a mere thing of the past, and the exotic subject is, in turn, irredeemably pluralized ("comme *des* Fils du Ciel"). The royal way leads only to an empty altar, and the (im)possibilities of this "as if" have in no way impressed themselves upon Loti. Emptiness reigns now that the sovereign has been "torn away from the dwelling place [*demeure*] where twenty generations of ancestors had lived beyond reach" (p. 171).

Because of this "unprecedented default," the inside of the imperial *demeure* now offers a perspective no different from that of its outside. All that is reserved for the colonial inhabitants of this desecrated palace is "the surprise of a funereal decay and a necropolis-like silence" (p. 169) or, in other words, a repetition of the gruesome monotony to be seen beyond its walls. Faced at all points with the infinite space that the invaders occupy, the colonial subject has only to proclaim, from the (empty) heart of the exotic, that for all intents and purposes the imperial city of his dreams is finished: "It feels done for, with no chance of renewal" ("on le sent fini, sans résurrection possible"; p. 327). Given this total penetration of the exotic space, the individual's hope of self-realization can be no more than a pale shadow of his original exotic dream, no more than a "petit rêve de souverain chinois" (p. 301).

No longer a place of inhabitation, the exotic has become a radically different sort of *demeure*—one that has not *demeuré*. As I will argue in the following pages, Segalen's belated attempt in *René Leys* at re-envisioning this imperial space bases itself upon the very impossibility of any such attempt: he will knowingly reproduce the sort of exoticizing desire that Loti's colonial vision of China has effectively nullified. With this strategic anachronism, Segalen points his work in the same ambivalent fin de siècle direction as a writer like Gozzano who, having turned his gaze away from the future and its alluring promise of a *vita nuova*, situates himself between an unoriginal present and what is as-

suredly only a past dream of originality, insisting all the while upon }
the necessity of dreaming both, together.

'René Leys' and the Politics of Metaphor

The gestures of the orator are metaphors—whether he is
displaying clearly between thumb and index finger the thing
well grasped, or touching it with a fingertip, his palm turned
toward the sky. What he touches, squeezes, severs, flattens,
these are imaginings: acts that in times past were real, when
language was gesture, and gesture action.

—Paul Valéry, *Autres rhumbs*

René Leys draws to a close. It is late autumn in 1911 and China's
millennia-old Empire is on the verge of being toppled. For *Segalen*, the
narrator of *René Leys*, a dream has come to its close; with the collapse
of the Empire, his project of penetrating the Imperial Palace—obsessively chronicled in a journal he had kept over the preceding ten
months—has been stymied once and for all. Coincident with this historical tremor is an event of a more personal nature: the death of René
Leys, a young Belgian polyglot who, with his claims of having immediate access to the Palace and its sovereign occupants, had hitherto
served as a providential mediator in *Segalen*'s attempt at gaining some
insight into "this full life, protocolar and secret and pekingese, that no
officially known truth will ever be able to suspect."[26]

The narrator is left to ponder the degree of truth in his young companion's stories about life inside the Palace. He finally decides that the
question of their "truth" must go unanswered. These stories were the
signs of a friendship he shared with the youth: that is all he wishes to
conclude. This friendship, he writes in the final entry of his journal,
ought to be affirmed without looking any further into the problem of
its actual foundation, "for fear of killing him, or killing it a second
time . . . or—this would be even more reprehensible—of suddenly
being called upon [*être mis brusquement en demeure*] to respond myself
to my doubt, and at last to pronounce '*yes* or *no*?'" (p. 239) To answer
"yes" or "no" could, in a New Imperialist world, only have the effect
of killing off everything that has to do with secret and alternative
worlds. Only by leaving the question open, undecidable, can this fatal
"notice of payment" (*mise en demeure*) be suspended.

Changing the sense of an ending from one of certainty to ambiguity
will be Segalen's way, or at least one of his ways, of preserving what

has passed away from the degraded finality of a world of "officially known truths." In this respect, *René Leys* stands as an early example of the modernist novel, which, with its appeal to undecidability, would establish itself at a doubtful distance from that succession of events we call "History," and it is to this aspect of the novel that most critics have devoted their attention. But *René Leys* is also something rather less than a modernist novel: it does say no, twice—once to the exotic possibility that the narrator seems to have salvaged by shrouding it with the veil of undecidability, and once again to the colonial reality that denies this possibility. In saying no to the possibility of his desire for the exotic, in killing off a second time what was already dead, the pre-modern Segalen acknowledges what his modernist alter ego must shrug off: a guilty allegiance to the historical process that he had once thought to distance himself from. In so doing, I believe, he also shows us what it is to say yes to the memory of everything that this insidious process has erased.

René Leys, like the *Immémoriaux*, raises the problem of colonialism and its effect on an exotic world. However, in the later novel Segalen focuses less on the disappearance of an alternative culture than on the destabilizing effect this cultural transformation has on the exotic subject. His friend Gilbert de Voisins remarks of *René Leys* that it was conceived as an ironic counterbalance to "ce sombre roman impérial," the unfinished *Fils du Ciel*. Voisins explains that the novel's irony stems from the fact that it was written "from the European point of view." He goes on to contend, however, that in adopting this perspective Segalen had a second, non-ironic intention: namely, to render "the colors and scents of Peking, the look of its crowds, its theaters, its low dives, to establish their sumptuous and truly imperial outlines, their charm and their surviving exoticism, despite the ugliness that with every passing day the European is bringing to it."[27] What Voisins has identified here clearly conforms to the traditional vision of exoticism that Segalen was trying to detach himself from in his *Essai sur l'exotisme*. This "exotisme survivant" is subject to entropy; it is open to the sort of impurities that the author of the *Essai* associated with a superannuated literary and existential practice. Has Voisins made a mistake, projecting his own aesthetic standards—of which Segalen strongly disapproved[28]—upon a writer engaged in the very different task of (re)constructing an "absolute" and "pure" exoticism?

I will argue that Voisins is essentially correct: he has identified the narratorial standpoint of the novel—and also, although in a necessarily indirect way, its authorial point of view. The novel puts into play an exotic vision that Segalen had apparently renounced in his *Essai*; committed as he was to the figure of the individual, however, Segalen could never completely distance himself from this now-untenable project. If the narrator's exoticizing position is problematized throughout the course of *René Leys*, it is not, we will see, done away with altogether. The exotic narrator *Segalen* is a voice that Segalen must, out of historical necessity, suppress; yet he feels it ethically imperative to preserve that voice. Only by marking out this posthumous space for himself can he at once admit to the disappearance of the exotic and the appearance in its place of an homogenizing modernity and yet persevere in contesting its uncontestable presence.

Segalen's desire is to enter into the heart of the exotic, Peking's Imperial Palace. As Loti had anticipated, after the evacuation of the allied troops, imperial power was restored and the Palace once again put off-limits to the outside world. The privileged site of Chinese sovereignty resacralized, the exoticist project of penetrating into the *Dedans* and gaining access to the marvels it contained again made sense, albeit a belated sense. The potential beauty of the mysterious Inside might once again be opposed to the "ugliness" of the modern colonizing-colonized world; *René Leys* and its narrator will obsessively zero in on this cradle of imperial values. A similar preoccupation with the entropic space of the exotic, interestingly enough, is absent from the diary upon which Segalen based his novel (the "Annales secrètes d'après Maurice Roy"): "The theme of nostalgia in the face of the empire's disintegration, which is so essential to the book, is found only in the novel."[29] This fact confirms the importance such nostalgia had in Segalen's conception of what the novel, as opposed to the real-life incidents it was based upon, was to signify.

This primary obsession, to be sure, is constantly being supplemented by an authorial irony that draws both the narrator and his hero René Leys into a complicated game of mirrors, which develops alongside the events that *Segalen* narrates in his journal (in a style that is necessarily clichéd, because exemplary of an outmoded literary tradition). As the reader progresses through the journal, he or she becomes ever more aware of the degree to which the narrator and René Leys are constructions, constructing each other in their conversations and constructed by the notebook that *Segalen* keeps. Indeed, at the end of the journal, the reader is invited to follow its author as he reads it over—

an act that, according to Jean Verrier, turns *Segalen*'s notebook into Segalen's self-referential novel and consecrates undecidability as its dominant trope.

For a critic like Verrier, in search of the novel's modernist essence,
the materiality of Peking proves, in the final analysis, inconsequential
in the face of what he interprets as the author's decision to inhabit literature. Commenting on the narrator's fascination with maps, especially his large-scale plan of the Imperial Palace, Verrier notes that "the
plan, the thing figured is . . . more important for the narrator than a
'real' penetration into the 'real' city, for the reason that this 'real' (the
signified Peking) is no more than an 'illusion of the real,' a fiction in
the novel *René Leys*, and conversely, it is the figuration, the path followed on the plan, the path of writing, which is the real."[30] In this reading, Peking ceases to be what it was for the Loti of *Derniers jours*, an
organic city "dying century by century, district by district, the way old
trees wither branch by branch" (p. 207). It has become, like Swift's Lil-
liput, no more than "a perfect square," and equally fictional. Although
René Leys undoubtedly does take this u-topic turn, the turn that asso-
ciates "reality" and *écriture*, it is one that Segalen will keep turning back
on (itself). Not by chance is the narrator's scale drawing of the *ville in-
terdite* pointedly identified as "a European plan, seemingly complete,
exact, to the hundredth, in color, crammed with transcribed names—
a plan drawn up in a hasty and puerile way by the allied troops, during
their full occupation of the Palace in 'nineteen hundred'" (p. 105); the
literary "figurations" of both narrator and author emerge from, and depend upon, this historical ground plan. It is this inseparable conjuncture of literature and politics that a thoroughly modernist reading of
René Leys must overlook and that we must now begin to outline.

René Leys was written in 1913–14 during Segalen's second sojourn in
China (revised in 1915–16, the novel was, like so many other of his writings, first published posthumously [1921–22]). Yüan Shih-k'ai was at
this time attempting to consolidate his power as president in order to
restore a native Chinese Empire in place of the deposed Manchus. He
died in 1916 without effectively realizing this dream, and China was
plunged into decades of anarchy as warlords took charge of various
parts of the country. During the years immediately following the
1911–12 revolution, however, Yüan's power base and the legitimacy of
his claims seemed well grounded to many observers. Indeed, Segalen,
who had for a time served as personal physician to Yüan's son, himself

published two laudatory articles on the new president in the popular magazine *Lectures pour tous* (dated 1 October 1913 and 15 June 1914); they are essential documents in understanding his politics—and his reactionary belief that, in the absence of a "protocole ancien," a new and necessarily modernized protocol could still embody the imperial values he so admired.[31] In choosing how much to conserve of their past in the face of the inevitable renovation brought about by the "Europeanization" of their country, the Chinese people had, Segalen asserts in the second article, "as sufficient guarantee, the powerful and personal work already accomplished by Yüan Shih-k'ai" (p. 67). In Yüan, Segalen thought he had found someone who was capable of establishing an ideal balance of old and new, rather like the "monarch of genius" whom Conrad in a 1905 essay entitled "Autocracy and War" (later collected in *Notes on Life and Letters*), imagined putting himself "at the head of a revolution without ceasing to be the king of his people" (p. 101).

Ironically enough, this second article was based on an interview with Yüan that took place in the Imperial Palace—the very *locus sanctus* into which *Segalen* hopes to penetrate, for all that he appears to have given up on this desire from the very outset of his journal.

Je ne saurai donc rien de plus. Je n'insiste pas; je me retire . . . respectueusement d'ailleurs et à reculons, puisque le Protocole le veut ainsi, et qu'il s'agit du Palais Impérial, d'une audience qui ne fut pas donnée, et ne sera jamais accordée . . .   (p. 13)

(I will know nothing more then. I don't insist; I withdraw   . respectfully, moreover, and backwards, since that is the way the Protocol has it, and since it is a matter of the Imperial Palace, of an audience that was not given, and will never be granted . . .)

This initial withdrawal is a preliminary admission that a certain type of book will not, and cannot, be written—a book that would in some way be directly connected to the exotic heart of imperial China and at a significant remove from "insipid contemporary China" (p. 142). Of course, the narrator of *René Leys* does not abandon his project quite so readily; he will continue to pursue the capital "Présence" (p. 15) of what has apparently been renounced from the beginning—although, as we will see, at the price of having it repeatedly diminished in his eyes.

As can be gathered by examining a few instances of the frequent play between majuscule and minuscule letters in the text, the exotic stature of the imperial *Protocole* is threatened on at least two fronts. On the one hand, the mysterious nature of the Palace is greatly reduced whenever it is considered in everyday terms, as a mere object of common knowledge. After his native professor Wang informs him, in textbook fashion, of the functions of those who inhabit the *Dedans*, *Segalen* shows a certain impatience with the clarity of Wang's account: "This arithmetical protocol is relatively unmysterious," he remarks ("ce protocole arithmétique est assez peu mystérieux"; p. 37). On the other hand, the *Protocole* also loses its capital prestige if situated in the context of Euro-Chinese diplomatic relations—that is, if viewed in terms of a *Weltpolitik* that circumscribes and constricts the exotic, as happens when *Segalen* does actually enter a liminal part of the Palace as part of a French cortege. "This Protocol comes at the right time," he affirms on the eve of that longed-for event ("ce Protocole vient à son heure"; p. 101). But the official and limited nature of this incursion deprives him of all the satisfaction that he had anticipated from it; in fact, it turns out, the content of the *Protocole* has been severely curtailed in order to spare French feelings. Having been informed that once the audience is finished, "one will bow three times and withdraw moving backwards," the narrator exclaims: "This, then, is what has become of the thrice three recumbent prostration of old! I imagine that the amount of kowtowing written into this protocol [*les courbettes inscrites à ce protocole*] has caused a lot of diplomatic sweat to run" (p. 102). Once again the *Protocole* has been reduced to an insubstantial *protocole*, more suited to a comic description than the sort of esoteric narrative that *Segalen* hopes one day to write.

Dissatisfied with his official entry into the *Dedans*, *Segalen* returns to his domicile and, immediately taking out his plan of the Palace, gazes longingly over it. This avid gaze, one divorced from any deed, is an emblem of the narrator's limitations as an exotic subject. He can do nothing to lessen the distance between himself and the Palace. The only "actions" that draw him closer to the imperial space with which he phantasmically identifies are self-contained gestures of passivity— as, for instance, his tendency to lie down facing south in accordance with the "imperial rule." This gives him the feeling "of living *parallel* [*vivre* parallèlement], in all the cold and measured rigor of the term, parallel to the hidden life of the Palace, which like me is facing south" (p. 47). This supine parallelism, his fervid scrutiny of the plan, and the "Founder's glance" ("coup d'oeil de Fondateur"; p. 67) that he casts from one of the city's ancestral bell towers are all examples of how the narrator's exoticist project has been reduced to his own incapacitated body—rather similar in this to Huysman's des Esseintes in *A rebours* (1884) who, "while not moving at all," is nonetheless able to procure for himself "the rapid, almost instantaneous feelings of a sea voyage" (p. 32).

Despite his best efforts, *Segalen* cannot even carry out the necessary first step of exoticism: disengaging oneself from European society. Attempting to achieve a *Loti*-like "solitude," he has housed himself in an outlying quarter of the Ville Tartare, but his neighbor turns out to be a vulgar Frenchman, Jarignoux, who has "gone native" the better to carry out his business affairs (a grotesque twist on *Loti*'s final conversion to the Ottoman cause at the end of *Aziyadé*). Indeed, Jarignoux has solidified his position by taking a native wife, thus discrediting the erotic strategy that facilitated *Loti*'s encounters with the exotic—one that, in any case, the strangely celibate *Segalen* shows little interest in pursuing.

The narrator's inactivity is matched, on the other side of the Palace walls, by the absence of any imperial figure with whom to identify: the Emperor Kuang-hsü, who was to have been the "Personnage" of *Segalen*'s book, has already been dead for three years, and the Dynasty is moribund. The narrator frequently laments this fact toward the beginning of his notebook:

—Enfin, tout ce qui s'est passé [au Palais] à quelques années près, est évidemment d'un autre âge. Mais tout est fini. Le *palais* actuel est aussi muré que l'autre, et ne contient plus qu'un grand vide, et pas une majesté. —Pas de 'successeurs', pas d'héritiers. —Des simulacres. . . .

Au fait, je suis bien démodé à m'inquieter ainsi du *Palais*. Il est déjà 'monument historique'. Il n'enferme plus rien de vivant.   (p. 49; my italics and ellipsis)

(In any case, everything that went on [at the Palace], no more than a few years ago, is evidently of another age. It's all over. Today's palace is just as walled up as the other and contains nothing more now than a great emptiness, not grandeur. No "successors," no heirs. Just simulacra. . . .

In fact, troubling myself in this way about the Palace, I'm really out-of-date. It's already a "historical monument." Nothing living is shut up in there.)

In this apparently irreversible passage from the *Palais* of his dreams to the *palais actuel*, the anachronistic position of the narrator is textually inscribed, and the likelihood of his inclusion in a degraded *nous*, along with Jarignoux, intimated. J. E. (*Jarignoux Européen*) is the alter ego of *je*, one who operates in the Capital the better to accumulate capital; as his stock goes up, other degraded capitals—parodies of the "majuscule impériale," such as the "Paradise of Widely Circulating Novels" ("Paradis des Romans à Gros Tirage"; p. 76)—take their place in the place of the exotic.

If this situation is to be averted, the narrator's passivity will have to be supplemented by an heroic activity. *Segalen* comes into contact with his young hero, René Leys, as a result of a last-gasp effort to "pénétrer dans le 'Dedans'"; he decides to take René Leys on as his professor, the better to acquire some knowledge of "the difficult 'Northern Mandarin'" that might help him gain entry into the Palace. The youth's extraordinary grasp of Chinese culture and languages is the ground of probability out of which his subsequent, improbable adventures can emerge. *Segalen*'s new professor of languages quickly turns into a "Professeur"—a person who, it soon appears, has access to the Palace and is willing to re-present it for his student's benefit.

The hero function detaches itself from the narratorial position, and a dialogue, one that will prove mutually delusive, ensues between the two men; this dialogue takes the place of the exotic story that *Segalen* initially wanted to live/tell. René Leys, son of a Belgian grocer ("le Père Epicier"), comes to assume for *Segalen* the activist qualities that he himself does not possess: René Leys's amatory success with the empress ("le Phénix"), for instance, complements the narrator's unfulfilled desire to possess, *à la Loti*, a Manchu woman. The heroic nature of René Leys cannot, however, come to light until his biological family has been effaced. Only once the grocer-father, epitome of all the insipid bourgeois values that Segalen associated with republicanism and colonialism, returns to France will the youth begin to recount his adventures; only then will he begin to "exotericize" the *Dedans* for his eager listener and thereby revive the latter's exotic dream.

René Leys becomes for *Segalen* an authority on life in the Palace; their association—which, in a curious way, is analogous to that of an ethnographer and his native informant[32]—creates a supplement of knowledge in excess of that possessed by the journalistic world of money/information. Theirs, as the following dialogue makes clear early on, is a privileged point of view transcending the sort of common knowledge that orders day-to-day existence in contemporary China. René Leys has just told his student about an attempt against the Regent's life; *Segalen*, who had already read about it "in the public papers," shows little interest at first. When René Leys asks him whether he knows who discovered the bomb, the narrator replies in the negative—with a pessimistic finality that echoes the opening sentence of his notebook: "No,

I know nothing about it. Nobody knows anything about it. I read in the papers that 'the police are investigating and believe they have the culprits.' So one will never know anything about it."

But René Leys promptly takes the place of this "nobody" (*personne*) who knows nothing about the incident:

—La Police? —Et René Leys prononce le mot avec un mépris tout . . . parisien. La police est arrivée . . . trop tard aussi. C'était déjà découvert.

Je prête un peu l'oreille. Mon professeur se déciderait enfin à m'apprendre un peu plus que ne m'en ont enseigné les journaux?   (p. 51)

("The Police?" —And René Leys pronounces the word with a contempt that is altogether . . . parisian. "The police arrived . . . too late as well. It had already been discovered."

I pay a little more attention. Would my professor finally make up his mind to tell me a little more about it than the newspapers have taught me?)

René Leys eventually reveals to the narrator the existence of a "Police Secrète"—one that more effectively ensures the safety of the Empire than the risible "police." *Segalen* had already heard, or thought he heard, about the existence of this Secret Police from his native professor Wang, but in the youth's account it becomes an idea to which he can enthusiastically attach himself: a supplemental ground upon which the exotic Capital might still stand, a "P.S." extending beyond the journalistic confines of contemporary China.

Segalen's belief in the veracity of René Leys's stories about life in the Palace stems in great part from the faith in vision that we saw to be a cornerstone of Loti's aesthetics ("on n'imagine pas, sans l'avoir vu . . . !"). Indeed, the first intimation that *Segalen* has of his young professor's in-sight comes as a gloss on the word *voir*. Having confided to René Leys his idea of writing a book about the late Emperor Kuang-hsü, *Segalen* goes on to state that his great regret is to have arrived in China a few years too late:

—Je coudoie tous les jours des gens qui, le temps d'une audience, sont entrés là, et ont pu l'apercevoir. Je doute, d'ailleurs, qu'ils aient su bien *voir*.

—Je l'ai vu, prononce mon Professeur, avec un respect soudain . . .   (p. 34)

("Every day I rub shoulders with people who got in there, for the span of an audience, and were able to catch a glimpse of him. I doubt, though, whether they were really able to *see*."

"I saw him," declares my Professor, with a sudden respect . . .)

Those Europeans who actually "saw" the Emperor, *Segalen* insinuates, were limited in their outlook to the sort of gregarious vision that we

saw at work in Loti's *Derniers jours*. In *René Leys* this degraded vision
is embodied by Jarignoux who, as the Empire collapses, will snigger:
"It's a pleasure to see such a beautiful, and rich, country open itself up
to the light of progress!" (p. 202) By contrast, although René Leys's
imagination is as grounded in a visual impressionism as Loti's, it does
not appear to be subject to the same historical limitations. His excep-
tional stories have the authority of a privileged vision: "That's peremptory. That's *seen*," the narrator enthuses (p. 48). They unfold with
"all the self-evident logic of the facts" ("la logique éclatante de l'évi-
dence").

Over the course of *Segalen*'s journal, René Leys's evidence accumu-
lates and, eventually, becomes *évidée*; his stories will be emptied out by
the turn of events—political events that come to annex the apparent
autonomy of the "P.S." and draw it back into the logic of another, less
appealing, (hi)story. The hollowness of the imperial story that René
Leys has produced, with the help of the narrator, will become especially clear near the end of the journal when revolutionary tumult over-
takes Peking. The fabricated nature of the young professor's evidence
is, however, alluded to throughout in various ways, as, for example,
in the play between majuscule and minuscule letters. Let us examine
one more such instance of this play—an important one, both because
it deepens our understanding of the process of (mis)comprehension
that enables the two men to "capitalize" upon each other, formulating
and reformulating the content of an imperial story, and because it
raises the question of history that will eventually undo the "tangled
hierarchy" of hero and narrator and destruct their mutual (re)con-
struction of an exotic *Protocole*.

Having casually admitted that the Phoenix, his purported imperial
lover, was the woman who unburdened him of his virginity (*pucelage*),
René Leys goes on to voice his worries about the rebel Sun Yat-sen,
whom the narrator had mentioned some three months earlier to his
apparently uninterested professor. *Segalen* consoles the youth:

—Non, mon cher. Ne vous alarmez plus. Sun-Yat-Sen! Vous n'y pensiez même
pas, l'autre jour, quand je vous en ai parlé! Avouez-le: je vous ai mis à l'oreille
cette puce cantonaise. Dangereux? Tenez: comme cela.

Et de mon ongle du pouce droit, j'écrase sur celui du gauche un parasite
imaginaire. Je termine en soufflant:

—Que la Dynastie en fasse autant, et voilà l'insecte et sa démangeaison ré-
volutionnaire passée . . . et de nouveau de longs jours de règne et de bonnes
nuits . . . d'amour. Au reste, vous ne m'avez jamais parlé des vôtres qu'en

termes si poétiques qu'il m'a fallu inventer le réel. Pourtant, vous n'êtes pas là qu'en Esprit. Du côté 'chair,' que se passe-t-il?

—Il y a le protocole, répond, sans rougir apparemment, le jeune homme ainsi mis en cause.

Je voudrais bien, sinon répéter ce Protocole, qui, dans ses gestes principaux, me semble remonter à la plus haute antiquité, du moins en connaître les nuances . . .   (pp. 164–65)

("No, my dear boy. Don't be alarmed. Sun Yat-sen! You didn't give him a thought, the other day, when I spoke to you about him. Admit it: I put this cantonese flea in your ear. Dangerous? Here: watch this."

And with my right thumbnail, I crush an imaginary parasite on my left. Blowing [it away], I conclude:

"Let the Dynasty do the same, and there's an end to the insect and his revolutionary itch . . . and, once again, long days of rule and pleasant nights . . . of love. Besides, you've never told me about yours except in such poetic terms that I've had to invent the real. And yet you're not there only in Spirit. 'Flesh'-wise, what goes on?"

Having been implicated in this way, the young man answers, apparently without a blush, "there's the protocol."

I would really like, if not to rehearse this Protocol, which, in its principal movements, I believe goes back to the earliest antiquity, at least to get acquainted with its nuances . . .)

Having disposed, with an imposing rhetorical gesture, of Sun Yat-sen and contemporary politics, Segalen returns to the object of his exotic desire. His professor's stories have left him in a capital state of anticipation; if they are to prove more than *jeux d'Esprit*, however, they will need further substantiation. *Segalen* thus provides René Leys with a new hermeneutic tool—the *côté 'chair'*—with which to interpret the *Dedans* for him and reveal it as something more than a poetic invention. René Leys then supplies a complementary term, the *protocole*; this *protocole*, in the youth's initial formulation, applies only to the limited domain of the "fleshly" that *Segalen* had specifically asked about. The narrator, however, seizes upon the term and makes of it an exotic *Protocole* more in keeping with the capitalized *Esprit* that was his own point of departure. It is, however, impossible for *Segalen* to "repeat" this Protocol; he is but a narrator in search of a hero and thus able only to (mis)comprehend the person who apparently does act it out. For this reason, *Segalen* will never be truly satisfied; all he is left with at the end of this little exchange is another poetic term that needs further "fleshly" clarification and narratorial (mis)comprehension.

Other factors complicate this unstable interpretive process yet fur-

ther. *Segalen*'s capacity for (mis)comprehension is, for instance, reinforced by René Leys's increasing skill at imitating the narrator's Capital
style of writing. Looking at an example of the Belgian youth's pen-
manship, *Segalen* notes a significant change in it: "The writing is still
indecisive, but with strokes, an emphasis, majuscules that were certainly not drawn in this way before" and that are clearly borrowed from
the older man's handwriting ("je sais à quelle écriture il vient tout juste
de les emprunter: à la mienne"; p. 154). René Leys's newfound ability
to use the "majuscule impérialissime," in turn, appears to confirm his
potential for realizing even more expansive, heroic actions: "It's not
only his majuscules that are straightening up and taking a virile turn"
(p. 161), the narrator glowingly insinuates, referring to his professor's
supposed amorous escapades with the empress.

The mutually delusive, and potentially unending, constructions of
narrator and hero give way, however, under the pressure of historical
circumstances. The fictionality of René Leys's story becomes ever more
obvious as a new, weightier form of evidence appears on the exotic
scene. The first time that the youth is discovered in flagrante delicto
occurs after the arrival of Yüan Shih-k'ai in Peking. This event, which
signals the fall of the Empire and for which Jarignoux has prepared a
disbelieving *Segalen*, completely subverts René Leys's contention—
supposedly based on "confidential telegrams received from Hankow"—that Yüan has just been stationed a thousand kilometers from
Peking. The narrator himself witnessed the arrival of Yüan, though
there is nothing heroic about this vision since it was had in the company of the very "crowd" that the exotic subject so desires to keep apart
from (p. 208). Arriving home that day, *Segalen* is possessed of irrefutable evidence—he knows what everybody knows because he has seen
what everybody has seen. As yet unaware of this turn of events, René
Leys confides to him, citing information culled in yet more secret telegrams, that Yüan has, as ordered, arrived at Hankow. *Segalen* is forced
to contradict him:

—Eh bien, moi qui n'ai reçu aucune dépêche confidentielle, je vais t'annoncer
sous le sceau du secret absolu que Yuan Che-k'aï est dans nos murs . . .
   Il prend un air très fermé . . . Je ris avec un peu d'aigreur:
—Jure-moi de n'en rien dire aux cinq cents personnes qui l'ont vu arriver
tout à l'heure à la gare . . .   (p. 209)

("Well, look, me who hasn't received a single confidential telegram, I'm going
to inform you under the seal of absolute secrecy that Yüan Shih-k'ai is within
our walls . . .")

He adopts an impassive expression . . . I laugh somewhat bitterly:
"Swear to me that you won't say anything about this to the five hundred people who saw him arrive at the train station just now . . .")

Confronted with this sarcastic rebuttal, René Leys attempts one last recuperative fiction, but it sounds fatally hollow: *Segalen*, he counters, has actually seen Yüan's double! Unable to complete his improbable story, the youth faints, succumbing to another of the syncopes to which he is prone. René Leys's syncope here marks his fall from heroic grace to the biological state of a man-child who has nothing left to say ("il redevient enfant"—*infans*: incapable of speech). In his place, the real-life Yüan emerges, his own fall from favor in 1908 finally reversed (a fall that, interestingly enough, the narrator had earlier referred to by the rhetorical figure of apocope; p. 84).

The narrator's definitive entry into "these days that we are living" (p. 189) coincides with his emergence as a *colonial* writer. The *Segalen* who describes Yüan's arrival in Peking can, I would suggest, be identified with the Segalen who gave such an enthusiastic assessment of Yüan in the articles for *Lectures pour tous*. At this point the political outlook of narrator and author coincide; the fall of the Empire effaces the possibility of an exotic vision and the narrator must adopt another, to our ears, less palatable discursive position. In any struggle between the liberal principles of "this perfect cretin," Sun Yat-sen, and a potential *chef* like Yüan—a "mandarin of the Ancien Régime"—there could be little doubt upon whose side an erstwhile exotic subject like Segalen/*Segalen* would pin whatever hopes remained to him.[33] A real politics, politics of the real, emerges at the point where the possibility of exoticism disappears. The death of René Leys coincides with the birth of "this hideous Peking, already almost a republic" (p. 232); no longer "the habitat of my dreams," revolutionary Peking is completely finished for Segalen.

The finality of this state of affairs is, in fact, inscribed in the very place that had been, for the narrator and his hero, the space of exotic possibilities: namely, the "P.S." Jumping outside the time of the notebook (1911), the postscript of *René Leys* simply affirms: "Ecrit à Pei-king du 1ᵉʳ novembre 1913 au 31 janvier 1914." What this nod to history signifies is that there can be no discursive supplement that does not take place, or have its place, in post-revolutionary time. From its beginning, the exotic position of the narrator was an entirely nostalgic one, at odds with an epoch in which the only pertinent authorial choice would seem to have been whether to assume the burden of a degraded political discourse or to withdraw into the shelter of "poetic language."

Just before the definitive end of the book, however, the central act of *René Leys* takes place: *Segalen* re-reads his manuscript. The text's turning-in upon itself generates a complex *mise en abyme* in which the problem of undecidability (what, if anything, in René Leys's account was actually true) is ensconced and endlessly repeated. Only by an act of re-reading can *Segalen*, and the reader of *René Leys*, determine the amount of truth in the young Belgian's stories; since the notebook lacks, and will always lack, the "truth" about René Leys, however, the only conclusion open to the re-reader in this respect is that the text has been written, that it is *écriture*. This revaluation of the book, in which it ceases to be the straightforward chronicle of *Segalen*'s various and sundry encounters with a young Belgian by the name of René Leys and takes on the mantle of a self-referential text, is undoubtedly one result of reading *René Leys*—perhaps, for our textually oriented generation, the most relevant result. And yet, in its unwillingness to accredit the sort of reading a contemporary like Gilbert de Voisins performed on *René Leys*, the modernist interpretation fails, I think, to address those issues at the novel's exotic heart.

To re-read *René Leys* is also to consider exoticism in the light of the definitive recoding it has undergone on first reading: the narrator's project has been superseded by colonial reality and hence can never again be read as an authentic possibility. "Everything is so calm in Peking at present," *Segalen* remarks at the outset of his notebook (p. 20). This pervading calm, in which the Imperial Palace might still seem the timeless habitation of "a many-sided, altering, and always renascent hero"[34] like Kuang-hsü or René Leys, is broken with the coming of the revolutionary storm. To begin (again), from this endlessly repeatable ending, is to see the tragic inadequacy of any and all such heroes and the impossibility of those exotic vistas initially present to *Segalen*. A curious phrase in the narrator's entry for 8 October 1911 then takes on a significance that was quite simply not present before. Prefacing his account of a conversation with René Leys, *Segalen* notes: "He responds, with an air of mystery that I sense has already been penetrated, entirely penetrated [*percé à jour, au grand jour*]" (p. 181). The interest of this remark, which is followed by a long dialogue about the origin of the name "Pei-king," resides in the fact that, upon first reading, the reference to a mystery that has been "percé à jour" makes no sense:

the narrator is still under the spell of his hero, still engaged by the exotic possibilities that his youthful interlocutor is opening up to him. On re-reading, however, this phrase (which so loudly echoes the ending of Loti's *Derniers jours*) makes all the sense in the world—the modern post-revolutionary world in which Segalen wrote *René Leys*, a world from which the exotic and its singular mysteries have been obliterated once and for all.

But our exotic story does not end quite here. To re-read *René Leys* is, certainly, to know that this story that was to have begun has in fact already come to its definitive end; yet, re-reading the novel in the light of this "once and for all," we must also read it under the sign of a *once again*—for in the wake of this ending, we are nonetheless beginning, once again, what must, in the end, be once again obliterated. And having arrived at this point, we find ourselves in the position of the author himself: Segalen, who chooses to begin after the end of that which he had hoped to come before; who, in writing *René Leys*, chooses to kill off a second time what was already dead, thereby giving the appearance of life to what initially had none.

The significance of this willfully nostalgic "appearance" can be inferred, I believe, from Giorgio Agamben's superb analysis of the *Immémoriaux*.[35] Agamben argues that Segalen's project in his first novel is to represent a world grounded in orality, performance, and myth. In attempting to speak about this original culture (culture of origins), however, Segalen necessarily speaks from the vantage point of his own society and must therefore have recourse to a medium, literature, that is at an absolute remove from this origin: the remove of writing. Lacking what is anterior to it, literature can never achieve its goal of returning to, by representing, this more original culture. The two worlds, the new and the old, are separated by a chasm that cannot be bridged; to seek after what came before is to keep coming up against this insuperable distance.

Vitally aware of this distance, Segalen will thus approach his subject matter not in terms of presence but of absence: paradoxically, the only way for him to communicate with the exotic world of Maori culture will be to record an absence, to remember (*Andenken*) the origin as that which has already been forgotten. In order to do so, he must recreate the unbridgeable gap that divides his writing from what is other than it. As Agamben explains, "The origin must be forgotten, erased (*oublier* [to forget], *oblivisci*, belongs, like *oblinere*, to the technical vocabulary of writing and means etymologically: to cross out [*raturer*]), in order that, thus abolished, the origin can be commemorated and assumed as foundation by a literature badly in need of origins" (p. 172). Inseparable from the erasure that it undergoes—indeed, that it has already undergone—this immemorial origin is accessible to Segalen's writing only once it has been abolished. Only thus can it then be remembered—or, more precisely, (mis)remembered—since in re-presenting this absent origin we can do no more than conjure up the appearance of what is irrevocably gone, the unlikely likeness of what has already been obliterated.

If the *Immémoriaux* establishes the anterior ground of a writing (and colonizing) culture, *René Leys* fulfills a more limited, historically defined, task: to trace out the prehistory of one (exemplary) modern writer, the writer of *Stèles*, of the *Origines de la statuaire de Chine*, of the interviews with Yüan; to provide, that is, the genealogy of those poetic, archeological, and political discourses that all originate from the exhausted ground of Segalen's exoticist project. Indeed, the novel's ambiguous dedication ("à sa mémoire / V. S.") alerts us, from the outset, that what is at stake in *René Leys* is above all a personal act of memory. The "sa" could, to be sure, refer to the real-life Maurice Roy, or to his fictional double René Leys. There is, however, another alternative: "V. S." himself, the exotic subject *Victor Segalen* whose desire for the mysterious and the unknown will, through the course of the novel, be dispersed by a colonial reality already present from before the beginning. To read, and to re-read, *René Leys* is to (mis)remember what history has once and for all effaced: an exotic world and the individual who would there have found his longed-for *demeure*. Just as for *Segalen* the re-reading of his manuscript must be proof against the cynical possibility raised near its end, under a revolutionary sky ("my bad mood invading and besieging the Palace itself, I even begin to doubt my desire to have ever desired entering it!"; p. 228), so too for the author of *René Leys* its writing attests to the continued pertinence of what has nonetheless been entirely written out of modernity's "nouveau protocole."

Toward the end of his journal, *Segalen* remonstrates that "one must not turn one's back on the mysterious and the unknown. The rare moments when myth consents to grab you by the throat . . . to seek entry among the everyday facts of life . . . .; the hallucinated minutes that can nonetheless be measured with a watch, whose ticking then resounds over years: none of this ought to be neglected" (p. 215). These unknown mysteries have, no doubt, their points of intersection with what the twentieth century has come to valorize as the *unheimlich*, but the myth in question here is also a more dated one, having to do less with Freud than with Loti. *René Leys* recalls, with a piety that its ironical tone only serves to confirm, an alternative world that has already ceased to be anything more than a dream. In writing this book, Segalen will put himself at a double, and equivocal, remove from the exotic and its mysteries—one that not only pushes him yet further away from the object of his desire but draws him back toward it in what is now the only possible way, a way that leads through the impossible, the im-memorial.

Rewriting the exotic through the antithetical lens of a colonial sub-ject, assuming the untimely and discredited voice of the individual, Segalen resembles no one so much as Valéry's orator who, with a rhe-torical gesture, a metaphor, memorializes "acts that in times past were real." Stepping back from a colonialism that he cannot step outside of, Segalen records through his imaginings (*imaginaires*) the disappear-ance of what has already disappeared, thereby bestowing upon this "valeur première" the only existence that can now be ascribed to it—and the only existence, perhaps, that was ever worthy of it: an unreal one. As with all rhetorical productions, the primary sense of this ora-tor's gesture is political: taking up the burden of an unreal past is the example he sets and the end to which his equivocal practice of meta-phor would persuade us. In this assertion of what has already been retracted, in this recantation/re-cantation of the exotic, the author of *René Leys* directs us along an unviable path leading back, once again, to a world that is no longer ours—and that is ours to remember.

Chapter 5

A MAN OF THE LAST HOUR

JOSEPH CONRAD AND THE TRAGEDY OF EXOTICISM

> I can't call myself a child, but I am so recent that I may call myself a
> man of the last hour—or is it the hour before last?
> —J. Conrad, *Victory*

• *Forward and Back: Into the East with Conrad and Russell*

In 1920 Bertrand Russell, fresh from a disillusioning tour of Bolshevist
Russia, arrives in Republican China. Yüan Shih-k'ai's attempt at unit-
ing the country and proclaiming himself emperor having already mis-
carried before his death in 1916, the political situation has quickly de-
generated into a bitter civil war. The north is under the dominion of
various rival warlords, while Sun Yat-sen's Kuomintang has established precarious control over the southern provinces. Despite the cli-
mate of anarchy Russell encounters, his eight-month stay in this strife-
ridden country will leave him with a more positive impression than
had Lenin's Russia, where he went, as he says, "hoping to find the
promised land" but, notwithstanding his socialist allegiances, discovered only "a close tyrannical bureaucracy, with a spy system more elaborate and terrible than the Tsar's."[1] Russell's relative enthusiasm for
"Young China," which he sets out in a thoughtful political tract entitled
The Problem of China (1922), takes us in two different ideological directions: back to the individualistic tradition of nineteenth-century exoticism, and forward to the twentieth century's dramatic resurrection of

the exotic Other under the cover of an appeal to new values—revolutionary and collective—that, if realized, would deliver us from the impasse of an intolerable modernity.

China appears to Russell as a place where the individual can still exercise the autonomy proper to him. In China, Russell argues,

the individual does not feel obliged to follow the herd, as he has in Europe since 1914, and America since 1917. Men still think for themselves, and are not afraid to announce the conclusions at which they arrive. Individualism has perished in the West, but in China it survives, for good as well as for evil. Self-respect and personal dignity are possible for every coolie in China, to a degree which is, among ourselves, possible only for a few leading financiers.

(pp. 215–16)

The Great War has written an end to the individual, just as for Walter Benjamin it has ushered out the likelihood of an "authentic experience": from the ashes of this holocaust arise both the undignified masses and the individual's negative residue, both the "herd" and the "few leading financiers" who exercise their usurious control over it. As Max Horkheimer will put it a generation later, from the (apparently) quite different perspective of "critical theory," the liberal pursuit of self-interest leads to the disappearance of the (bourgeois) individual: "In our era of large economic combines and mass culture, the principle of conformity emancipates itself from its individualistic veil, is openly proclaimed, and raised to the rank of an ideal *per se*."[2] Partially compensating Russell's sense of loss is the "fact" that this deadeningly modern conformism has yet to make its appearance in China—just as Horkheimer's distaste for mass society is in part counterbalanced by his appeal to "the real individuals of our time," "the martyrs who have gone through infernos of suffering and degradation in their resistance to conquest and oppression" (p. 161).

This negative reaction to mass society, and the subsequent turn toward an "elsewhere" that as yet stands exempt from the evils of "our civilization," is clearly a repetition of that which greeted the twin revolutions at the turn of the nineteenth century: the Great War stands in for the Revolution, and another generation sets out in search of "new hope" abroad, buoyed by the thought of a more "authentic" way of life and for the most part oblivious to the unoriginality of their position. However, this neo-exoticist impulse will more often than not be supplemented by another nineteenth-century ideological project: international socialism/communism. Although a goodly number of these latter-day exotic subjects will continue to valorize an unsullied indigenous culture, the majority come to place their hope, not in any "traditional civilization," but in a new and better society of the future that will emerge both transformed and strengthened from its inevitable, and already ongoing, contact with the degraded world of "industrialism," "imperialism," and "Americanism" (to use a few of Russell's favorite epithets).[3] This, at least, is the hope raised in *The Problem of China*: "If they are not goaded into militarism," Russell prognosticates, the Chinese "may produce a genuinely new civilization, better than any that we in the West have been able to create" (p. 220).

Although it may perhaps determine the efficacy with which an indigenous culture is able to combat the contagion of a now-global modernity, the original worth of this culture, even its manifest superiority—"the Chinese are gentle, urbane, seeking only justice and freedom . . . [and] they have a civilization superior to ours in all that makes for human happiness" (p. 175)—is no longer the primary consideration. The exoticist project's engagement with the cultural past makes way here for the dream of a radically different future. Of the authors so far considered, only Verne showed (as will Pasolini) a commitment to this "genuinely new" future, but Verne's progressive liberalism came to a fin de siècle standstill because of his reluctance to think beyond the figure of the individual. What nineteenth-century socialism and, a fortiori, twentieth-century communism project, by contrast, is the creation of a new subject capable of responding to mass society on its own (plural, global) terms; we see this project at work, for example, in Malraux's novels about China, which are directed toward "the replacement of the individual hero by a *collective* protagonist," the revolutionary community.[4] Modernity and its degraded present, if they cannot be bypassed—as was the original project of exoticism—are, following this alternative political path, to be passed through and beyond.

Two very different responses to the postwar crisis of values thus co-inhabit Russell's text—the one entropic (valorizing what "still" is), the other progressive (accenting what "will" be). Although the latter predominates throughout, it is clear that Russell's commitment to the "international socialism" that he preaches is partial at best—distinctly attenuated, reformist and not revolutionary. His hopes for redirecting the rising tide of modernity toward a more enlightened future hinge for the most part upon the new possibilities that advanced technology, despite its abuse by the forces of "industrialism," has opened up to the world. Above all, he argues, the Chinese of the future must "learn to become technical experts and also to become skilled workers" (p. 261). Education and industrial development are the key points in a political program that repeatedly shies away from the radical changes that his socialist project presupposes. Indeed, the imperative of creating new values would seem for Russell to be indissociable from that of conserving an older set of values: "Perhaps something may be preserved," he insists, "something of the ethical qualities in which China is supreme, and which the modern world most desperately needs" (p. 224). The limited scope of his reforms and the persistent stress he places on indigenous "ethical qualities" are obvious signs of Russell's unwillingness to adopt a point of view that would relegate the individual to the backpages of history.

The difficulty that Russell has in thinking the collective on its own terms, without reference to the disappearing figure of the individual, comes out most vividly when he speaks of the need for a council of sages to rule China. "The genuinely progressive people throughout the country," he states, must "unite in a strongly disciplined society, arriving at collective decisions and enforcing support of those decisions upon all its members" (pp. 258–59). Russell's appeal to "genuinely progressive people," for all that it recalls the dictatorship of the proletariat or some other such form of group rule, also emphatically points back in the direction of the individuals who would make up this "collective." The path forward into a positive future depends upon the continued existence of what that future shall have surpassed; only because China is a place where "the individual does not feel obliged to follow the herd" can Russell foresee there a (necessarily collective) resolution to the ills of modernity. His optimistic position, in short, depends upon this uneasy conflation of an individual- and a group-oriented politics.

In a letter of 23 October 1922, an aging Joseph Conrad warned Russell that this proposed council of sages "would become a centre of delation, intrigue and jealousy of the most debased kind," going on to add that "no freedom of thought, no peace of heart, no genius, no virtue, no individuality trying to raise its head above the subservient mass, would be safe before the domination of such a council and the unavoidable demoralisation of the instruments of this power."[5] Here Conrad takes sides against a form of power that he sees as entirely inimical to certain fundamental values. In defending the cause of "genius" and "individuality" against that of social change, he is, of course, adopting a reactionary position and yet one that is nonetheless more radical than Russell's inasmuch as it acknowledges, if only to warn against, the qualitative difference between individual and collective action; once brought into line with the latter, the former undergoes an essential transformation. That this change will be for the better is the hypothesis of a truly socialist politics; that it can only be for the worse is the supposition of a writer like Conrad for whom any non-traditional collective takes on the negative features of a debased bureaucracy and a subservient but readily agitated herd. In these modern mass formations, the individual as such counts for little or nothing; as the crowd psychologist Gustave Le Bon had put it a generation before, "In a crowd men always tend to the same level, and, on general questions, a vote recorded by forty academicians is no better than that of forty water-carriers."[6] Whether considered as a positive or as a negative phenomenon, this "equality" is what Russell must overlook if he is to pursue the optimistic path of reform, although as his correspondence shows he was by no means secure in his position: he would, indeed, admit to Conrad that the latter's pessimism probably conformed more to the facts than his own "artificial hopes for a happy issue in China."[7]

Notwithstanding these doubts, Russell's career as a social reformer would extend well into the century, and if I have lingered over his portrait of "Young China," it is partially in order to anticipate some of the issues that I discuss at length in the following chapter on Pasolini's grandiose hopes for the "Third World." As far as the subject of this chapter is concerned, however, no such neo-exoticist horizons were to emerge in the wake of the First World War and its devastation. Unable to embrace Russell's revolutionary hopes, and unwilling, in his confrontation with modernity and mass society, to remain in the tragic state of tension that characterizes the great works of his middle period, late Conrad will come to uphold the integrity of values such as "individuality" and "genius" that a work like *Heart of Darkness* had already effectively hollowed out. This unproblematical return to his former beliefs is evident, for instance, in the brief preface that Conrad wrote in 1922 for a book of travels by his friend Richard Curle. Collected in his *Last Essays* (pp. 84–92), this seldom-mentioned piece is worth looking at here since it is his most concentrated and theoretical account of what it means to write about exotic locales in an age when "our very curiosities have changed, growing more subtle amongst the vanishing mysteries of the earth."

In his reading of Curle's *Into the East*, Conrad sketches a deeply pessimistic analysis of the "spirit of modern travel" that he feels the book embodies. Nowadays, he notes, "many people encompass the globe"; they go rushing through the world with blank notebooks and even blanker minds, incapable of realizing what such "infinitely curious and profoundly inspired men" as Hugh Clapperton and Mungo Park experienced in their journeys through darkest Africa (p. 89). The time for voyages, and books, like those of Marco Polo "is past": little or nothing remains to be done in the way of traveling "on this earth girt about with cables, with an atmosphere made restless by the waves of ether, lighted by that sun of the twentieth century under which there is nothing new left now, and but very little of what may still be called obscure" (p. 88).

Conrad insistently assures his reader that the days of "heroic travel" are gone, "unless, of course, in the newspaper sense, in which heroism like everything else in the world becomes as common if not as nourishing as our daily bread." Formerly exotic settings have long since been despoiled of "their old black soul of mystery"; soon they "will be bristling with police posts, colleges, tramway poles." Curle would seem to be perfectly suited to the task of chronicling this "marvellously piebald" world: "He is very modern, for he is fashioned by the conditions of an explored earth in which the latitudes and longitudes having been recorded once for all have become things of no importance, in the sense that they can no longer appeal to the spirit of adventure, inflame no imagination, lead no one up to the very gates of mortal danger" (p. 90). Appealing to the "spirit of adventure," inflaming the imagination, leading one's reader up to "the very gates of mortal danger": such are the possibilities still open to those writers not yet fashioned by "the conditions of an explored earth."

But where, we might well ask, does the author of these lines stand in relation to this ongoing process of decline? Conrad's slightly condescending tone toward the younger Curle would certainly lead us to believe that he considers himself to be something rather less than "very modern." No doubt. And yet I would suggest that this preface gains its full resonance only if we consider this portrait of Curle as first and foremost a piece of displaced autobiography. Shunted off onto the generation of writers that follows in his tracks is a problem that, from the beginning, fashions Conrad's own work as a writer: the problem of a truly global modernity. Everywhere and in everything, this modernity cancels out whatever might once have differed from it, reducing both the earth and those who inhabit it to a single common denominator. As David Simpson has argued, convincingly to my mind, Conrad

writes from within an undifferentiated world: "Conrad has reduced all
the potentially dialectical elements in the antitheses of primitive and
civilized societies, whereby each might function as an image of what
the other is not, to a state of monotonous, undifferentiated oneness.
. . . The fetishized world of the colonial nations has imposed itself
upon the far-flung corners of the earth, creating a commerce in the images of its own alienation."[8] Within the global space of this "monotonous, undifferentiated oneness," goods take the form of commodities,
fetishized, mechanically reproduceable, and we ourselves come to
seem no more than the interchangeable parts of a mass society whose
fate is inseparable from the impersonalized machinations of the bureaucratic State.

In Conrad, then, the dialectical encounter between primitive and
civilized worlds, between an outside and an inside, that was at the
heart of nineteenth-century exoticism is determinedly absent. The
New Imperialist crisis that I have been chronicling in this book is Conrad's point of departure as a writer, and for this very reason, as Simpson goes on to say, he "does not tend to show us the genesis of this
process of [colonial] exportation; to do so would be to introduce the
energetic antithesis of innocence and corruption which he clearly
means to avoid." To write from within an undifferentiated world
means forgoing the sort of "energetic" ideological oppositions that
were at the heart of the exoticist project. The difference between innocence and corruption, or between savagery and civilization, is from
this perspective no difference at all; it is entirely unreal.

But Simpson's claim needs to be nuanced in at least two ways, both
of which I hope to expand upon in this chapter through a discussion
of Conrad's evolution as a writer from 1895 to 1900. First, there are indeed many signs of such "energetic antitheses" in his first novels, although Conrad is unable to join them into a coherent whole. The failure of his early works to achieve this heroic coherence is a symptom of
that undifferentiated perspective which is already his, from the time
he first takes pen to paper, but with which he will only come to grips
in *Heart of Darkness* and *Lord Jim*. In these works, the matter of guilt and
innocence is no longer at issue; it can never again be a real issue for one
who takes a worldwide modernity as his point of departure. But, and
here is the second (and all-important) nuance that must be attached to
Simpson's claim, the passage from exotic difference to colonial indifferentiation is nonetheless not forgotten in these more properly Conradian works. The "energetic antitheses" of exoticism continue to

haunt the world of Conrad's novels, in spite of his by-now complete awareness of their inadequacy to the present. Conrad de-energizes these oppositions, hollowing them out and yet nonetheless conserving them in this weakened form; they inhabit the text as absence, as what has been canceled out of an indifferent world girt round by wires and enlightened by the sun of disenchantment. The creation of this absence will occupy us in the following pages: the tragic absence of that "hour before last" without which, I have been suggesting, the "last hour" of our modernity cannot (begin to) be thought.

The Crowds of the Anxious Earth: (Rewriting) The Individual in Decline, 1895–1900

> "What's good for it?" He lifted up a long forefinger. "There is only one remedy! One thing alone can us from being ourselves cure!" The finger came down on the desk with a smart rap. The case which he had made to look so simple before became if possible still simpler—and altogether hopeless. There was a pause. "Yes," said I, "strictly speaking, the question is not how to get cured, but how to live."   —J. Conrad, Lord Jim

Conrad's early novels, which we, along with the vast majority of Conradians, may think of as the products of his "artistic immaturity,"[9] subscribe—albeit uneasily—to the traditional vision that generated nineteenth-century exoticism. Gauguin's "native of old" is assuredly present in Almayer's Folly (1895) and Outcast of the Islands (1896): indigenous females, mysterious and potentially salvational objects of desire; sovereign figures who conjure up the image of what Conrad would much later refer to (in the preface for Into the East) as those "real chieftain[s] in the books of a hundred years ago." After briefly examining these novels, I will go on to show, paying special attention to his shifting representation of individuals and crowds, how this already vacillating belief in the exotic collapses in the Tales of Unrest (1898) that follow upon his first two novels. Conrad's attempts at finding a discursive resolution to this situation lead him, on the one hand, to the historicist vision of "solidarity" that shapes the Nigger of the 'Narcissus' (1897) and, on the other, to the memorialistic strategy that he adopts in Heart of Darkness (1899) and, most notably, in Lord Jim (1900). The story of Conrad's evolution as an exotic writer does not, obviously, end with the two Marlow novels, but the literary and political matrix of subsequent works like Nostromo (1904), The Secret Agent (1907), or Victory

(1915) ought, I believe, to be traced back to the tragic insight that he develops there. In different, though intimately related ways, they testify to the same cultural malaise that the author of *Lord Jim* had diagnosed as incurable—a diagnosis that seems to leave Conrad with no room to operate but which in fact proves the precondition of his essentially posthumous enterprise.

Gareth Jenkins has argued that in Conrad's early novels "natives are natives—colourful, exotic, essentially 'different'—and European life and language, which encapsulate and place this exoticism, are assumed to be superior."[10] Jenkins is, I think, at least partially correct. The omniscient narrator of Conrad's first novel, *Almayer's Folly*, is indeed committed to the representation of "savagery" in all its difference from the world of "civilization"—an autonomy assured by, among other things, the fact that colonialism in the Malayan peninsula is as yet a relatively limited phenomenon (Dutch control over the state of Sambir is said to be only "nominal"; the interior of "unknown Borneo" is consistently invoked as one of the remaining dark places of the earth). But the assumed "superiority" of European life and language is quite another matter. If it is fair to say that the Conradian narrator would like to valorize this civilization, it is nonetheless obvious, as any reader of *Almayer's Folly* (and *An Outcast of the Islands*) knows, that he more often than not ends up exposing it—or at least a particular version of it—to the light of a corrosive irony. This irony is in great part defused, however, by the narrator's positive emphasis on savagery: paradoxically, the unsullied existence of savagery ensures the continued possibility of that truly "superior" civilization in which the narrator still places, if only with the greatest of difficulty, his Old Imperialist faith.

What must be avoided at all costs in the manichean world of Conrad's Malayan novels is an indifferent mingling of these two distinct spheres. It is just such a confusion that initially characterizes the half-caste Nina Almayer: brought up in the colonial world of Singapore and then "thrown back again into the hopeless quagmire of barbarism," she had, we are told, "lost the power to discriminate." The two worlds appear all too similar to her:

Whether they plotted for their own ends under the protection of laws and according to the rules of Christian conduct, or whether they sought the gratification of their desires with the savage cunning and the unrestrained fierceness of natures as innocent of culture as their own immense and gloomy forests,

Nina saw only the same manifestations of love and hate and of sordid greed chasing the uncertain dollar in all its multifarious and vanishing shapes.

(p. 43)

David Simpson cites this passage as evidence of the lack of differentiation that the "configured structure of imaginative commerce" has exported to the far-flung reaches of the globe.[11] As I have argued, this "lack of differentiation" will soon come to dominate Conrad's experience of the exotic; here, though, the case is not quite so desperate. If at this early point in the novel Nina has indeed lost the power to differentiate savagery and civilization, the same cannot be said of the narrator: that Europeans and Malayans pursue many similar ends merely proves that, as he says elsewhere, "there are some situations where the barbarian and the, so-called, civilized man meet upon the same ground" (p. 67). The original division that is constitutive of exoticism still holds true, even if one of its terms, the "so-called civilized," has been covered over with the shroud of irony and rendered, for the moment, inoperable.

The "savage cunning" of Nina's Malay kinsmen is no illusion: it is a quality that makes a difference, as Nina herself comes to see. Their "savage and uncompromising sincerity of purpose" will appear preferable to the "virtuous pretences of such white people as she had had the misfortune to come in contact with" (p. 43). Given the opportunity, the half-caste chooses the side of her "savage" mother over that of "a feeble and traditionless father," Almayer. That Nina is still capable of making such a choice is the novel's exotic presupposition—one effectuated by the arrival on the scene of a heroic native male, "the ideal Malay chief of her mother's tradition" (p. 64). A quintessentially romantic figure, whose father, significantly enough, is the *independent* Rajah of Bali, Dain Maroola wins Nina over with "the rude eloquence of a savage nature giving itself up without restraint to an overmastering passion" (p. 69). At the end of the novel, having escaped Sambir, the Dutch, and the enraged but powerless Almayer, the two will produce an heir for the Rajah—a son whose birth signals an extension of the Other's line into the indefinite future.

The difference that separates the world of the Malay from that of the European becomes especially clear if we consider one of the novel's central thematic motifs: vision. In *Almayer's Folly* Conrad opposes Dain's way of seeing to Almayer's in a manner that might well be characterized as Wordsworthian. In Book Twelve of *The Prelude*, Wordsworth speaks of a time when he was under the "absolute dominion" of "the bodily eye, in every stage of life / The most despotic of our senses."[12] It is this "despotism" that characterizes Dain's exotic world: concerning his initial encounter with Nina we are told, for instance, that "from the very first moment when his eyes beheld this—to him—perfection of loveliness he felt in his inmost heart the conviction that she would be his; he felt the subtle breath of mutual understanding passing between their two savage natures" (p. 63). Almayer's vision, on the other hand, is a badly flawed version of what Wordsworth (in "I Wandered Lonely as a Cloud," among other places) called the "inward eye"—that internalized vision by which the Wordsworthian subject is rescued from and redeems the power of the first, despotic eye. Rather than enlightening the exotic realm of the senses, however, Almayer merely projects upon it his own murky desire for material possessions. Entirely given over to "the commercial imagination," he can envision nothing more "in his mind's eye" than "the rich prize in his grasp" (p. 65); an adventurer like Lingard can only become "a hero in Almayer's eyes" because of "the boldness and enormous profits of his ventures" (p. 8).

Because of the failure of Almayer's vision, Conrad cannot, in a Wordsworthian manner, pursue a dialectical reconciliation of this opposition in favor of the "inward eye" of civilization. Rather, he must preserve the integrity of Dain's savage vision until such time as the two ways of seeing can effectively be brought together. In point of fact, though, one character in the novel is already capable of seeing with both an inward and a bodily eye: the half-caste Nina, whose face is early on described as being "turned towards the outer darkness, through which her dreamy eyes seemed to see some entrancing picture" (p. 16). But the reconciliation of inside and outside that Nina thus figures is not one Conrad can embrace, because her double vision is for him only another symptom of a hybrid condition that can no longer see any real difference between the worlds of savagery and civilization. It is a product of her *métissage*, and as such a sign of the disappearance of the truly exotic—a sign that must, ultimately, be erased if the original project of exoticism is to remain possible.

In order for the story to reach its exotic conclusion, Nina must forget the ambivalent, indifferentiating vision to which she is at first subject. She must give herself entirely over to the "outer darkness." In this respect, it is no doubt significant that Conrad transformed the original model for Almayer, Olmeijer, from a half-caste into a man of pure European stock; as Ian Watt points out, "this has the effect of dramatising the conflict in Nina's loyalties between her European father and her Malayan mother."[13] Figuring Nina's *métissage* as primary, rather than secondary, facilitates what for Conrad is the necessary task of erasing the (modern) condition of hybridity that she embodies; by virtue of her genetic proximity to the purely exotic, she can the more easily be thought of as effecting the dramatic return to savagery that her status as a half-caste would seem to have precluded.

Despite the air of exotic primitivism in *Almayer's Folly*, which the end of the novel would appear to consecrate, Conrad's sympathies are, ultimately, on the side of what I have termed imperialist exoticism, which assumes, as Jenkins puts it, the superiority of civilization over savagery and affirms the desirability of drawing the bodily eye up into the realm of mind. But, as the narrator's frequent outbursts of irony bear witness, this distinction was becoming increasingly difficult for Conrad to maintain. Imperialist exoticism posits a form of contact between the worlds of Same and Other that does not end with the victory of Flaubertian *bêtise* and the effacement of cultural difference in the name of a gregarious colonial bureaucracy; it depends upon the idea of a heroic individual capable of effecting the genial reconciliation of savagery and civilization that an older paternal figure like Tom Lingard is said to have achieved. To have attempted directly to represent this positive experience would have led Conrad to question the viability of his Old Imperialist beliefs in the age of the New Imperialism—and this, of course, will be the rock upon which his novel about Lingard, "The Rescuer" (begun in 1896 and abandoned three years later), runs aground. Instead, Conrad chooses to sidestep the issue and engage in a narrative that derives most of its strength from the exoticizing mode of exoticism. In privileging savagery at the expense of a civilization about which he was becoming increasingly cynical, Conrad succeeds, at least provisionally, in securing a field of action where a truly imperial subject might still, at some point in the future, exercise the heroic sovereignty expected of him.

Because he can hold out this possibility of a properly imperialist vision, Conrad is able to present Almayer's own flawed way of seeing as an anomaly: rather than being typical of a new colonial state of affairs, Almayer's "commercial imagination" is a quirk. The half-finished building that he has constructed in anticipation of the British Borneo Company's takeover of that part of the island—in anticipation, that is, of the coming of the New Imperialism to Sambir—proves no more than a folly in an (Old Imperialist) world where colonialism has its limits. If, at the end of the novel, this building becomes Almayer's dwelling place, it is his alone—a madhouse that is more an emblem of his own decadence than a sign of the imminent, and eminently reprehensible, colonial ascendancy his murky vision anticipates. Conrad must sacrifice Almayer, mark him off as a pathological case, an anti-hero, if he is to maintain the possibility of a heroic successor to the imperialist tradition that an adventurer like Lingard embodies. And yet no worthy successor to Lingard will emerge in Conrad's next novel, *An Outcast of the Islands*—a fact that no doubt strengthened the author's sense that his original exoticist project was misguided.

Looking back on the *Outcast* in his "Author's Note" (1919) to the novel, Conrad remarks that "it brought me the qualification of 'exotic writer'": "For the life of me I don't see that there is the slightest exotic spirit in the conception or style of that novel. It is certainly the most *tropical* of my eastern tales" (p. xiii). In fact, tropical scenery is about all that is left of an "exotic spirit" that can barely find a place in the novel: the world of savagery has been reduced to a state of nature, more or less emptied of its cultural content (a strategy closely related to the one we saw at work in the *Mariage de Loti*). Exotic nature—brooding, menacing, sublime—survives, in the midst of a narrative that even more so than *Almayer's Folly* fails to live up to its exoticist presuppositions.

Since the problems the *Outcast* raises and attempts to deflect are the same as those that troubled Conrad's first effort, we need not linger over it here. Worth pointing out, though, is the fact that its protagonist, Willems, assumes a role diametrically opposite to that of Almayer. Whereas the latter, his "inward eye" corrupted by visions of lucre, obviously fails to match the imperatives of a properly imperialist exoticism, Willems, in his tortured attachment to and repulsion from the "primitive woman" Aïssa, is a man who cannot live up to those of exoticizing exoticism; he cannot abandon his own inwardness and take up residence in the despotic realm of the senses. Although he briefly glimpses the outside world into which Dain and Nina escaped, Willems proves incapable of following through on his transgressive vision, mostly because of his "clear conviction of the impossibility for him to live with her people" (p. 152). Willems's self-deluding racism is the pathological flaw that disables him as the subject of an exoticizing exoticism; it prevents him from giving himself over to the Other, despite his desire for it in the person of Aïssa.

Presumably, a better man than Willems would have succeeded in detaching himself from his prejudices, or not have held them in the first place: this is one conclusion that the reader can draw from Conrad's often desultory account of the outcast's downfall. But the narrator lays down the foundation for a different interpretation, one based upon what I will be terming a *historicist* vision that willfully situates the exotic in the past, cutting it off from the degradation of the present. This historicist vision figures the past as free from the malaise that governs a present in which mediocrities like Almayer or Willems are typical rather than anomalous. With the building of the Suez Canal, we are told early on in the novel, the mystery of the sea was destroyed: "Like all mysteries, it lived only in the hearts of its worshippers. The hearts changed; the men changed. The once loving and devoted servants went out armed with fire and iron, and conquering the fear of their own hearts became a calculating crowd of cold and exacting masters" (pp. 12–13). There is no trace of this historicism in *Almayer's Folly*, and very little in *An Outcast of the Islands*: its presence, though, signals the possibility of the impossibility of continuing on as if a recourse to the exotic were still a present option in an age when hearts had changed and men had become part of a "calculating crowd." In the following examination of his *Tales of Unrest* and *The Nigger of the 'Narcissus,'* I will take a closer look at the dissolution of the exotic in Conrad's work and the simpleminded historicism—as simpleminded, in its own way, as Willems's racism, although perhaps more agreeable to the modern ear—with which he at first tried to combat this collapse. That Conrad found a way of putting this vision to a more complex, and politically more interesting, use in his "elegiac romances" *Heart of Darkness* and *Lord Jim* is the argument of this chapter's concluding section.[14]

The Malayan peninsula of his youth, Conrad asserts in his late essay "Geography and Some Explorers," made up part of "the old Pacific mystery, a region which even in my time remained very imperfectly charted and still remote from the knowledge of men" (p. 18). His first novels, although set in the past, remain committed to extending this "time" into our own day and age; the exotic "mystery" they invoke apparently remains unsolved. Almayer's folly and Nina's *métissage*, to be sure, point to a very different situation, but their fallen world is one that can still be wished, and written, away through a recourse to a form of narrative closure similar to that we find in a writer like Captain Marryat—whose novels, as Conrad himself noted in the 1898 essay "Tales of the Sea," invariably end in inheritance and marriage. The inadequacy of this resolution, which is already pretty well absent from the *Outcast*, soon impresses itself upon Conrad: his "time," and the uncharted world it once contained, has been displaced by a modernity that has no time for such mysteries. What he once lived can now only be remembered; perhaps, indeed, it was never anything more than the memory that it has become. Between 1896 and 1899, Conrad begins to probe both this hiatus that separates a desired but no longer possible exotic past from a repugnant but unavoidable colonial present and the nature of that bridge which his memory (de)constructs between them.

As Frederick Karl has noted, during the period immediately following the publication of *Outcast of the Islands* in 1896, Conrad was "caught at the conjunction of several literary styles":[15] he would experiment with at least three styles, each of which entailed a different approach to the figure of the individual, whose decline Conrad could no longer overlook. In "The Rescuer," he attempted to pursue the exotic vein of the early novels; the notorious difficulties he had in finishing this manuscript (abandoned in 1899, it would get taken up again some fifteen years later and eventually be published as *The Rescue* in 1920) derive in great part from his wish to portray Tom Lingard, a "simple, masterful, imaginative adventurer,"[16] as a viable alternative to the inadequate proto-colonial subjects who had taken center stage in his first two novels. "The Return," on the other hand, is characterized by an archly cosmopolitan prose that attempts to match its, for Conrad, unusual subject matter; his account of Alvan Hervey's marital problems hesitantly opens up onto the world-weary perspective of fin de siècle decadentism. In seemingly direct contrast to this story, *The Nigger of the 'Narcissus'* puts into play, as Karl says, "a more 'natural' style, though without the irony that would become characteristic of his middle career" (p. 401). The lack of irony signals the *Nigger* as Conrad's most positive fictional portrayal of the individual, whose modern decline, it is insinuated, can be arrested through an allegiance to and dependence upon a traditional community, the ship's crew; but the often-remarked "polyphonies" in this text deprive it of the ideological certitude that Conrad there aspires after.[17] The problem of the individual will, he discovers, require a quite different sort of (lack of) resolution.

Conrad was certainly aware of this shift in his work after the first two novels. In his "Author's Note" (1919) to the *Tales of Unrest*, he speaks of the brief story "The Lagoon" as marking "in a manner of speaking, the end of my first phase, the Malayan phase with its special subject and its verbal suggestions." For the moment, the exotic alternative disappears from Conrad's horizon—to be replaced by the explicitly colonial scene of "An Outpost of Progress," the refined atmosphere of "The Return," and the shipboard setting of the *Nigger*. The exotic disappears; or, rather, it makes one last appearance, in a register of loss that anticipates its treatment in *Heart of Darkness* and *Lord Jim*. If, Conrad remarks, "anybody can see that between the last paragraph of An Outcast and the first of The Lagoon there has been no change of pen, figuratively speaking" (p. v), it is equally obvious that something quite different is at stake in "Karain: A Memory": "I had not gone back to the Archipelago, I had only turned for another look at it" (p. vii). The Malayan peninsula can no longer be returned to; it can be apprehended only across a distance that is not spatial but temporal—recorded by a look that, in its secondariness (*another* look), must inevitably betray what was seen before. The "memory" of the man who narrates this story cannot reach its object, the exotic world of the native prince Karain. The space marked in the story's title by a colon, while it joins their two worlds together, also separates them definitively.

Karain, in reality no more than "a petty chief of a conveniently isolated corner of Mindanao," once offered the story's narrator the comprehensive vision of cultural alternatives that nineteenth-century exoticism thrived on. He stands for an entire way of life distinct from "ours": "He seemed too effective, too necessary there, too much of an essential condition for the existence of his land and his people, to be destroyed by anything short of an earthquake. He summed up his race, his country, the elemental force of ardent life, of tropical nature. He had its luxuriant strength, its fascination; and like it, he carried the seed of peril within" (p. 7). With its anaphoral insistence, this passage captures the sort of sovereign vision, or vision of a sovereign, that a writer like Loti craved. Filling the stage "with barbarous dignity" (p. 8), Karain embodies his culture and represents his people—"that crowd, brilliant, festive, and martial" who help make up the "gorgeous spectacle" of exoticism to which the narrator and his fellow adventurers bear witness (pp. 4, 7). "An adventurer of the sea, an outcast, a ruler," Karain retains the power "to awaken an absurd expectation of something heroic going to take place" (pp. 8, 6).

What does take place, of course, is something rather less heroic than might have been expected; Karain produces not deeds but words—a story within a story, a memory within a memory. He tells his shipboard audience about the life-sapping spell he finds himself under: he has come to be haunted by the unrestful shade of a dead friend whom he once betrayed. The tale at an end, one of his English listeners, Hollis, breaks the spell, returning Karain to his former self by giving him a "charm" made out of a Jubilee sixpence bearing "the image of the Great Queen" (p. 49). That this episode reveals (on the part, one suspects, of both Hollis *and* Conrad) a condescending attitude toward native superstition is an obvious and banal point; more interesting is the fact that the renewal of Karain's exotic power coincides with his (unwitting) inclusion in the world of money/information—a world in which the figure of the sovereign is no more than an image subordinated to the purposes of commerce. It is at precisely this moment of ambiguous renewal that the narrator loses track of Karain; what becomes of him is left up in the air (although we are led to believe that quite possibly he is "making it hot for the caballeros" who rule the Eastern Archipelago). But the capacity for action that has here been given back to Karain prepares the ground for a similarly counterfeit sovereignty that, as we will see, Conrad's *Lord Jim* explores in depth. Although his fatal leap from the *Patna* has forever put in doubt "the sovereign power enthroned in a fixed standard of conduct" (p. 50), Jim nonetheless goes on to reassert that power in the tropical solitude of Patusan.[18]

This, however, is to anticipate matters. It is not so much Karain's tale, and its problematical resolution, that need concern us here as the last pages of the story, where the narrator's evocation of an exotic past is explicitly situated in the degraded present of writing ("now"). Some years after parting company with Karain, the narrator meets one of his fellow adventurers, Jackson, in the Strand: "His head was high above the crowd . . . he had just come home—had landed that very day! Our meeting caused an eddy in the current of humanity. Hurried people would run against us, then walk round us, and turn back to look at that giant" (p. 53). Jackson stands out from the urban crowd by virtue of his recent contact with a world outside it. He appeals to the narrator, whose exotic tale about Karain will be inspired by this meeting with Jackson, in the same way that Lingard appealed to the omniscient narrator of *Outcast of the Islands*: "The breath of his words, of the very words he spoke, fanned the spark of divine folly in his breast, the spark that made him—(the hard-headed, heavy-handed adventurer—stand out from the crowd, from the sordid, from the joyous, unscrupulous, and noisy crowd of men that were so much like himself" (p. 273). Lingard, though, is a man among men: the "crowd" in which he plays a significant part is, if unscrupulous and sordid, also joyous, and compatible with his heroic individualism. The narrator of "Karain," by contrast, finds himself in a very different sort of crowd, one that (as the last lines of the story make clear) puts into question the present reality of his and Jackson's shared experience of the past.

In this anonymous "current of humanity," from which only the gigantic Jackson still stands out, or seems to, we have one of the first appearances in Conrad of what will become perhaps his preferred metonym for the global indifferentiation of modernity: the crowd, a "bad" crowd entirely lacking in any of the positive qualities that characterized other, traditional, group formations of men (Lingard's joyous and unscrupulous crowd of adventurers; Karain's brilliant, festive, and exotic crowd). For Conrad, as he makes clear in "An Outpost of Progress" (written after *Outcast of the Islands* and before "The Lagoon"), the herd mentality of this modern, essentially urban crowd is identical to that governing the new colonial subject.

With its biting and omniscient narratorial voice, a voice not yet marked by the nostalgia pervading *Heart of Darkness*, "An Outpost of Progress" represents Conrad's most direct literary attack against the New Imperialism and the impoverished minds that serve it. The colonial traders Kayerts and Carlier, both "incapable of independent thought," are exemplary of the individual's rapid decline in an age of mass society:

They were two perfectly insignificant and incapable individuals, whose existence is only rendered possible through the high organization of civilized crowds. Few men realize that their life, the very essence of their character, their capabilities and their audacities, are only the expression of their belief in the safety of their surroundings. The courage, the composure, the confidence; the emotions and principles; every great and every insignificant thought belongs not to the individual but to the crowd: to the crowd that believes blindly in the irresistible force of its institutions and of its morals, in the power of its police and of its opinion. But the contact with pure unmitigated savagery, with primitive nature and primitive man, brings sudden and profound trouble into the heart. (p. 89)

Conrad puts forward a double thesis in this passage. First, the "civilized" individual is not an independent being but, rather, the epiphenomenon of an obtuse collectivity. Conrad's thinking here shows a marked resemblance to that of Gustave Le Bon, who a few years before, in his study *The Crowd* (1895), had loudly proclaimed the new predominance of *la voix des foules*: "The destinies of nations are elaborated at present in the heart of the masses, and no longer in the councils of princes" (p. 15).

If this collective voice had drowned out every other, then our situation would indeed be dismal. Fortunately, and here is where Conrad's second thesis comes in, this is not (at least not yet) the case. Mass society has an outside: "pure unmitigated savagery" exists and is capable of disaggregating the herd, bringing "sudden and profound trouble" into its heart; indeed, this outside is, presumably, the point from which Conrad-as-narrator is able to launch his direct critique of mass society. But should this "savagery" disappear (and the presence of Makola, the "civilized nigger," signals this as an imminent possibility), then all likelihood of that absolutely necessary contact with a troubling outside would cease. In such a closed and enclosing society, there would be no more openings for a truly individual action—or even, as in the case of Kayerts and Carlier, reaction.

This is the dramatic sense of closure that comes to dominate much of fin de siècle literature, and to which Conrad too will, in his own way, accede. The problem these writers confronted was that of preserving a degree of autonomy for the individual in a world from which the possibility of such autonomy seemed absent. In *A rebours*, for instance, Huysmans has his hero, des Esseintes, try living out Baudelaire's idea of the artist—solitary, childless, but nonetheless "his king, his priest, and his God"—in an out-of-the-way place to the south of Paris, where "the uproar of foul crowds" ("le brouhaha des immondes foules"; p. 37) has not penetrated. And yet this convalescent retreat from mass society results in nothing more than an *immobilité* that, ultimately, provides neither cure nor satisfaction. Far from resolving the problem of decadence and the individual's looming disintegration "in the century's vile and servile throng" ("dans la turpide et servile cohue du siècle"; p. 335), des Esseintes's retreat merely ends up confirming the (impossible) necessity of *mouvement*—as we see in the ending, with its dilation back out into the fallen world of the metropolis.

Conrad, clearly, does not valorize this futile retreat into the self, and yet his work is in large part determined by the same sense of closure that so predominates in an author like Huysmans. The dilemma is clear: if his second thesis proves untenable, then all that remains for him is to chronicle, à la Flaubert, the *bêtise* of a "civilized" world—the sort of world introduced in his most ostensibly fin de siècle piece of writing, "The Return." Yet it is precisely in the midst of this *bêtise*, where the inadequacy of the "civilized" individual becomes most apparent, that we catch a glimpse of another approach to the dilemma—one that matches the problematical turn to memory we witnessed in

"Karain" and that draws out the essentially *hypocritical* nature of this turn.

Alvan Hervey, self-righteously appalled by his wife's aborted attempt at leaving him and their unsatisfactory but socially respectable marriage, engages her in a long, and imminently shallow, argument meant to sway her from the paths of scandal. Arguing for the status quo, he has occasion at one point to recall their past:

"Now, a scandal amongst people of our position is disastrous for the morality—a fatal influence—don't you see—upon the general tone of the class—very important—the most important, I verily believe, in—in the community. I feel this—profoundly. This is the broad view. In time you'll give me . . . when you become again the woman I loved—and trusted . . ."

He stopped short, as though unexpectedly suffocated, then in a completely changed voice said, "For I did love and trust you"—and again was silent for a moment. She put her handkerchief to her eyes.   (p. 164; ellipses in original)

This change of voice, to my mind, is the central event of the story. Here, memory has reworked the past (whether or not Hervey actually did at some point love and trust his wife is beside the point) and intruded upon the atrocious insincerity of the present. This is not to say that the change marks a return to sincerity, but merely that it registers another moment that is both different from the first, ongoing moment of hypocrisy and yet inseparable from it. Hervey's change of voice is, thus, doubly hypocritical: his initial hypocrisy is not displaced but merely supplemented. Although it disturbs the present, this memory-induced change of voice remains complicitous with the degraded strategies of persuasion that it at once reveals and participates in. Hervey's change of voice, in other words, anticipates the Conradian problem of the lie in which, as Marlow says in *Heart of Darkness*, resides "a taint of death, a flavour of mortality" (p. 82). For Conrad it is this mortal hypocrisy that must be grasped if anything is to come out of the sense of "one's own mediocrity and the world's corruption and degradation" that, as Edward Said has rightly argued, characterizes the vast bulk of late-nineteenth-century British and Continental literature.[19]

"Pure uncomplicated savagery" can never(more) be disengaged from the colonial context that disables it as a present reality. If savagery and the sovereign individual resurface in Conrad, they will do so only in such a way that their hollowness remains in evidence. Marlow, for instance, is attracted to what he calls the "original" Kurtz, and his first, proleptic vision of the man seems to conform to his idea of Kurtz as an exemplary individual, removed from the degradations of the Central

Station: "As to me, I seemed to see Kurtz for the first time. It was a
distinct glimpse: the dugout, four paddling savages, and the lone
white man turning his back suddenly on the headquarters, on relief,
on thoughts of home" (p. 90). This original exotic vision of Kurtz cannot, however, be realized: what Marlow eventually finds at the Inner
Station is, as we have seen, the "atrocious phantom" of a sovereign
individual and indigenous peoples who offer not the relief of "pure,
uncomplicated savagery" (p. 132) but the subtle horror of a "crowd of
savages" (p. 134). In the heart of difference rises up the gregarious figure of the Same—a "wild mob" (p. 146) that resembles what it is supposed to be most different from. With this resemblance Marlow's superimposition of an untimely exotic vision onto the colonial scene becomes glaringly visible; the figure of indifferentiation haunts every
invocation of difference. This disclosure of Marlow's hypocrisy is the
revelation of Conrad's own, and it is in the giving voice, a changed
voice, to this duplicitous vision that his distinction as a writer, and his
potential as a thinker of our modernity, resides.

What Conrad discovers in writing the *Tales of Unrest*, then, is that
any invocation of the difference that was originally to have constituted
the exotic can, from the perspective of one who is firmly situated
within the confines of mass society, be grounded only in a revocation
of that difference. The "murmuring stir" of Karain's "ornamented and
barbarous crowd" (p. 4), which seemed at the beginning to hold out
the promise of real difference, proves in the end—an end that precedes
the beginning of the story, an end that is the precondition of its telling—no more than a literary (re)construction. Amid the "sombre and
ceaseless stir" of the urban crowd in which the narrator of "Karain"
finds himself immersed (p. 54), the (re)constructed nature of the exotic,
and of the individual who was to have realized himself by crossing over
into it, becomes apparent. Their reality is retroactively erased in the
face of a global indifferentiation that forms, as Simpson has argued, the
point of departure for much, if not all, of Conrad's writing. And yet
this moment of memorialization by which Conrad returns to the scene
of cultural difference troubles, although it cannot displace, the indifferent world in which he must write.

This initial erasure and subsequent re-vision of the past will gen-
erate the "elegiac romances." Characteristic of what I have termed
Conrad's historicism, by contrast, is a view of the past as that which
has been, alas, eclipsed but whose objective reality is not thereby put

into question. It is this historicist faith that engages Conrad in *The Nigger of the 'Narcissus'*; this work appeals to historical (temporal) difference in the same unproblematical way that the first novels invoke geographical (spatial) difference.

I have already pointed out a preliminary instance in *Outcast of the Islands* of Conrad's historicism: there, although the mystery of the sea was said to be a thing of the past in our own cold and calculating age, we were nonetheless led to believe that it could be remembered as it was. Present degradation does not, by this account, affect past glory: Conrad's historicist strategy valorizes the past—a past that has been effectively disengaged from the present in all its corruption. This valorization serves a tacitly dialectical purpose. The past becomes the preserve of positive values that, at some point in the future, we may hope to recover. As Giuseppe Sertoli puts it, in an account of Conrad's historicism to which I am much indebted here: "The past, rescued, shows up again, in the future, as that which must be re-established in order to leave decadence behind and avoid the end."[20] If steam, to cite one of Conrad's favorite historicist dichotomies, has replaced sail, by virtue of sail's difference from steam (the difference between a heroic craft and a degraded technology) the essence of sail can someday be restored, even though in all likelihood its superficial form shall have been substantially altered. The insight of "Karain," on the other hand, is that the past cannot be remembered without its very essence being put into question. It is the past's complicity with, rather than its difference from, the modern world that Conrad must come to terms with before he can write *Heart of Darkness* and *Lord Jim*—although, to be sure, the memorialistic strategy he adopts in these novels would be unthinkable without traces of the simpleminded historicism that guides a work like *The Nigger of the 'Narcissus.'*

If in his fiction Conrad quickly gives up on the unproblematical valorization of the past that he promotes in the *Nigger*, this historicist outlook will nonetheless continue to dominate, though with an increasing sense of futility, much of his nonfictional prose. One such instance, taken from "Autocracy and War," is worth citing here because it provides a vivid idea of how the historicist model is meant to work in the *Nigger*. Conrad there affirms of the French Revolution that it was "except for its destructive force . . . in essentials a mediocre phenomenon" (p. 86). The Revolution, which, as Jonathan Arac has remarked, was "the historical experience that imprinted the urban crowd on all modern sensibilities,"[21] functions in this essay as the inaugural event of a destructive modernity radically different from the constructive tradition it has replaced but not sullied. Separating off a constructive past from a destructive present allows Conrad to offer the admittedly slim hope of a real return to this past and its values: at the end of the revolutionary tunnel could be glimpsed, he affirms, "the idea of a Europe united in the solidarity of her dynasties which for a moment seemed to dawn on the horizon of the Vienna Congress through the subsiding dust of Napoleonic alarums and excursions" (p. 103). However, this renewal of a venerable idea, Conrad laments, was rapidly extinguished; the dynastic unity of nations gave way to the abstract unity of modern States led by political chiefs who, unlike the sovereigns of old Europe, would remain "fatherless, heirless." The optimistic moment of Conrad's analysis, which asserts that we had a chance to leave the revolutionary present behind and return to a more organic way of life, is thus, in the end, overcome by a dark pessimism that foresees no further chance for any such historicist recuperation of the past.

Conrad here aligns himself with a long list of conservative thinkers who, faced with the undeniable but (they hoped) merely provisional displacement of traditional society, would in the interim choose to valorize the figure of the individual as a bulwark against modernity. Romantic individualism evolves as a form of compensation for the destruction (the *hypothetical* destruction) of organic community and its replacement by what critics of the Revolution condemned as a society of and for the masses. As Arac has argued with reference to Conrad, "The pressures of mass society demand in response a strongly assertive constitution of individuality which may permit a later reconstitution of community" (p. 78). For some nineteenth-century writers, this "strong individuality" becomes an end in itself; Segalen clearly falls into this category. For others, such as Conrad, it remains only a means of conserving—with an eye to its future recuperation at the level of community—a realm of values they saw as having been lost with the Revolution.

In *The Nigger of the 'Narcissus,'* Conrad attempts to think this means entirely in terms of the end that it serves; the narratological matrix shifts from the geographical to the historical, and from the isolated individual to the once and future collective. Significantly described in its preface as "an unrestful episode in the obscure lives of a few individuals out of all the disregarded multitude of the bewildered, the simple and the voiceless" (p. xvi), the *Nigger* is Conrad's most concerted effort at thinking beyond, or before, the figure of the individual—at inserting, or re-inserting, him within a community organized in accord with values that held sway in the past. Once his fate has again been attached to that of the traditional community, the individual can no longer hope to avoid the fate of that community: if the individual on his own can stay clear of the present and its degradation (that, at least, is what nineteenth-century exoticism posits), once reinserted into a traditional community he too must be subjected to its inevitable breakup. The risk to which Conrad here puts the individual by linking his fate to a community whose time has passed is justified by his historicist faith that this community will be capable of reconstituting itself in a "new/old" future, having passed through the alienation of the present. The tale of loss and restoration that the *Nigger* enacts doubles the historicist meta-narrative that provides the novel with its ideological ground. The narrative, in other words, does what history has not yet done, and yet must do: it effects the return to a past order after that order has been shattered; it does away with the present disorder, revealing it as nothing more than an interregnum.

I will now briefly show this historicist narrative at work by charting the progress of one of the novel's central images: the "crowd"—a crowd that crops up obsessively in the *Nigger*, notwithstanding the author's own famous description of the circumstances under which it was written ("writing in a solitude almost as great as that of the ship at sea the great living crowd outside is somehow forgotten"[22]).

At the beginning of the novel, the crew of the *Narcissus* is referred to as a good "crowd," one that can be "mustered," brought to order. Two men, the Captain and old Singleton, represent this order—the one politically, the other in a more overtly symbolic way. The Captain is "the ruler of that minute world," a sovereign figure embodying the central authority that for Conrad binds the traditional community together. Singleton's relation to the Captain parallels Michel Strogoff's to the Czar. His unquestioning fidelity to the figure of authority establishes his own authority and makes of him an individual distinct from and yet, in this distinction, representative of the rest of the crew: "Taciturn and unsmiling, he breathed amongst us—in that alone resembling the rest of the crowd" (p. 41). However, if in Verne's novel historical process was necessarily occluded, here it proves essential to the unfolding of the plot. Singleton's heroic distinction is marked off as a thing of the past: he is "a lonely relic of a devoured and forgotten generation" (p. 24). If the novel is to progress toward a future in which the values embodied by Singleton can be regenerated, it must confront a

world without value, one in which "the grown-up children of a dis-
contented earth" (p. 25) have usurped the place of an in some ways
infantile and primitive father (Singleton, we are told, "resembled a
learned and savage patriarch"; p. 6). Strogoff's displacement in space,
which takes him into the realm of the Other in order that the realm of
the Same might be further consolidated, here turns into an essentially
temporal displacement: a voyage out of the past and into the alienation
of the present, which is to result in a future recovery of this past.

What must be dialectically restored is the story's point of departure:
the "good" crowd that "mustered in" the novel. What must be passed
through is the "bad" crowd, in which collective action gives way to collective reaction, legitimate authority to the demagoguery of a usurper.
As Ian Watt has pointed out, "Conrad's treatment of the psychology of
the crew of the *Narcissus* is . . . similar to . . . Gustave Le Bon's *La Psychologie des Foules*."[23] In its journey through the present, the crew of the
Narcissus loses touch with the order that originally constituted it and
takes on the sort of negative features that Le Bon saw as typifying all
mass formations. With the appearance of this "bad" crowd, the individual disappears from sight: "In the collective mind [*âme*] the intellectual aptitudes of the individuals, and in consequence their individuality, are weakened. The heterogeneous is swamped by the homogeneous, and the unconscious qualities obtain the upper hand."[24] This
"unconscious" crowd is, Le Bon asserts, capable of both heroism and
violence; however, in either case, its predominance results in the fall
from conscious action to blind reaction, the sacrifice of the individual's
autonomy to a collective "soul" and, simultaneously, the emergence of
a leader (*le meneur*), who fascinates the crowd, of which he is himself
only an epiphenomenon, by miming the very individuality that each
of its members has lost.

Thus, Le Bon—and thus Conrad, with one important difference.
Conrad's organicist ideology (whose essential contradictions I pointed
out in Chapter 2) allows him to posit the existence of a traditional collective whose "psychology" would be qualitatively different from the
one that motivates Le Bon's crowds: a positive community dependent
upon the exemplary conduct of each of its members and ordered according to a hierarchy that finds its supreme embodiment in a single
figure of authority. By virtue of his belief in this community, Conrad
can, in the *Nigger* at least, assume a dialectical perspective that is markedly absent from Le Bon—one that foresees a restoration of the "good"
crowd and an end to the dominion of the masses that both he and Le

Bon pessimistically identified as the central characteristic of their own age.[25]

Le Bon's negative analysis of the crowd certainly applies, though, to the crew of the *Narcissus* once its original order begins to erode. Its behavior becomes increasingly hysterical and the influence of the Captain and Singleton—those exemplary figures of the past—gives way during the present crisis, the crisis of the present, to that of their decadent doubles, Donkin and Wait. By-product of the crowd, the "fascinating Donkin" ends up representing it: "independent offspring of the ignoble freedom of the slums full of disdain and hate for the austere servitude of the sea," he knows how to conquer "the naïve instincts of that crowd" (pp. 11, 12). From Conrad's traditionalist perspective, Donkin is the individual—or, rather, the facsimile of an individual—who must be made to bear the guilt for the crew's fall into the present; the task of historicism is rendered all that much easier if some one person can be held responsible for the degeneration of the clean, white forecastle into a "black cluster of human forms" bent on destruction. Just as Donkin mimes, and undermines, the legitimate authority of the Captain, Wait provides a symbolic counterpoint to the primitive Singleton. He "fascinated us," the narrator notes (p. 46); his heavy eyes sweep over them, "a glance domineering and pained, like a sick tyrant overawing a crowd of abject but untrustworthy slaves" (p. 35). But if Wait's domination helps draw the crew into a decadent present—"through him we were becoming highly humanised, tender, complex, excessively decadent" (p. 139)—his character is nonetheless profusely ambivalent. Unlike the clear-cut opposition that holds between Donkin and the Captain, the difference separating Wait from Singleton is hardly, as it were, one of black and white; indeed, he will come to assume many of the same almost metaphysical qualities ascribed to that "lonely relic."

The proximity of these two characters, who should be opposed as black to white, as present to past, signals the existence of a blind spot in Conrad's historicist strategy, one that produces many of the often-remarked and by-now glaring "polyphonies" in the novel. Interesting as these may be, a discussion of them would not be to the point here. Rather, we need only keep to the novel's most basic narrative line and remark how neatly the strategy appears to dispose, at least when it comes to Donkin, of the social disorder that it cannot help but confront. The process set in motion by Donkin eventually leads to a brief uprising in which the ever more agitated crew comes into its own as an "unconscious" force, a body of men whose every vestige of individuality has been momentarily lost: "the crowd took a short run aft in a body" (p. 123), directing its fury toward the Captain and his mates. Their run, of course, will not be a long one: the Captain soon reasserts his authority, shaking a finger at the crowd and thereby initiating the first phase of its coming (back) to order. The onrushing group of men becomes "the impressed and retreating crowd" (p. 137), and the threat posed by Donkin's angry masses is definitively put to rest; the crisis of the present is over, at least on this explicitly political front. The victory over Wait's troublingly metaphysical illness is, of course, a rather more uneasy one, and the reader of the *Nigger* is left to ponder whether Wait's excessive decadence has indeed been swallowed up once and for all by the sea or has taken on even more cosmic proportions—like those stars, which, remote in the eternal calm, glitter "hard and cold above the uproar of the earth . . . more pitiless than the eyes of a triumphant mob, and as unapproachable as the hearts of men" (p. 77).

Notwithstanding these doubts, by the end of the novel, the narrator can return to the *Nigger*'s point of departure—asserting, as if the crisis had never occurred (and, indeed, from the perspective of a redeemed future, modernity must seem no more than a blink in the eye of history): "You were a good crowd. As good a crowd as ever fisted with wild cries the beating canvas of a heavy foresail; or tossing aloft, invisible in the night, gave back yell for yell to a westerly gale" (p. 173). The cost of this encomiastic return to the "good" crowd, though, is the narrator's separation from the once-again-orderly crew of which he was a part: as many critics have pointed out, [26] after the *Narcissus* enters port, the "I" is obtrusively divorced from the perspective of an "us." Contemporaneous with the appearance of this isolated individual is the *reappearance* of a problem that seemed to have been left behind for good and that now presents itself in a different and more ominously modern form: "Tall factory chimneys appeared in insolent bands and watched her [the *Narcissus*] go by, like a straggling crowd of slim giants, swaggering and upright under the black plummets of smoke, cavalierly aslant" (p. 163). This is the real future that opens out before the narrator, now cut adrift from a pre-industrial community that only his memory can restore ("you *were* a good crowd"): the historicist narrative enacted in *The Nigger of the 'Narcissus'* is, in these last pages, itself historicized, placed in the context of a modernity that disrupts the novel's reassertion of traditional community. The voyage of the *Narcissus* toward a restored future only leads back, and thus forward, into the continued degradation of the present.

In his excellent article on the *Nigger*, Sertoli shows at great length how the historicist strategy that Conrad there attempts to put into effect is itself continually undermined by what he calls the "text." Conrad's positive affirmation of (bourgeois) social values—of a past salvaged and proposed as a restorative, a means of overcoming the decadence of modernity—can, Sertoli argues, be achieved only through a repression of historical contradictions; we witness the return of the repressed at the (unconscious) level of the "text," where apparently black and white distinctions—for instance, those between Nature and Culture, or between Singleton and Wait—break down and turn in upon themselves. Sertoli's deconstruction of Conrad is certainly convincing. I suggest, however, that in the final pages of the novel Conrad performs a more or less identical operation upon himself and his beliefs. In disengaging his narrator from the "good crowd," he undoes what the historicist strategy had purported to do; the singled-out narrator can only remember the community he would valorize, in a place that denies such memories the objective weight they must possess if they are to achieve their dialectical end. The guiding light of *The Nigger of the 'Narcissus'*—that decadence can be overcome by a restoration of the past—here fails. If the textual ambiguities brought out by Sertoli make this point against Conrad's own intentions, the final turn to memory bears witness to Conrad's own capacity for that "self-critical lucidity" Sertoli attributes to the "text" alone.

Both the inadequacy of the historicist strategy that was to have allowed him to think a way outside of mass society and the purely commemorative nature of his enterprise have become apparent to Conrad. *Lord Jim*, in line with this "self-critical lucidity," abandons the historicist vision—or, rather, situates it, and the past it upholds, firmly within the bounds of the present that both gives rise to and delegitimizes it as a strategy. *To the destructive element submit yourself*: the values put forward in *The Nigger of the 'Narcissus'* are those in which Conrad placed his faith, and yet in order to conserve them he will now have to reveal their complete inadequacy to his own time, or to any other. The existence of the past he valorizes is of no matter in the present that denies it, "except, perhaps, to the few of those who believed the truth, confessed the faith—or loved the men" (p. 25). That this "truth" is a fiction, utterable only amid "the undying murmur of folly, regret, and hope exhaled by the crowds of the anxious earth" (p. 164), is the sole insight by which it can (never) be regained. The distinction between innocence and corruption that provided the ground for Conrad's historicism gives way to the vision of a world in which such distinctions have no force: Conrad abandons narratives of ideological resolution, adopting instead an engaged form of nostalgia that continues to put into question a modernity to which it can no longer put an end.

A Mere Fiction of What Never Was:
Conrad, D'Annunzio, and 'the Desire of the Impossible'

> Paradise and groves
> Elysian, Fortunate Fields—like those of old
> Sought in the Atlantic Main—why should they be
> A history only of departed things,
> Or a mere fiction of what never was?
> —W. Wordsworth, "Prospectus" to the *Excursion*

Around the time he begins mapping out *Lord Jim*, Conrad writes a revealing letter to his politically engaged socialist friend R. B. Cunninghame Graham. In it, he expresses a profound absence of faith in any and all ideological resolutions to the problems facing humanity:

Sometimes when I think of You here, quietly You seem to me tragic with your courage, with your beliefs and your hopes. Every cause is tainted: and you reject this one, espouse that other one as if one were evil and the other good while the same evil you hate is in both, but disguised in different words. I am more in sympathy with you than words can express yet if I had a grain of belief left in me I would believe you misguided. You are misguided by the desire of the impossible—and I envy you.[27]

To live in the undifferentiated world Conrad describes is to be unable to distinguish right from wrong, one cause from another. The courage, beliefs, and hopes of his friend are unfounded, and hence "tragic"; the ground that would differentiate one course of action from another is lacking, and Cunninghame Graham's stand is doomed to inadequacy, ever taken in by the lure of seeing something good in what is uniformly evil, a redeemed future in what has none.

Conrad's portrait of the human condition here seems to aspire after the finality of metaphysics—to identify the essence of humanity without regard to its historical existence ("what you want to reform," Conrad points out to his friend, "are not institutions—it is human nature"). But Conrad's remarks take on a different import if we resituate them in the context of the ideological impasse at which he had arrived; these apparently metaphysical considerations then acquire a historical direction and can be read as a decadentist response to the decline away from value that he would come to identify with global modernity. That is to say, the absence of faith he expresses here also signals a loss of faith: it has *become* impossible for him to differentiate one cause from another, to credit a "fixed standard of conduct" that would justify his beliefs. Modernity is that time in which the impossibility of grounding one's actions in a "just" belief comes to light, once and for all. In this world no such belief can hold true, for the ground of difference upon which it depends has disappeared; we are left only with sympathy— a sympathy that, if it goes beyond words, can do nothing to combat the evil that inhabits every last one of these words.

Having placed Conrad's remarks in this decadentist light, we must in turn reconsider the "tragic" nature of his friend's will to action. Cunninghame Graham's courageous yet inadequate efforts can under these circumstances only be the stuff of an emphatically *modern* tragedy. They are the product of a time of indifferentiation and, for this reason, will never attain to that real difference after which they seek; the differential ground whereupon an authentically tragic destiny might unfold has already vanished. As Paolo Valesio points out, "From the beginnings of modernity to the present time, tragedy 'declines' to drama—that is to say, it loses a solid connection with myth, with ritual, with religious faith. Unveiled, then, in its cruelly ironic nudity is the *minuteness* of tragedy in the face of the passing of time, the weakness of its battle against the evil and the malaise of time (*il male del tempo*)."[28] As the (apparently) solid ground of myth, ritual, and religious faith gives way to modernity, the impossibility of achieving a tragic destiny becomes the only source of tragedy. Although he bathes in this source, Cunninghame Graham is entirely unaware of it: his eyes are closed to the minuteness of his enterprise, its merely "dramatic" nature. Blind to the "weakness" that marks him out as the protagonist of a modern tragedy—that is, of a drama that must ever fall short of tragedy proper—he will continue, unknowingly, to err in the name of a strength he does not possess.

It is this "weakness" that Conrad will so patiently attend to in *Lord Jim*, rendering the sheerly dramatic nature of our modern will to action manifest and yet insistently directing us back to that strength away from which we have declined. Taking as his point of departure the indifferentiation of a colonial world, he will go on to reappropriate the problem of difference and the space of the exotic—knowing that to do so can only be to expose their impossibility in our own and any other time. Like Segalen or (as we will see) D'Annunzio, he commits his hero to a life of error, a life that cannot possibly be lived: Jim's is a posthumous existence—one that ineluctably falls short of the past it recalls and that dissolves in ignominious combat with the present in which it has no real place. To any strong-minded thinker such pessimism must seem empty indeed: thus D. H. Lawrence, who laments "this giving in before you start, that pervades all Conrad and such folks—the Writers among the Ruins."[29] But for one like Conrad, who has confronted the inadequacy of ideological thinking and the "misguided" solutions it espouses, this surrender must be grasped, like a destiny—a destiny that need not assume the sterile trappings of the metaphysical despair he broaches in the letter to Cunninghame Graham.

Conrad's resignation, it turns out, will be the necessary condition of starting not anew, but again. He will re-sign himself to what has become no more, and no less, than a memory, thereby affirming "the desire of the impossible" as such. For this writer among the ruins, having seen the inadequacy of those "misguided" actions by which his friends and his enemies would battle against the malaise of (our) time, has not ceased to envy their courage, their beliefs, and their hopes. And for this reason he has knowingly chosen the path of error: a path leading back to that away from which it has forever declined, even as it pursues its dramatic course through the labyrinth of a modernity without end.

As we have seen, Conrad's early novels are marked by an open narratorial commitment to "obscure adventurers" like Lingard, who at the beginning of *The Rescue* is indirectly likened to the Rajah Brooke, "a true adventurer in his devotion to his impulse—a man of high mind and of pure heart, [who] lay the foundations of a flourishing state on the ideas of pity and justice" (p. 4). For Conrad, however, these noble ideas are precisely what has been excluded from a New Imperialist world; the benign despot Lingard is bound to fail when confronted with the sordid reality of his colonial successor Travers, who with unintentional acuity puts the case rather well: "The existence of such a man in the time we live in is a scandal." Conrad's failure to complete this novel in the late 1890's is one glaring signal that it had become impossible for him to commit himself as he would have wished to a man like Lingard, who, "knowing nothing of Arcadia," as he puts it in *An Outcast of the Islands,*

dreamed of Arcadian happiness for that little corner of the world which he loved to think all his own. His deep-seated and immovable conviction that only he—he, Lingard—knew what was good for them was characteristic of him, and, after all, not so very far wrong. He would make them happy whether or no, he said, and he meant it. His trade brought prosperity to the young state, and the fear of his heavy hand secured its internal peace for many years.

(p. 200)

But Lingard, Conrad will soon have to confess, is as "tragically" wrong as his friend Cunninghame Graham—in a superficially different way, to be sure, but one that is at heart entirely similar: in following different paths, both are equally "misguided," and both arrive at the same erroneous place.

Jim, who, as Marlow says, "captured much honour and an Arcadian happiness (I won't say anything about innocence) in the bush," at once differs from and yet ends up resembling his Old Imperialist predecessor. From the very first pages he is, unlike Lingard, delegitimized as a hero. As Fredric Jameson has pointed out in a discussion of the following passage,[30] the anonymous narrator of the novel's first chapters is careful to stress Jim's *bovarysme*:

On the lower deck in the babel of two hundred voices he would forget himself, and beforehand live in his mind the sea-life of light literature. He saw himself saving people from sinking ships, cutting away masts in a hurricane, swimming through a surf with a line; or as a lonely castaway, barefooted and half-naked, walking on uncovered reefs in search of shell-fish to stave off starvation. He confronted savages on tropical shores, quelled mutinies on the high seas, and in a small boat upon the ocean kept up the hearts of despairing men—always an example of devotion to duty, and as unflinching as a hero in a book.   (p. 6)

Not only the heroism Jim aspires to but an entire alternative world, one in which a confrontation with savagery might still take place, figures here as part of the same exotic, and wholly bookish, fiction. All of the distant regions Jim eventually does visit prove, by contrast, "strangely barren of adventure" (p. 10); the men he works with "did not belong to the world of heroic adventure" (p. 24). There can be, for Jim, only one world; the other world of Patusan that he will meet with in the second half of *Lord Jim* has, from the beginning, been excluded from the novel as a real possibility.

All that remains to Jim is the daydream, a purely phantasmic relation to life that is not active but passive, incapable of realization if put to the test. As Marlow remarks in *Chance*, "Two men may behave like a crowd, three certainly will when their emotions are engaged": during the crisis aboard the *Patna*, it is precisely this herd-like impulse to which Jim succumbs, after a necessarily ineffective resistance. His initial response is one of "passive heroism" (p. 104); he abstains from helping the other crew members in their ignoble efforts at abandoning ship. And yet this heroism cannot be activated. Jim is, despite himself, a part of this unheroic crowd, incapable of acting on his own putatively heroic initiative. His fatal leap from the *Patna* is the only action he is effectively capable of—a degraded one that is, from the standpoint of the individual and the traditional naval community to which he supposedly belongs, inexplicable, forever casting in doubt "the sovereign power enthroned in a fixed standard of conduct." Only after it has been invalidated as an authentic possibility can the fiction of this "sovereign power" be played out. Jim's heroics in Patusan, where he approaches what Marlow calls "greatness as genuine as any man ever achieved" (p. 244), are fated to ring false; for all that he "look[s] as genuine as a new sovereign" (p. 45), he must, because of his failed beginnings, eventually reveal himself as one whose metal/mettle has been falsified by some infernal, and New Imperialist, alloy. When, in the closing chapters of the novel, Gentleman Brown and his "crowd" (p. 356) break into the Arcadian realm of Patusan, the hegemony of a degraded and gregarious power over the apparently "rehabilitated" hero will once again be symbolically confirmed.

The power that Jim comes to exercise in Patusan is no more real than the place itself—a territory located at an impossible remove from the now-global reach of civilization: "The stream of civilisation, as if divided on a headland a hundred miles north of Patusan, branches east and south-east, leaving its plains and valleys, its old trees and its old mankind, neglected and isolated, such as an insignificant and crumbling islet between the two branches of a mighty, devouring stream" (p. 226). One of "the lost, forgotten, unknown places of the earth" (p. 323) in a world where everything has become known and every last scrap of land "significant," fictional Patusan is the only place where Jim can escape his inadequate self and (re)live an imperial story. Like the heroic individual, this exotic space is no more than a dream and yet bookended, as it were, by the real—by an ending that confirms the novel's demystificatory beginning—such dreams amount to something more than the fiction they must nonetheless remain. Their presence in *Lord Jim* puts in doubt, although it can never vanquish, the very doubt that has rendered them absent. The exotic gesture of *Lord Jim* is thus a hypocritical one, blinding itself to its own self-evident inadequacy: having made sure that his readers know Jim can never escape the world of the *Patna*, Conrad, through Marlow, "rehabilitates" his hero, extending both the scope and the tone of that "ambiguous redemption" we saw him undertaking on the behalf of Kurtz.

Marlow is able to see Jim for what he never was: "The mystery of his attitude got hold of me as though he had been an individual in the forefront of his kind" (p. 93). This revival of the exotic subject proves inextricably linked to the act of writing. Marlow's first mention of Jim's impossible future occurs at a significant point in his oral narrative: the trial over, he has taken Jim back to his bedroom so that the youth can be "alone with his loneliness." While Jim mulls his destiny over in silence, Marlow takes pen to paper and begins to write incessantly: "No sooner in my chair I bent over my writing-desk like a medieval scribe, and, but for the movement of the hand holding the pen, remained anxiously quiet" (p. 171). The place of writing also turns out to be the place of resuscitation, for it is precisely at this point in his narrative that Jim's "Arcadian happiness" is first mentioned (p. 175); the act of writing has freed Marlow to begin approaching the topic, the exotic topos, that has already been ruled out of the world without difference in which he and his hero find themselves.

Jim's heroic story begins in the wake of this representation of the act of writing. Only after the playing out of this scene can something different, something novel, emerge from Marlow's narrative: Jim "left his earthly failings behind him and that sort of reputation he had, and there was a totally new set of conditions for his imaginative faculty to work upon. Entirely new, entirely remarkable. And he got hold of them in a remarkable way" (p. 218). What this "entirely new" state of affairs amounts to, of course, is a nostalgic (re)construction, a memorialistic return to the tradition of nineteenth-century exoticism, or what Marlow might have called "the illusion of my beginnings": an alternative space in which the posthumous figure of the individual re(at)tains its validity. Exotic memories offer the only remaining novelty in a world where "there is nothing new left . . . and but very little of what may still be called obscure."

Because of its inadequacy to the present, this nostalgic vision of difference must, to be sure, eventually collapse in on itself. The fiction of two worlds, the old world and the new, gives way in the end to the vision of indifferentiation that was its point of beginning: having "retreated from one world, for a small matter of an impulsive jump," Jim now experiences "the other, the work of his own hands, [falling] in ruins upon his head" (p. 408). This fall at the end of the novel confirms Jim's original commitment to a world, his one and only world, in which retreat and redemption are no longer possible. The intimacy that Marlow and Jim establish after the trial, as one writes and the other prepares himself for action, serves to defer this final closure, opening up a textual space in which a return to the illusion of a beginning might seem possible. Perhaps remembering that distant night, Jim himself, when his new world has been folded back into the old, tries to write, but he soon gives up the attempt (p. 409). In laying down his pen, perhaps he intimates what Marlow himself will soon discover: that writing must also at some point acknowledge the impossibility of its desire, must reveal that it has already been enclosed by the very closure it defers. Marlow's account of Jim's last days in Patusan, which extends from chapter 36 to the end of *Lord Jim*, is a written one: what writing (re)creates, it also necessarily abolishes. With one, and the same, stroke of the pen, the dilatory space of exoticism appears and disappears, revealing itself, tragically, as no more than a fiction, a mere fiction of what never was.

In *Conrad in the Nineteenth Century*, Ian Watt concludes his fine account of *Lord Jim* with a discussion of whether the word "tragedy" can be usefully applied to the novel (pp. 346–56). The answer to this question, of course, depends entirely on one's idea of tragedy, and Watt runs the novel through several familiar definitions (Hegel, Schopenhauer, Unamuno) as a sort of critical litmus test. None proves totally convincing. I suspect *Lord Jim* falls short of every orthodox definition of tragedy—a point Watt himself seems to confirm when he shifts the terms of discussion away from the question of tragedy in order to portray the novel as a nostalgic affirmation of the aristocratic ideal of personal honor. *Lord Jim* is too melodramatic, too modern—indeed, too much of a novel—for it to match in any rigorous manner the traditional criteria of tragedy.

Yet there is a closeness, a proximity (or approximation), to tragedy in *Lord Jim* that forces us into thinking about the novel in these terms. Marlow himself specifically characterizes Jim as "tragic" and, in doing so, provides us with yet another possible definition: Jim and his indigenous female companion, Jewel, Marlow assures us, had "mastered their fates. They were tragic" (p. 316). To master one's fate: let us, for the moment, take this as our definition of "tragedy." For Jim, such mastery can be grasped only in a locale remote from civilization; Patusan is the scene of Jim's tragedy, the only place where he can catch up with and master the fateful identity that has eluded him in his own world. But the inadequacy of Marlow's vision of Jim and Jewel will soon become vividly apparent. The events that occur after Marlow's visit to Patusan show that he has spoken too soon; they show up his vision as merely provisional, lacking in the finality to which it aspired. Jim and Jewel's mastery is undone when their true fate—that which is fatal to them—breaks into the "tragic" situation that Marlow's yarn underwrites and his subsequent written narrative must undermine. The fate of the hero, and of the exotic world in which he was to have realized himself, proves entirely contrary to the one that Marlow initially envisioned for Jim and Jewel: the nonheroic world in which Jim can never be master of his fate catches back up with him in the person of that melodramatic nemesis, Gentleman Brown.

The theatrical space of this modern tragedy proves, then, a sort of waiting room, a zone of deferral that must eventually reveal its identity with the merely "dramatic" world of the present. Marlow is forced into rewriting his "tragic" hero as something less than the master of his own fate—a cruelly ironic revision that the novel's anonymous narrator had already effected a first time in the opening chapters of the novel. Exotic Patusan, which appeared to offer the hero the possibility of an Other space in which to realize a potential for tragedy denied him in his own world, collapses back on itself. For Conrad, such alternatives could no longer be disassociated from what they might once have appeared as counters to. In an undifferentiated world, no real distance can be established between the two worlds of Same and Other, and for this reason the fate of Jim's modern tragedy is always to fall short of the tragedy that he invokes: he cannot really separate himself from his own world, yet it is precisely this separation that must take place if what he does is to be "tragic," fate-mastering.

This discussion of Marlow's definition of the "tragic" helps us to see the genealogical connection between tragedy and the exoticist project: that Other world in which the exotic subject would seek refuge from the degraded realm of the Same, thereby realizing himself as an individual, can be identified up to a point with the space of excess that the tragic hero, leaving the realm of measure behind him, must enter if he is to live out his solitary encounter with fate. As François Hartog has noted, commenting on the function that despotic Persia plays in the *Histories* of Herodotus, "Tragedy can only unfold in a world where *hubris* has a place. Now, the city, precisely, insists on denying and rejecting the action of *hubris* and instead favors moderation [*mesure*], whereas despotic power is the locus par excellence of *hubris*."[31] Just as the tragic protagonist in Herodotus differentiates himself from the everyday world of measure (the city) through an act of hubris that can take place only outside it (despotic Persia), so too would the exotic subject transgress the limits of his own society and pass over into a world where sovereign action remains possible.

As Hartog goes on to point out, though, the geographical and cultural division that Herodotus effects between the world of the city and that of the hero (Greece-Persia, democracy-despotism) already marks a decline away from the properly tragic, a secular attenuation of it. The differential ground of tragedy proper is not "this-worldly," as in Herodotus, but "other-worldly"; solidly connected, in Valesio's words, to myth, ritual, and religious faith, tragedy explores the abyssal ground between man and the gods. There is tragedy when the realm of the sacred irrupts into the life of the city; the tragic hero, exceeding the measure of humanity, puts himself on the same footing as this divine force, agon-izing with the destiny that he has come to confront. In Herodotus, by contrast, tragedy is made to serve the purposes of history: the difference between the sacred realm of excess and the human space of measure has been rewritten in political terms as a tale of war between two geographically identifiable territories—a secular displacement of the clash between two worlds that produces tragedy proper. The sacred disappears from the realm of the city—a significant rupture in the organic continuity of Greek society—and with it, too, does the very possibility of tragedy.[32]

The vision of difference the exoticist project would promote in its reaction against the modern world of measure is, even more so than that of Herodotus, a secular vision, but one that is still, in its own way—a way that has forever declined away from its tragic origin—relatively powerful. However, with the coming of a global colonialism that puts into question the very idea of geographical and cultural difference, the exotic simulacrum of an original, tragic difference itself comes undone. The gods disappeared from our world; this was the first, sacred disenchantment. The New Imperialist revelation of the Same in the place of the Other is one aspect of a second, secular disenchantment that follows in its place and that characterizes our modernity. To confront this modernity is to feel the insignificance of the world in and of itself; the secular world, to which we once attached a significance, finally reveals itself as nothing more than what it is—a place in the place of the sacred, empty of all transcendence, banal. The tragic aspect of our encounter with modernity must reside solely in the insignificance of that encounter; the vacant/vacated place in which we find ourselves offers no point of difference from which to contest our fate. We are tragic only by virtue of our inability to be tragic—our failure to impose even a secular meaning upon our lives and thereby, in the words of Marlow, to master our fate.

What I have just paraphrased is a theory of modernity at work in many great writers of the past two centuries, Conrad included. The work of Flaubert is an exemplary instance of this theory. His writing never fails to uncover the banality of our experience; he immerses his reader in a world that reduces life to the status of a still life, a *nature morte*. In a novel like *Education sentimentale* (1869), for instance, the "use-value" of experience is shown to be the very thing everywhere missing from the life of its "hero," Frédéric Moreau. Frédéric's world is one in which loves, memories, and hopes have become mere commodities, stamped with an always fluctuating "exchange-value," but lacking in any deeper significance. Remaining true to his theory of the all-consuming nature of modernity, Flaubert will (unlike, say, Balzac) doggedly refuse to posit an authorial/authoritative vantage point outside the commodified world of the novel from which Frédéric's "experience" might be read as "inauthentic." Such judgments can have no place in Flaubert's novelistic universe because there the illusion of a life has already taken the place of life itself. Aware of this transformation, we can nonetheless replace the illusion with nothing more substantial, since the banality of the modern is everywhere and in everything. Our insight into the degraded state of affairs that modernity inaugurates can, thus, only be ironical: lacking a ground, this ironical awareness unceasingly folds back into the fallen reality that it is unable to contest.

There is no small amount of irony in *Lord Jim*; however, the novel also gives ample evidence of a pious concern with the past—with that time, in other words, which alone makes possible, which *preconditions*, our ironical awareness of modernity and its banal malaise. This attention to the past, which supplements an ironical vision of the present, is characteristic of allegory.[33] As Walter Benjamin once remarked in *The Origin of German Tragic Drama* (1928), "Allegories are, in the realm of thoughts, what ruins are in the realm of things" (p. 178); they turn the reader back to what once was—or, rather, to what no longer is as it once was. The allegorical text does not envision the recovery of the past that it contemplates. Dilating back toward this past, it remains firmly attached to the degraded moment of the present; it is, as Benjamin says, "at home in the Fall" (p. 234). Allegory approaches the alterity of the past from the perspective of a present that ruins and masks (or fictionalizes) what has come before it. With a melancholy gaze, the allegorist "revives the empty world in the form of a mask, and derives an enigmatic satisfaction in contemplating it" (p. 139); an equivocal figure, he situates himself *both* between the past and the present *and* entirely to one side, the fallen side, of this opposition. Through his work, we envision the path that lies before us but that we cannot take, or can take only in a dream. Ultimately, led neither back to the past as it was nor forward to a future free of the evil of (our) time, we are thrown once again upon the literal ground of the present that we never left and in which our only mastery of fate must lie precisely in a recognition that such tragic mastery has become impossible for us.

Following up on this idea of allegory and the static dynamism it creates, and drawing together a few of the threads of my discussion in this section, I will refer briefly here, by way of conclusion, to another fin de siècle text in which the problematical cluster of modernity, tragedy, and exoticism that occupies Conrad in *Lord Jim* is even more emphatically brought to the fore: Gabriele D'Annunzio's powerful play *Più che l'amore* (1905).[34] In his lengthy preface to this "tragedia moderna" (as it is subtitled), D'Annunzio identifies it as a rewriting of Aeschylus' *Oresteia* in the modern setting of post-Risorgimento Italy, "la terza Roma" (the third Rome: itself a pale simulacrum of what was itself only a representation of that first, originary Rome). It is hardly surprising that the play should fall short of its illustrious model; the point that needs making here, though, is that this failure to reach truly tragic dimensions is central to D'Annunzio's allegorical design. Vitally aware that to speak of "modern tragedy" is to speak in oxymorons, D'Annunzio writes a tragedy that insistently, and yet piously, falls short of tragedy proper.

As a brief plot summary shows, to impose tragedy upon the scene of the modern is to engage in (melo)drama. The hero, Corrado Brando, is an explorer who has recently headed a dangerous expedition into the hinterland of Italian East Africa; at the time of the play, he is back in Rome, futilely trying to squeeze funds out of a tightfisted and inglorious governmental bureaucracy in order to launch another expedition "over there" ("laggiù"). Corrado's humiliating need for money also leads him to a gambling house: that is, to the very antithesis of the exotic locale whither he so longs to return. His luck there proves no better than in the corridors of power, although his descent into this squalid inferno has one concrete result—the anything but heroic deed that stands in the place of tragic hubris: he murders and robs the moneylender-cardsharper who worsted him. Corrado's guilt uncovered, he dies in a shootout with the police.

The exotic world that should, as Giorgio Bàrberi Squarotti says in his comprehensive analysis of this play,[35] offer Corrado "a refuge from impotence, from decadence, from the humiliation of his present condition," turns out to be at an unbridgeable distance from the melodramatic world of this modern tragedy. What Bàrberi Squarotti calls the "hiatus of memory" separates the heroic Africa of Corrado's past from the degraded bourgeois society in which he now finds himself; the sovereign activity of the explorer can appear only in an "oneiric-memorialistic" mode that the play's "realist" milieu and actions cannot fail to undermine. The world of modern tragedy is a world without alternatives, a bureaucratized space in which the power of capital reigns supreme and from which the very possibility of heroic action has been abolished.

The exotic locale in which Corrado once (or so it is said) realized himself can now be nothing more than a dream—a phantasm that, as D'Annunzio himself says of his hero in the preface, has its only place in the past:

Sembra che perfino il fantasma della sua volontà sia già dietro di lui e che . . . pur tenendo rivolto il viso verso il fato, egli non faccia se non la commemorazione di ciò che è irrevocabile e la rappresentazione di ciò che non può esser più raggiunto.   (p. 1076)

(It seems that even the phantasm of his will is already behind him and that . . . even as he keeps himself turned toward fate, he is effecting only the commemoration of what is irrevocable and the representation of what can no longer be attained.)

The fate that awaits the hero and to which he is turned will and must be less than tragic; even as he moves toward it, however, he commemorates and represents what can no longer be present to him: the *irrevocable*. Corrado's past is irrevocable, in both senses of the word: at one and the same time, it can no longer be called back to the present and yet continues to make itself felt in the present as that which can never be done away with—entirely absent and yet present in this very absence.

Corrado's ability to grasp this phantasmic presence, to grasp its absence, its unreality, is all that marks him off from the world of domestic measure. It is all that distinguishes him from a world that, as Corrado points out to his friend Virginio (a hydraulic engineer and a sympathetic representative of the new civic order), is effacing the traces of its excessive alternative from the domain of reality: "In reality, you are canceling the signs of a venerable writing, in order to put in their place a brutish and off-color embankment, which expresses nothing and commemorates nothing [*che nulla esprime e nulla commemora*]" (p. 1116). The all-inclusive domain of the city is canceling out the signs of a writing that is itself only a sign of what came before it, a commemoration of that past already entirely absent from the world of the play. These signs and traces of what has passed away are the object that the tragic hero must attend to—by commemorating and representing, across the "hiatus of memory," what can no longer be grasped as it truly was.

It is precisely these irrevocable signs of the exotic past that the literal-minded Virginio cannot envision: "Ah," Corrado exclaims to his friend, "if only you had experienced just once that which I experienced when, beyond the River Imi, we entered into the unknown region, when we planted the Latin footprint [*orma*] on virgin ground!" (p. 1112) For Corrado, this footprint is no more than a trace (*orma*): absent from our own time, that "one time" when the "unknown region" might still have been entered can now be grasped only in its unreality. As an irrevocable trace, this time necessarily remains incomprehensible to those, like Virginio, who continue to think in terms of the reality they serve. Virginio cannot grasp the phantasmic, commemorative nature of Corrado's "experience" of the exotic; incapable of thinking its unreality, he can assume only that what Corrado speaks of is (still) real. In sympathy with what he interprets as the excessive, superhuman reality that his friend has momentarily fallen away from, Virginio continues to see in Corrado the embodiment of a possible heroism: "I can still feel the hero that is alive in your soul; and I discern only one impending necessity: that light be brought upon the cause of your act, that you have the means of transmuting your frenzy into heroism, of redeeming your crime with your prodigy. You need the Ocean and the Desert in order to become pure again" (p. 1214).

Corrado, on the other hand, knows that the majestic purity he evokes cannot be re(at)tained: the exotic mystery that he desires has been "percé à jour" and its darkness can be recalled only in the cold light of a New Imperialist day. His sordid fate awaits him not "over there" but here, in a modern city that has once and for all done away with its outside.[36] Corrado's every action must draw attention to the absence of the very heroism that he continues to call forth; it must confirm his distance from the Oceans and Deserts that would redeem him. An abyssal-abysmal distance now ineluctably separates him from the land of his *virtù*. "Primavista" is the name of this land (p. 1113); in the memory of this name resides Corrado's (modern) tragedy.

What D'Annunzio emphatically draws our attention to in *Più che l'amore* is, first, that the time for Corrado's heroism is over: there will be no new prodigy, no *trasmut-azione*. Second, and most important, the very nature of those prodigies that may have occurred in the past has changed by virtue of the hero's complete immersion in a present that delegitimizes his past: Corrado's history of departed things is at one and the same time a mere fiction of what never was, separated from its object by a gap that cannot be (truly) crossed. And here Corrado's nostalgia gains its allegorical dynamism. It is the emphatically rhetorical nature of Corrado's experience of the exotic that D'Annunzio wants us to take hold of. In order to commemorate the past away from which he has fallen, Corrado is forced to invent it; denying himself the sterile, and reactionary, pleasures of a nostalgia that affirms the real integrity of its object, he pursues nothing more or less than the traces of the exotic. As D'Annunzio notes in his preface to the play, the day of his tragedy is not so much one of "transfiguration" as of "heroic invention" ("invenzione eroica"). The tragic difference that D'Annunzio recalls through his hero is only an invention, a fiction; it is also, however, a strategic fiction, a rhetorical gesture (*inventio*) whose ultimate purpose is to persuade us, in the words of Jim's mentor, Stein, "to follow the dream, and *again* to follow the dream."

A discussion of the manifest differences between Conrad's novel and D'Annunzio's play would require a separate essay; my central concern in discussing these two writers together has been to point out their common emphasis on this commemorative *inventio* of both the geopolitical difference that nineteenth-century exoticism took for real and the sovereign individual who was to have realized himself in this alternative space. The realm of the exotic and the figure of the individual are for these writers posthumous (re)creations, whose tragic vacancy they are intent on exposing—in both senses of the word (displaying, unmasking). In the ambivalent expression of this vacancy, both authors come to terms with the contradiction that I have argued is central to the exoticist project: namely, that it cannot help coming after what it must come before.

A Marxist critic like Fredric Jameson has no difficulty picking out the contradiction that lies at the heart of a heroic individual like Conrad's Jim. He identifies Jim, whom Romance has "singled" out for its own, as the impossible union of what, in the age of "high capitalism," perforce remain separate: activity and value.[37] But if Jameson is able to identify Jim's founding contradiction, he is unable, I think, to admit its significance; he sees in the creation of Jim a necessarily failed attempt on Conrad's part, at once reactionary (drenched in the *mauvaise foi* of the bourgeois writer) and utopian (opening out onto the idea of a redeemed future), at resolving this unpleasant contradiction between activity and value. From Jameson's ideological perspective, one that requires of its faithful a firm belief in the topos of resolution, fin de siècle writers like Conrad or D'Annunzio stand condemned as the confused exponents of an ideological center that, despite their best (or worst) intentions, will not hold—condemned, that is, for believing in the possibility of the nostalgic, and essentially contradictory, fictions they have invented.

But it is precisely this sort of resolute thinking that the fin de siècle imagination has renounced. Writers like Conrad and D'Annunzio do not will themselves beyond the contradiction of their own time; they knowingly situate themselves at the impasse of an atomized modernity whose end they do not propose to think. Indeed, they exacerbate that contradiction by turning our attention toward an irrevocable past that both contests and complies with the degraded present in which they write. Whatever resolution to the problem of modernity that they might once have considered possible has become for them "the desire of the impossible." If, as Jameson remarks in *The Political Unconscious*, dialectical thinking is the "collective and 'comic' inversion of tragic thought" (p. 235), then Conrad and D'Annunzio are indeed tragic in their refusal to engage the perspective of some "genuine community" of the future, in which the global contradictions of our own time shall have been resolved. They envision no dialectical progress forward to truth nor any real return to the past whose absence they lament and in the name of whose memory they err. This tragic lack of a solution must forever prove distasteful to the proponents of a resolute thinking that desires, in the words of Perry Anderson, "to abolish modernity."[38] But for those willing to accept the inadequacy of such thinking to our own time, the work of these fin de siècle writers confronts us with a supremely ethical decision: to occupy the scene of decadence rather than attempting to overcome it; to abandon all hope for a radical cure to a malaise that has taken on global proportions; and to (re)create strategies for living with(in) this unending decline.

As I pointed out in Chapter 1, Gianni Vattimo's analysis of the postmodern condition leads in not one but two directions: back toward a consideration of the past, whose phantasmic dimensions I have been sketching out in this book, and forward—or, better, sideways—toward a positive appreciation of the hybridity and contamination that characterize our present condition. Although neither direction is to lead us out of modernity and its unpleasant contradictions, the decision to emphasize one over the other has obvious consequences: those who stress the second are likely to engage in a manner of non-dialectical thinking rather less "decadentist" than the one I have been describing, and promoting, here. They will be able to rewrite the irresoluble chaos of modernity in more affirmative terms—to look out upon "an horizon peopled with many, with infinite possible forms, open, as open as the destiny of the tragic hero appeared when faced with the 'many forms which the divine assumes.'"[39]

As Franco Rella, whom I have just quoted, puts it in his recent book *Metamorfosi*:

> The monstrous plurality, the frightful multiplicity of the modern, in which it is no longer possible to discern anything new, and that seems to stretch around us with its insuperable and undistinguishable buzzing, its shapeless swarming, can . . . be read as "inhuman" and "impossible," but also as infinite and unexplored possibility. This "uncertain and dangerous" space can reveal itself, then, as the most properly human of spaces, in which it is possible to have what Leopardi called . . . a new "experience of the truth."   (p. 111)

The modern can be read in more than one way, and if I quote this eloquent vision of "infinite and unexplored possibility" here in closing, it is because I am well aware of the extent to which I have excluded from my own argument the insights available to this other non-dialectical, yet possibilist, way of thinking. It is by far the more beautiful reading of our postmodern condition. It is also, however, a reading that tends, in its openly and assertively tragic beauty, toward the very path of resolution it has renounced: Vattimo's valorization of contamination as the only possible "*Ausweg* from the dreams of metaphysics"; Rella's forceful appeal to the unknown, to the infinitely possible, to a new "experience of the truth." Although they want no part in Jameson's comedy, these thinkers of postmodernity's second direction run the risk—inevitable, perhaps—of repeating in a minor key the old truths of their modern, all too modern forefathers. For those who have pursued the other direction—attending, with both an inescapable irony and a necessary piety, to the "departed things" that have been irrevocably lost to us—this tendency to betray the founding intuition of the postmodern, by insisting on a cure for the incurable and an end to the endless, can only seem as "tragic" as those tainted beliefs and hopes that Conrad spoke of in his letter to Cunninghame Graham—yet another "misguided" ideology for our own fin de siècle to envy, and to decline.

Chapter 6

A POSTSCRIPT TO TRANSGRESSION

THE EXOTIC LEGACY OF PIER PAOLO PASOLINI

> I plans un mond muàrt.
> Ma i no soj muàrt jo ch'i lu plans.
> Si vulún zí avant bisogna ch'i planzíni
> il timp ch'a no'l pòs pí tornà, ch'i dizíni di no
>
> a chista realtàt ch'a ni à sieràt
> ta la so preson.*
> —P. P. Pasolini, "Significato del rimpianto"

● Monsieur Courneau, impresario of the Grand Cirque de France, calls a press conference to announce his next sensational undertaking: the domestication of an eagle. This "civilized man" is about to engage "a prehistoric being" on the path of history and speech. As it turns out, however, all efforts to draw the eagle into his rational world prove futile: most frustrating of all, he cannot convince the taciturn beast to talk. Then Courneau hits upon a formidable idea: he will introduce the eagle to its Third World brothers. One by one, they come forward and voice their fondest hopes—in obsequiously perfect French. Monsieur le Crocodile du Congo wants to "study at Brussels and get his baccalaureate!" Monsieur le Chameau du Ghana, rather more ambitiously, aspires to be "conversant with all of European high culture, from Marx to Lévi-Strauss, and then to teach it in the capital of his own country!"

---

*"I mourn a dead world. / But I the mourner am not dead. / If we want to move on, then mourn we must / the time that can no longer return, no must we say // to this reality that has enclosed us / in its prison house."

And so goes the triumphant roll call, with only the Lion of Algeria (whose cage is empty) failing to answer the call. Despite all this fraternal persuasion, the eagle maintains its silence. Courneau pleads: Accept our world if only to refute it! Courneau rages: The OAS was right, better to have exterminated the brutes! Courneau falls to the ground in a dead faint.

At this point, urged on by the impresario's sympathetic subproletarian helper, Ninetto, the eagle condescends to speak:

VOICE OF THE EAGLE: Do you really want to know what I'm doing?
· · · · ·
M. Courneau sits himself back up, looking at the eagle as one would a godhead.
THE EAGLE: I'm praying!

In the light of this "revelation," Courneau's attempt at schooling the beast gives way to a painfully sincere attempt at grasping its innate religiosity. The Frenchman immerses himself in readings that he hopes will provide him with clues to understand this noble animal: Pascal, Rimbaud, the papal encyclical *Pacem in terris*. Although none seems quite adequate to the situation, Courneau nevertheless begins to undergo an inexplicable transformation: more and more he is coming to resemble what he had once hoped to domesticate. Eventually, Courneau takes his *imitatio aquilae* to the utmost extreme: impelled by a mysterious force, he leaves the confines of the Grand Cirque and ventures to the eagle's mountainous homeland. Once there, he gathers his forces and literally takes off, soaring up and away into the limitless azure.

This moral tale makes up the first part of a screenplay, *Uccellaci e uccellini* (1966), written by one of the most important figures in postwar Italian culture, Pier Paolo Pasolini (1922–75).[1] Here, Pasolini is poking fun at a position close to one he himself had maintained only a few years before: Courneau is a bitingly sarcastic portrayal of the Western intellectual attempting to come to terms—inevitably, his own terms—with the reality of the "Third World" (henceforth presented without quotation marks). We have already touched upon this topic in the introduction to the preceding chapter. In his enthusiasm for Republican China, Bertrand Russell anticipated a wave of twentieth-century intellectuals who, especially after the Second World War, were to take back, under the cover of an ostensibly progressivist ideology, the worn mantle of the "exotic subject." With the political "liberation" of former colonial territories, an escape from the capitalist prison house of the

"West" again seemed possible; a host of writer-activists, of whom Sartre can be taken as exemplar, would attempt to project themselves beyond their own corrupted society into new and decolonized promised lands of innocence and marginality.

Pascal Bruckner, in an engaging study of this Third-Worldist ideology, or *tiers-mondisme*,[2] identifies three primary modes by which Western intellectuals have cast themselves upon the beatific person of the Third World Other: solidarity, compassion, and mimeticism. In Courneau's second, "religious" moment, all three are significantly present. To use my own terminology, they cluster around the transgressive pole of nineteenth-century exoticism. The flip side of the exoticist coin—imperialist and transmissive—is equally present in this episode, in Courneau's first moment. Pasolini's insistence on the doubleness of Courneau's disposition toward the Other makes it clear that the moment of empathy is part of the same trajectory as the previous one of control. And here, Pasolini's critique hits the mark: the *tiers-mondistes*, with their dreams of an Other and better world, are still chained to the very epistemology of control from which they want to exclude themselves; the pre- and post-revelation Courneaux are, in the most vital of senses, one and the Same.

Pasolini's critique, however, has its limits—some easier to read in this episode than others. His pointed exemption of Algeria from the list of Third World "collaborators" is one obvious sign that he is still writing from the perspective of a limited (neo-)colonialism: the empty cage marks the scene of an effective resistance to (neo-)capitalist hegemony and furnishes the activist intellectual with an authentic point of reference for comprehending the Third World and its positive difference. It is not difficult to read this limit in the Courneau episode. Less easy to read is Pasolini's continued belief in the (alternative) reality of one of the most discredited of all ethnological tropes: the Other as "prehistoric being." The mocking identification of a person like Courneau with "civilization" might at first glance lead us to treat as equally ironical his description of the eagle, but the equation of the Third World with prehistory (and irrationalism) was, in fact, a constant of Pasolini's thinking throughout the 1960's—although his early hopes for the revolutionary potential of this prehistoric force were, by the middle of the decade, beginning to collapse in the face of an increasingly tragic awareness that modernity had already permeated every last recess of the "prehistory" he wished to valorize. The continued existence of this prehistoric limit in Pasolini's writings is one sign, among many others, of his inability to take the critique of *tiers-*

mondisme, which he broaches in the Courneau episode, to the fin de siècle conclusion that it anticipates: that the (neo-)exotic Other is itself an impossible dream, and the promise of transgression it offers nothing more (but nothing less) than a matter of rhetoric.

Pasolini's problematical, and largely infertile, encounter with the Third World is the subject of this concluding chapter. Besides providing an exemplary conclusion to my history of the exoticist project, the story of this encounter also has a sui generis interest, since it emphasizes a crucial aspect of Pasolini's work that has largely been ignored.[3] The story will be structured in the most simple of terms: before, during, and after. In the first section I establish the "prehistory" of Pasolini's *tiers-mondisme* (what led him to adopt this ideological position). I then go on—in a survey of the few Third World writings he did produce—to look at his aborted effort in the early 1960's at making the decolonized Other talk. Finally, I portray Pasolini after his (never complete) abjuration of *tiers-mondisme,* as he simultaneously sidesteps the conclusions to be drawn from his failed encounter with the Third World (continuing to valorize revolutionary pockets of resistance against an homogenizing mass society and to lament the imminent disappearance of prehistory) and reluctantly edges toward a position close to the decadentist one that I argue for in this book. Although the idea of the Third World and its essential difference from the "horrendous universe" of global capitalism continued to attract Pasolini right up to his death, he had long since abandoned the attempt at giving literary expression to this endangered idea. Rather than assume the vacancy, the sheer rhetoricity, of his neo-exoticist project, Pasolini could respond to the collapse of his transgressive dreams only with an absence of *oeuvres*—and it is this absence that we must now begin to interrogate more fully.[4]

Modernism and/in Mourning: A Prehistory of Pasolini's Tiers-mondisme

Ma io, con il cuore cosciente

di chi soltanto nella storia ha vita,
potrò mai più con pura passione operare,
se so che la nostra storia è finita?*
    —P. P. Pasolini, "Le ceneri di Gramsci"

*"But I, with the conscious heart // of one who only has life in history, / can I ever again with pure passion act, / if I know that our story is over?"

In many respects, it is difficult to imagine a less decadentist writer than Pasolini. Not only was he consistently vociferous in his dislike of fin de siècle authors such as D'Annunzio but he had, by the end of the 1950's, also taken to identifying many of his contemporaries with the negative epithet "neo-decadentist"—a word that crops up often in his descriptions of the work of film directors like Michelangelo Antonioni and Federico Fellini. *L'avventura, La dolce vita*: such films are not, he tells the readers of his column in the Communist party weekly *Vie nuove* in 1961, truly vital because they effect "the critique of a society from within that very society."[5] At this point in his career, a limited critique of that sort strikes him as an insufficient gesture. Such work can, Pasolini contends, be justified only by "a perfect stylistic success." At best, decadentism is equivalent to aestheticism; at worst it proves a symptom of the *male incurabile* that (as he points out in his next column) infects all of Alberto Moravia's characters. To be sure, Pasolini adds, Moravia himself is exempt from the bourgeois malady he chronicles: Moravia maintains an ironical distance from his incurable characters. Pasolini would, however, never feel at ease with irony as a literary strategy because the distance it creates is perforce never total; in order for the ironical text to function, it must remain to a certain extent complicitous with its object. Pasolini's projected contact with an outside world of "health" was, as we will see, to be far more straightforward.

One cannot, though, speak of Pasolini during the early 1960's without taking into account the twenty-year path that led him to embrace the Third World as a radical solution to the problem of decadence. In this section I will lay the necessary groundwork for an understanding of Pasolini's *tiers-mondisme*, at the cost of a digression into his past. If we consider his earlier (and without question most important) literary production, we find that the "outside" that will eventually become so necessary for Pasolini is anything but present there; it proves, in fact, irremediably absent. For the decadentist-tinged poetry of his first literary decade, the 1940's, this should come as no surprise. The young Pasolini was careful to situate himself firmly within Italian literary tradition: if this poetry—much of it indebted to the hermetic school that flourished during the fascist *ventennio*—succeeds, it is, quite clearly, only at the level of "a perfect stylistic success." There is no question of an "outside" in this work (or, rather, the motif is raised in the traditional and non-secular terms of religious transcendence).

One point about the early poetry does, however, need to be brought out before we examine some of the works written during the next decade—works that form the more immediate genealogy of Pasolini's *tiers-mondisme*. The novelty of this poetry resides in Pasolini's decision to write not only in Italian but also in the dialect of his mother's home region, the Friuli (to the northeast of Venice). In these poems—most of which were subsequently collected in 1954 as *La meglio gioventù*— Pasolini gives literary form to what might well be considered the sheer orality of dialect, a dialect that he himself had to learn as an anthropologist would that of a culture under study. Far from being a mimetic attempt at re-presenting this language, however, his written dialect, in its extreme literariness, places itself at a clear remove from the dialect spoken by the inhabitants of the Friuli. Pasolini's Friulan, in other words, turns out to be a metaphor of "real" Friulan; as Rinaldo Rinaldi, the author of far and away the most compelling account of Pasolini's work as a whole, puts it, "His dialect is a register of writing used as a metaphor for the negation of writing."[6] By writing in dialect, Pasolini refers, metaphorically, to what is prior to that writing: to engage this spoken language is, inevitably, to put oneself at a distance from it, to evoke it in the form of what it is not—namely, writing.

Given its inevitably metaphorical form, the content of Pasolini's dialect poetry is also, of necessity, at a distance from what it purports to say; his "exotic" attachment to the Friuli—the identification of it as "my country," *me país*, as he calls it in the epigraph to *La meglio gioventù*— must, for this reason, be read as a conceit, a rhetorical artifice. It is the artificiality of such identification with the Other that Pasolini's *tiers-mondisme* will fruitlessly contest—a contestation that is, indeed, anticipated during Pasolini's last years in the Friuli when he will attempt, in the wake of what he called his "discovery of Marx," to use dialect as the vehicle for his new political activism. This move toward a language of immanence is, however, abruptly curtailed when, in 1949, Pasolini is expelled from the local Communist party on moral grounds (having to do with his homosexuality). Forced to leave the Friuli, he relocates in Rome and, after several years of intense poverty, emerges as one of the most prominent, and scandalous, figures on the Italian cultural scene.

During these years, Pasolini often has occasion to reflect on his Friulan experiences. Situated at the political center of Italy, in the seemingly very different world of postwar Rome, he can appreciate the Friuli for what it "is": an autonomous region, fundamentally untouched by those ravages of history so evident in the capital city. In his post-Friulan discussions of the Friuli, he comes to a first formulation of the position he would eventually take with regard to the Third World: he sees it as a world apart, with its people "living in a sort, as it were, of political substratum, a sort of rustic world-in-itself, noble in its own way, upon which has passed without damaging it, without winning it over or being won over by it, the external rule first of Venice, then, briefly, of Napoleon, of Austria, of Umberto's Italy, and, one might add, of Fascist Italy."[7] Resilient to historical change, the essential Friuli remains, despite all external interventions. What we might call "colonialism," in a very large sense of the word,[8] is here figured as something superficial, inessential. But as the Wordsworthian overtones of this passage bear witness (one thinks, obviously, of the "Preface" [1800] to *Lyrical Ballads*, with its praise of the "humble and rustic life"), Pasolini's vision of this world as a present alternative, or an alternative to the present, is very much belated—and one that his earlier writings, with their insistence on absence, had already displaced.

Within the theoretical perspective of the essays written during this decade (many of them collected in *Passione e ideologia* [1960]), this belated vision of an "outside" takes shape; the rustic world-in-itself becomes the scene of a possible experience, although for Pasolini, caught up in(side) the flux of a rapidly modernizing Rome, this possibility is fraught with nostalgia. Pasolini's theory emerges as a means of dispensing with this nostalgia: the personal voice, suffering through the trauma of exile from both the Friuli and the realm of political activism, is supplemented by the impersonal, and compensatory, voice of the critical essays, one that looks back upon an absent world as if it were present. As Rinaldi has argued, there is a significant gap between Pasolini's developing theory and his literary practice in these years:[9] his status as intellectual allows him to carve out a domain of certainty that both his poetry and his novels belie. It is this gap that, as the decade progresses, Pasolini will feel drawn to close.

The self-contained subproletarian world of Pasolini's Roman novels, which I can mention only in passing here, would at first glance seem analogous to the *rustico mondo a sé* that he was beginning to map out in his theory; indeed, in later life, Pasolini frequently insisted on such an analogy. But this yoking of urban and rustic worlds is very much an ex post facto gesture, one made possible only by forgetting the eminently modern insight that dominates his first novel, *Ragazzi di vita* (1955)—an insight that effectively negates all possibility of experiencing autonomous and uncontaminated worlds like that of the Friuli. As Giorgio Agamben has argued, modern poetry "does not found itself upon a new experience, but upon a lack of experience without precedents."[10] *Ragazzi di vita* is highly "poetic" in Agamben's modern sense: it takes this lack for granted, rather than embrace the continued possibility of an "authentic experience" (the approach of Pasolini's theory), or mourn its loss (the strategy, as we will soon see, of the poetry that he wrote during this decade).

Like Baudelaire's Paris, the urban peripheries of this novel are essentially modern: places, one might say, in which all use-value has been effaced in favor of its exchange-value—in favor, that is, of the simulacrum of value. The world of Pasolini's "street kids" (*ragazzi*) is very much of the present, but this presence reveals itself as entirely dependent upon, and situated within, the commodified realm of capitalism; if anything, their lives prove an intensification of modernity, a taking to extremes (or peripheries) of a world in which experience has once and for all been expropriated. Identifying this exacerbatedly modern (lack of) experience as characteristic of the *ragazzi* serves to problematize the conventional view that, as one critic puts it, they act out their lives "in the enchantment of prehistory."[11] The enchantment they are under is a thoroughly historical one, indissociable from modernity. Their ability to adapt to a fallen world, I would argue, is one that more and more discomforted Pasolini, as he himself came under the spell of a supposedly real and undefiled "prehistory."

The *poemetti* of *Le ceneri di Gramsci* (written from 1951 to 1956 and published in 1957) are of more immediate interest to us than the novels because of their obsession with a phantasmic past—not Gramsci himself but the ashes of Gramsci, the traces of an authentic experience. Poetry here turns away from a modernity to which it nonetheless remains attached: it assumes a memorial stature, setting itself the task of remembering a heroic world that has no place in our own. As such, it falls somewhere in between what Agamben, following Freud, has identified as the two related strategies of mourning and melancholy. The real object of mourning, he notes, is doubled by the unreal object of the melancholic, who possesses

the phantasmic ability to make an unappropriable object appear as if it were lost. . . . Covering over its object with the funereal ornaments of mourning, melancholy confers upon it the phantasmagoric reality of something lost; but since it is a mourning for an unappropriable object, its strategy opens up a space for the existence of the unreal and delimits a scene in which the subject can enter into relation with it [the unreal] and attempt an appropriation that no possession could match and no loss ensnare.   (*Stanze*, pp. 25–26)

The melancholic confers reality on an object that never was, mourning it, and thereby in a way giving life to its unreality. This is the essence of mourning itself since the real object, once it has ceased to exist, proves equally phantasmic, equally "unappropriable."

We can see this laceration of self and (real/unreal) object, one that history effects and writing records, at work in a poem like "Canto popolare" (1952), where an absolute distance is established between us ("noi")—the subjects of history—and the people ("popolo")—those who ingenuously repeat the past and who are not "blinded" ("abbagliato") by modernity because they are not exposed to its harsh light. These "people" are never drawn up ("tolto"), as it were, by the dialectic of enlightenment:

> . . . non abbiamo nozione
> vera di chi è partecipe alla storia
> solo per orale, magica esperienza;
> e vive puro, non oltre la memoria
> della generazione in cui presenza
> della vita è la sua vita perentoria.[12]
>
> (. . . we have no true
> notion of who participates in history
> only through oral, magic experience;
> and lives pure, not beyond the memory
> of the generation in which presence
> of life is his peremptory life.)

The world of "oral, magic experience" is at a painful remove from the subject who desires its "presence." For all that he longs to come into contact with this other world, Pasolini un-realizes it, placing it at an insuperable distance from his own. He remembers it at the cost of a laceration: historical man "non ha più che la violenza / delle memorie, non la libera memoria" ("now has only the violence / of memories, not memory's freedom"; p. 20). In *Le ceneri* what makes up for this absence is the belief that "our" world is not merely one of mourning but of hope: against the loss of this "libera memoria," this peremptory ground of experience, we can hope for a very different, redemptory sort of liberty.

The poet of *Le ceneri* is not, however, very interested in considering this future, which at once attracts and "repulses" him; the ethos of these poems is melancholic, directed toward a world anterior to "ours," one that has come before and yet remains with us, but only as trace—unreachable, if not in its absence. In "Le ceneri di Gramsci" (1954), Pasolini calls this trace "la forza originaria / dell'uomo, che nell'atto s'è perduta" ("the originary force / of man, which has been lost in the act")—a lost force that provokes both "l'ebbrezza della nostalgia" ("the rapture of nostalgia") and "una luce poetica" ("a poetic light"; p. 73). Poetry and nostalgia unite, as they always have, to reveal/conceal what is hidden to "us." This insight is presented less compactly in an exemplary stanza from a poem written the same year, "L'umile Italia":

> Più è sacro dov'è più animale
> il mondo: ma senza tradire
> la poeticità, l'originaria
> forza, a noi tocca esaurire
> il suo mistero in bene e in male
> umano. Questa è l'Italia e
> non è questa l'Italia: insieme
> la preistoria e la storia che
> in essa sono convivano, se
> la luce è frutto di un buio seme.
>
> (p. 48)

> (The world is more sacred where it is
> more animal: but without betraying
> the poeticity, the originary
> force, we must exhaust
> its mystery in human good and
> evil. This is Italy and
> this is not Italy: together
> the prehistory and the history, which
> are in it, live—if
> light is the fruit of a dark seed.)

Here, "prehistory" differs considerably from what it will soon become for Pasolini in its Third World incarnation; the realm of the sacred, of animal nature, is lost to "us" as darkness is to light, as something that we can have no "true notion" about. Its "cohabitation" (*convivenza*) with history is nothing more than a phantasmic one, an imaginary relation between the real and the unreal.

We must not turn away from what has come before us, yet neither can we re-present its originary force. To deliver that force over to the present would be to betray its "poeticity." The light of poetry grounds itself in an unre-presentable absence of light that is anterior to it; the poet looks back upon this absence, interrogating it with what Pasolini would so often refer to as an *amor da lonh*, a love from afar. The poet, through commemoration, seeks access to an origin that is always-already inaccessible: it might well be argued that this is the essential(izing) project of the European poetic tradition.[13] Whatever one's definition of poetry, however, this is the central project in Pasolini's *Ceneri*. With an approximating language that simultaneously draws near and pushes back, Pasolini's overwhelming impulse in these poems is to articulate an unbridgeable gap: between the sacred, animal world of nature and a secular, human world; between a heroic people whose metonym is Gramsci and the ashen inferno of modernity.

A potential ambiguity inhabits Pasolini's idea of *convivenza*, however. For the poet of *Le ceneri*, the prehistoric is present only as phantasm, as an object to be mourned in the world of light and history; to bestow upon the prehistoric a real content would be to betray its originary force. It would, we can add, be to grasp (fetishistically) what is by essence ungraspable. But it is precisely this reality that Pasolini—increasingly unhappy with the prospect of mourning and equally uncomfortable with that extension of mourning we identified as modernism (a position that takes the absence of experience for granted)—will attempt to embrace, at the cost, as he had foreseen, of betraying "la poeticità." The *glas* of melancholy, as it were, has sounded too early for Pasolini's liking, and he will seize upon the apparent possibilities of mutual presence that a word like *convivenza* opens up despite the nostalgic intentions of (his) poetry. A period of relative optimism begins, in which his work attempts to conjure up first historical, and then prehistorical, alternatives to capitalism—openings of the sort that he had already theoretically envisioned in some of the essays of *Passione e ideologia*. During his brief *tiers-mondiste* period (roughly, 1958–63), Pasolini is buoyed up by the possibility of political and literary transgression, on both the domestic and the international front. He begins to explore the futural dimension that was almost entirely absent from the world of the *Ceneri*[14]—a world where, as he puts it in "Picasso" (1953), remaining "inside the inferno with a marmoreal / will to understand it" appeared to offer the only chance of "salvation" (p. 30).

On the one hand, he adopts, or re-adopts, the traditional terms of the class struggle when speaking about the possibility of political change within Italy: modernity, he will claim, can be surpassed through a qualitative leap forward—as we see, for instance, in his account of the difference between "dissent" and "revolution." Dissent, he explains to the readers of *Vie nuove* (30 November 1961), is essentially religious, irrational, caught up within what it contests; however, all moments of dissent (and here he identifies three types: the heretical, the anarchical, and the humanitarian) prepare the way for the "qualitative leap," the "betrayal," of Marxism: "With this leap 'religiosity' loses every historical characteristic—irrationalism, individualism, metaphysical prospectivism—and acquires entirely new characteristics: rationalism, socialism, laical prospectivism." This epochal shift will establish "another culture," "another and entirely new point of view" ("un'altra cultura," "un altro punto di vista totalmente nuovo"), from which the ills of modern society will have disappeared.[15]

It is in his second novel, *Una vita violenta* (1959), that Pasolini tentatively begins to explore this new horizon, effecting a partial break with the dilatory modernism of *Ragazzi di vita* through a turn in the novel's second half to the ideological assertion and narrative resolution called for by the anti-modernist poetics of social realism. However, Pasolini's commitment to the process of closure that grounds this poetics, as it does Marx's own master narrative, never solidified, for at least two reasons: first, the disturbing irony of conferring one's hope for the future on an outworn aesthetic form—the (nineteenth-century) novel—could not have escaped him; second, he was becoming increasingly convinced that the onset of neo-capitalism, of the age of technocracy and consumerism, had indefinitely postponed a revolutionary *salto di qualità* in the industrialized world.

In the wake of Adorno and the Frankfurt School, Pasolini saw neo-capitalism and its culture industry as effectively puncturing the positive telos of Marxism, a telos that he himself was somewhat belatedly, and hesitantly, adopting as the ideological credo of his art; under these conditions, whatever critique the artist might make of Italian society would necessarily prove only a moment of dissent, ineluctably bound to and trapped within the very system being contested. Pasolini's engagement with the traditional novel leads him, then, into the same impasse that he would so bitingly portray in his account of the neo-decadentists: whatever the novelist writes reveals itself as a product of modernity rather than a possible resolution to it. Thus, although the first years of the 1960's are marked by one announcement after another of various novelistic projects, by the middle of the decade Pasolini is forced to admit that he has "renounced" the novel.[16]

By this time, his poetic vein is also temporarily exhausted—arriving, although from a rather different direction, at the same neo-capitalist dead end. If his next collection of poetry is in many ways an extension of *Le ceneri* (just as *Una vita violenta* grows out of *Ragazzi di vita*), one fundamental difference resides in Pasolini's efforts to figure what had hitherto been the object of his melancholy as really present. Reworking the material of the previous collection, *La religione del mio tempo* (1961), establishes a direct contact between the poet and the "prehistoric" world that he had previously contemplated *da lonh*: Pasolini separates himself from the alienated historical subject of the *Ceneri* ("noi") in an attempt at opening up another point of view from a trans- or extra-historical perspective. The individual subject, it now transpires, can come into contact with Other worlds: in "La ricchezza" (1955–59), for instance, Pasolini the dandy ("il raffinato") assimilates himself to the urban "subproletariat," because they are

> entrambi fuori dalla storia,
> in un mondo che non ha altri varchi
> che verso il sesso e il cuore,
> altra profondità che nei sensi.
> In cui la gioia è gioia, il dolore dolore.
>
> (p. 188)

> (Both outside of history
> in a world whose only passageways lead
> toward sex and the heart,
> whose only depth comes from the senses.
> In which joy is joy, and sadness sadness.)

This alliance with the "frutti / d'una storia tanto diversa" ("fruit / of such a different story") is what Pasolini will seek to effect in the coming years, trying to operate outside the historical framework in and by which he nonetheless still feels himself engaged.

But in his earlier poetry he had already so effectually buried Italy's peasantry (*contadini*) and subproletariat under the ground of an unattainable "prehistory" that his literary efforts to recuperate a *convivenza* on the domestic front inevitably fall short of their goal, striking the reader as a painfully awkward projection of reality onto some phantasmic object—in other words, as essentially rhetorical. And it is precisely this sense of rhetoric that Pasolini most wants to avoid. Dissatisfied with these results and yet wishing to elaborate his vision of an alternative present, Pasolini extends his gaze beyond the boundaries of Italy to the emerging Third World and comes to the conclusion (in

"Alla Francia" [1958]—an epigram inspired by Sékou Touré, then-president of Guinea):

> Forse a chi è nato nella selva, da pura madre,
> a essere solo, a nutrire solo gioia,
> tocca rendersi conto della vita reale.
>
> (p. 259)
>
> (Perhaps he who is born in the forest, of a pure mother,
> born to be alone, to nourish joy alone,
> will be the one to take real life into account.)

Pasolini turns away from Europe and the all-embracing world of neo-capitalism, in search of the once and future alternative—a poetic program that he announces at the end of one of the closing poems in *La religione del mio tempo*, the "Frammento alla morte" (1960):

> Sono stato razionale e sono stato
> irrazionale: fino in fondo.
> E ora . . . ah, il deserto assordato
> dal vento, lo stupendo e immondo
> sole dell'Africa che illumina il mondo.
>
> Africa! Unica mia
> alternativa . . . .
> . . . .
>
> (pp. 304–5)
>
> (I have been rational and I have been
> irrational: right to the end.
> And now . . . ah, the desert deafened
> by the wind, the wonderful and filthy
> sun of Africa that illuminates the world.
>
> Africa! My only
> alternative . . . .
> . . . .)

That this fragmentary invocation to the new world is couched in a self-consciously Romantic style; that Pasolini must produce his alternative vision in a language that reeks of nineteenth-century exoticism; that he must ignore the clichéd nature of his project if he is to invest it with any degree of "authenticity": these are obvious ironies, signaling the a priori sterility of his neo-exoticist undertaking. It is this hopeless vacancy that Pasolini will discover in his literary and existential encounter with the Third World. This vacancy, we might add, is itself inscribed in the poem's final ellipsis: the future that would complete the present cannot be uttered; the words that would heal the poet's *male incurabile* are irretrievably absent from the discursive realm, covered over by a set of periods, each of which marks the same thing. That same thing is the end of the line.

La Negra Luce: Savagery, Enlightenment, and Pasolini's Third World

> I switch on the light in a dark room: certainly, the illuminated room is no longer the dark room, I have lost that forever. And yet isn't it a question of the very same room? Isn't the dark room in fact the sole content of the illuminated room? That which I can no longer have, that which infinitely recedes back and, at the same time, hurls me onward is only a representation of language, the darkness presupposing the light; but if I abandon the attempt at grasping this presupposition, if I turn my attention to the light itself, if I receive it—that which the light then gives me is the *same* room, the non-hypothetical darkness. The sole content of a revelation is what is closed inside of it, the veiled—light is only the coming to pass of the darkness to itself.
>
> —Giorgio Agamben, "Idea della luce"

The existential importance of Pasolini's encounter with the Third World at the beginning of the 1960's cannot be underestimated; during the last fifteen years of his life, it will serve as a haven from the increasing burden of his scandalous celebrity and the seemingly ineluctable advance of neo-capitalism in Italy. After the Friuli (1940's) and Rome (1950's), Pasolini's geographical point of cathexis becomes the Third World: although rather too neat, this triadic progression more or less fits the biographical facts. But despite the critical role of the Third World in the later part of Pasolini's life, the literary harvest of this third "season" is surprisingly meager, from both a quantitative and a qualitative perspective. All that will follow upon the Friulan and Roman masterworks are a few decidedly minor (in the worst sense of the word) texts.

Enzo Golino's recent study of Pasolini is revealing on this point: in a book of 275 pages, covering in one chapter each zone (novel, tragedy, journalism, and so on) of his literary output, we find near the end an impressively titled chapter on the subject of Pasolini's *tiers-mondisme* totaling 3 pages.[17] This is not to say that a critical injustice has been done and needs to be redressed: Golino has been scrupulously correct in his allotment of space, especially since his book does not deal with Pasolini's work in film, where the Third World is indeed often present as a picturesque, but rarely thematized, backdrop. If we wish to discuss the issue of Pasolini's writings and the Third World in a less perfunctory way, we must take a different starting point than did Golino: not the presence of a Third World *oeuvre* but its almost complete absence; not the success of Pasolini's search for new and more genuine discursive and political values abroad but its radical failure. It is this sort of "negative" reading that I will propose here, one that centers around a short preface he wrote in 1961 for an anthology of Black writers and around what is no doubt Pasolini's most ambitious work in this vein, the never-filmed African screenplay *Il padre selvaggio* (first drafted in 1962 and published in 1975).

The romantic fantasy of liberation, which forms the ideological backbone of a nineteenth-century project like exoticism, continues to haunt our own time, conjuring up vistas of an Other way of life that would "cure" our endlessly lingering malady. As a decade, the 1960's provide perhaps the most startling, and startlingly naive, revival of this transgressive fantasy. At the same time that Pasolini is scouring the Third World for possible alternatives to neo-capitalism, for instance, a critic like Foucault offers his readers (in a 1963 article entitled "Preface to Transgression") the alluring prospect of a liberated discursive future in which the prison house of language/modernity gives way to an entirely different epoch, one whose transgressive writing we have already begun, though just barely, to read on the penitentiary walls: "In spite of so many scattered signs, the language in which transgression will find its space and the illumination of its being lies almost entirely in the future [*est presque entièrement à naître*]."[18]

Foucault's project, of course, is an explicitly anti-humanist one: the Other language that lies in wait for us, at some point in the future, will no longer revolve around the alienated, and alienating, figure of "man." But here Foucault's purported anti-humanism gives its game away: the dreamed-of transgression leads us nowhere if not to that most "human" (and modern) of places—namely, the "future." In thinking transgression and alterity in terms of an emancipated future, the early Foucault—and this is one of the more salient points in Derrida's well-known critique of *Madness and Civilization* (1961)[19]—reveals his commitment to that human, all too human, world whose historical closure he groundlessly foretells. To continue thinking about the future, and to argue its point of view, is to remain within the boundaries of what an anti-humanist ideology purports to exceed.

The early Foucault's dreams of transgression are worth mentioning here not only because they are signs of the Zeitgeist but also because they contrast rather starkly with those of his contemporary Pasolini. Pasolini's commitment to the idea of a "future" comes as no surprise, given his avowedly humanist and socialist point of view: the object for him is not, ultimately, to go "beyond" man but to redeem man by going "beyond." The Third World holds out a promise that this project can be realized. But, as we will see, it is precisely Pasolini's commitment to humanism and an alternative future that draws him into making an untenable, and dehumanizing, distinction between "prehistoric" and "historical" man. Once this distinction has itself broken down, all that will remain to this fervid humanist is the knowledge that the object of his desire is truly a thing of the past—and in this bitter renunciation of the future, ironically enough, Pasolini turns out to be a much more thoroughgoing visionary of the end of man than Foucault ever was.

But this is to anticipate matters. At the beginning of the decade, a Third World in the throes of decolonization offers Pasolini a much-desired window onto the future—as he makes especially clear in "La Resistenza negra," a little-known piece written as the preface to a 1961 anthology of Black literature. Although by no means a monumental document, especially compared with Sartre's influential "Orphée noir" (1948),[20] this preface contains what is perhaps Pasolini's most extended theoretical statement about the Third World and as such offers an ideal starting point for our discussion.

The main thrust of this preface is to identify Black poetry with that heroic moment in European history, the "Resistance"—a moment of "hope" that has for "us" already slipped into the past and thus been rather sadly placed within quotation marks. The Black Resistance, on the other hand, has not finished, "and it does not seem as if it will finish as it has finished here for us, with the clericals and De Gaulle in power" (p. xv). What has happened "here" but not in "Africa" (which Pasolini identifies with "the entire world of Bandung") is the "split between resistance and Resistance"—that is, between a political movement whose primary goal is national independence and a more far-ranging struggle whose "true objective is 'social justice.'" It is this fusion of historical and "meta-historical" struggle that characterizes the emerging Third World and allows for an unexpected renewal of those "hopes" no longer open to the inhabitants of "our" world, where neo-capitalism has managed to co-opt the authentic subject of historical change, the proletariat. "Africa" is, in short, a new revolutionary concept, "the concept of an extremely complex subproletarian condition as yet unused as a real revolutionary force" (p. xxiii).

In this place/concept, the Resistance can still be thought of as something real; it has not yet, as it were, been enclosed by quotation marks (although the reality of this Resistance would seem possible only at the cost of putting "Africa" itself within those troubling quotation marks that at once affirm and yet un-realize the object they enclose). Because of its firm basis in reality, Pasolini argues, the poetry of the Black Resistance is typified by a "look to the future" that is no longer characteristic of European poetry. "Our poetry," he affirms, "no longer looks toward the future; it is forced to retire into [*ripiegarsi*] its own specific problems, into regurgitations of the past: to define itself in the new situation in which action no longer seems to have a sense" (p. xvi). Whereas "we" are compelled toward the past, folding back into ourselves and what has already been written, for the "Black Resistance" future-oriented action, and an activist poetry, still has a sense. The literary and political work of the Third World is not defined, nor confined, by our "new situation"; if "we" have lost our power to resist the forces of neo-capitalism and a modernity whose end "we" can no longer envision, the same (or the Same) cannot be said for "Africa."

And yet, as Pasolini is also at pains to point out, the poetry brought together in this anthology nonetheless remains tied to the very past away from which it is directed: a pastiche of styles, it is a hybrid poetry, characterized by the "coexistence of a culturally anterior language, already stylistically 'fixed,' and a newborn language, as yet stylistically without any tradition" (p. xvi). What this "newborn," untraditional language of the future might consist in is left to our imagination. The identity of the "culturally anterior" language is, however, obvious: "it is that of European decadentism." A stylistic canon for much African poetry, it turns out, is "uninterrupted poetry" ("la poesia ininterrotta")—a genealogical line that extends back from surrealism to romanticism (pp. xvi–xvii). Ultimately, the fact of this poetic continuity works against the interruptive aims of the Resistance, putting into question the proposed break between colonialism and an emancipated, decolonized world.

Pasolini's sentiments toward this traditional, "decadentist" language and its continued presence in Third World writing are clearly ambivalent. On the one hand, he acknowledges that such continuity is the very soul of literature: "The more these sources are both recognizable and assimilated in a poet, the greater, I would say, is that poet's worth, also when it comes to innovation" (p. xvii). On the other hand, this literary process of assimilation runs against his neo-exoticist grain, since it is inevitably a sign of cultural contamination. Given this complicity with what has already been said, how can Black poetry ever be expected to wipe the ideological slate clean of its colonial past and fully partake of the innocent, "newborn" language that it supposedly augurs?

Perhaps, at least such will be the central assumption of Pasolini's *Il padre selvaggio*, this necessary leap into a new future and over the contaminated present is conceivable only by means of an abrupt return to "Africa" as it was before colonialism—that is, through a return to "prehistory" (and, by extension, "savagery"; as he reminds the readers of *Vie nuove* on 18 March 1961, the worlds "of the bee, of the rose, of the savage, are worlds outside of history, eternal in themselves, without prospects if not into the depths of the sensitive").[21] The revolutionary concept of the Third World subproletariat turns out to be inextricably linked for Pasolini with the category of the "prehistoric"—of a natural, indeed animal, way of life whose vitality has yet to be undone by the sort of historical complications that characterize "civil" society: "It is highly symptomatic that the ones who are fighting for social justice should be those peoples who are as far from industrial civilization as can be imagined: subproletarians who are, with respect to that civilization, thoroughly prehistoric" (p. xxiv). Ultimately, perhaps, only a force that stands outside history might be resilient enough to resist successfully the onward march of a modernity from which "social justice" is so terribly absent.

Pasolini's appeal to a totalizing category like the "prehistoric" is but the most extreme instance of the "strong" dialectical way of thinking that characterizes his *tiers-mondisme*: only as an homogeneous whole does the revolutionary concept "Third World" offer him the hope of a "scandalous" rather than a predictable resolution to the process of decolonization. The task of reappropriating a new future from the clutches of the neo-capitalist Same can be carried out only by an Other totality. However difficult to overlook, the historical and cultural diversity of the Third World must nonetheless be downplayed or ignored if the revolutionary space is to emerge in all the seamless unity that his differential criteria demands. Pasolini's cult of difference, ironically enough, leads him to search out only one thing in the Third World, although it has various, if interchangeable, names: "the subaltern," "the peasant world [*il mondo contadino*] the whole earth over," "the world of the subproletariat that consumes with respect to a capitalism that produces," and in its most drastic yet revealing incarnation, "the prehistoric." Differences are elided in the name of this one difference that alone can ensure the conceptual integrity of his *tiers-mondiste* alternative: such is the monolithic imperative that dominates Pasolini's encounter with "the entire world of Bandung."[22]

Pasolini himself was acutely aware of the stylistic difficulties connected to the empirical problem of producing this totalizing vision in the face of asynchronous historical and cultural development within the so-called Third World. How can we represent the reality of the prehistoric without reducing it to the sort of phantasmic, and essentially rhetorical, construct we encountered in his work of the previous decade? Pasolini's criticism of the way certain of the anthologized poets attempt to celebrate the "alternative of vitality" is enlightening in this regard:

In the previous culture of a people, the one that history has surpassed, there is always this reserve of vitality that in the poet, living as he does inside of history, cannot help turning into rhetoric. Naked Blacks dancing around the fire are like subproletarians from Rovigo huddled around a flask of wine or peasants from the south of Italy playing the guitar: pure objects of rhetoric (when they are brought up to the "learned" [*culto*] level, naturally, and not understood and mimed stylistically right inside of their very being . . .).

(p. xxi)

How can the writer return to this necessary "reserve of vitality" if, from the perspective of history (and of writing itself), the prehistoric has always-already been surpassed? The writer's every attempt to assert the prehistoric in all its reality serves only to un-realize it, to reveal it as nothing more than a rhetorical category that takes its place not under the sign of truth but of persuasion.

Or rather, and here Pasolini adds a parenthetical kicker that more or less completely undoes this insight into the purely rhetorical nature of a totalizing category like the "prehistoric," its decline into rhetoric occurs only once it is brought up to the "learned" level. There are other levels at which the project of representation can come to terms with the reality of the prehistoric, at which it can be stylistically understood and mimed in its very being, stripped of all rhetorical masks. But in order for this to happen, the writer must himself be as absent as possible from his own Third World work: his inevitably "learned" presence must be effaced if he and his readers are to reach these other levels. For the source of revolutionary hope to appear in all its non-rhetorical immediacy, it must be allowed to speak for its "uneducated" self—without, as it were, the obvious intervention of a Monsieur Courneau.

The central problem that Pasolini's Third World *oeuvre* must overcome, then, is heterogeneity: the twofold disruptive presence of history in the Third World and of a "learned" writing self in the text. That this problem is an irresoluble one goes, I think, without saying, but that certain geographical sites and certain modes of writing are more amenable than others to this project is equally clear, especially if we compare Pasolini's enthusiasm for "Africa" with the surprisingly tepid prose of a work like *L'odore dell'India* (1962)—a collection of newspaper articles written about his voyage in late 1960 to India, which I will only mention in passing here and by way of introduction to *Il padre selvaggio*.[23]

The diaristic form of the travelogue holds little appeal to Pasolini, for it cannot fail to draw attention to the very figure whose "learned" (and interpretive) presence has to be downplayed if the reality of the Third World is to emerge in all its integrity. Pasolini's I/eye finds itself at the center of what it ought to be absent from. By way of compensating for this unwanted centrality, Pasolini adopts a markedly neutral position—one that, as Rinaldi points out, hardly jibes with the revolutionary and poetic claims of his *tiers-mondisme*: "The tone is, in a word, even in those instances where the mythic release would be easiest (think of the final pages, with the crossing of the Ganges, the funeral rites), flat, a little sly, scarcely animated by any inquisitive interest."[24] If Pasolini here passes up a golden opportunity to portray the Third World in the heroic terms one might expect of him, it is in great part due, I suspect, to his misgivings about the subjective nature of the travelogue. In this context, positive representations of the Third World might well appear less the description of some alternative reality than the projection of a "learned" self whose polemical claims would serve only to disrupt and rhetoricize the object they privilege.

This formal problem is, in turn, matched by one of content: only with the greatest of difficulty can Pasolini fit India into his *tiers-mondiste* mold. Unflattering portraits of the Indian bourgeoisie (pp. 75–98) or the anything but "peasant-like" Sikhs (pp. 127–28) are but a few signs of his unwillingness to acknowledge the obvious cultural heterogeneity of India. Moreover, thousands of years of Indian civilization, not to mention over a decade of national independence, must be glossed over if India's identity with the supposedly ongoing Third World "Resistance"—"the appearance upon the scene of history of the underdeveloped peoples, from India, to Indonesia, to Africa" (p. 101)—is to seem at all plausible. The great number of leveling affirmations in this travelogue bears indirect witness to Pasolini's need for an unfissured Third World totality: he will consistently figure India in terms of uniformity ("the terrible monotony of India"; p. 141) or pandemic poverty ("the enormous Buchenwald that is India"; p. 118).

This homogenizing strategy goes hand in hand with what might at first strike one as his rather strange insistence on the continued and pervasive presence in India of the traditional caste system, "that atrocious shadow which they have only just left" (p. 103). The caste system points us back to that most extreme, and privileged, category of Pasolini's *tiers-mondisme*: namely, the prehistoric. This "atrocious shadow" must, for Pasolini, be something more than a mere phantasm: only the fact that Indians are "like people who have lived for a long time in the darkness and suddenly find themselves brought back into the light" can guarantee India's difference from the world of a fallen history. The continued presence of this shadow functions as a necessary evil—a darkness that Pasolini, from the standpoint of his own enlightenment, can only criticize but which nonetheless holds out the promise of an Other way of life for those still capable of experiencing it.

As we will soon see, this is precisely the dialectical role that Pasolini assigns to the prehistoric in *Il padre selvaggio*; in *L'odore dell'India*, however, this traditional force inaugurates nothing—partly because the travelogue is intrinsically committed to the perspective of enlightenment, partly because even India's "prehistory" cannot be disentangled from the vagaries of its long history. Indian tradition comes to us, we are told, only "through the various static milieux created by subsequent foreign rulers," and thus its conservation "is in reality a degeneration" (p. 103). As such, it offers little interest or hope to a writer in search not of "degeneration" but of history's regeneration through an encounter with what is outside and Other than it.

The novelist Alberto Moravia, Pasolini's frequent traveling companion and a writer who shared his friend's neo-exoticist faith in the prehistoric, provides an extremely clear summation of what is, from this (absurd, to be sure) perspective, "wrong" with India: the Indian subcontinent is a place where "history has, let's put it this way, misfired, but in which it is nonetheless present in an obsessive, indeed overwhelming manner." By way of a positive contrast to this "obsessively" historicized India, Moravia offers the example of Africa, "a continent as yet poised between prehistory and history."[25] Not surprisingly, it will be to this Africa in transition that both Moravia and Pasolini feel themselves most drawn in their travels and their writing (although Moravia's interest in the prehistoric is always less a matter of revolutionary hope than of aesthetic contemplation, and for this reason Africa will continue to be a source of personal satisfaction to him long after Pasolini has given up on its revolutionary potential).

Writing about Africa in 1963, Moravia gives a succinct definition of the "prehistoric" that offers a perfect gloss on Pasolini's own use of this category in *Il padre selvaggio*. For Moravia, the "prehistoric" is essentially twofold: both a natural and a cultural phenomenon. In the first case, it is "the actual conformation of the African landscape," whose principal character "is not diversity, as in Europe, but rather [a] terrifying monotony."[26] In the second, it is the stuff of primitive religion: "Prehistory in Africa exists not only in the conformation of the landscape but also in the universal presence of the one truly autochthonous religious belief—magic. In Europe the world of magic survives in modest and enigmatic remnants, like scraps of flotsam in the sea after a shipwreck; but in Africa one is all the time aware that the world of magic is still complete, intact and in working order" (p. 10). This African culture is itself a form of nature because it "springs from unchanging biological necessity, not from the ever-changing evolution of history" (p. 54). Taken together, this prehistoric nature/culture, Moravia argues, is still very much the heart of "authentic Africa"; although he looks with dismay upon everything that conjures up the image of history (for instance, the modern and "unnatural" African city, "full of uprooted people"), Moravia is nonetheless comforted by the fact that "the smaller agglomerates, the tribe and the African village, remain positive, human realities."[27] Only because of this prehistoric presence does Africa appear to him, as one of his more sympathetic commentators puts it, as "the place in which it is possible to recuperate an undegraded certitude about existence."[28]

If the African continent still holds out for both writers a promise reneged upon in Europe (and in India), the two differ in their estimation as to just how easily it may be approached. For Moravia the task of grasping this exotic difference poses no great difficulty, since the prehistoric mirrors his own "original" truth, that "simple nature" which was once his: "Decadent culture caught onto a simple nature, as was my own originally, like a sort of illness. It was as if I had caught small-pox while frequenting places that were new to me. Like an African who comes to Europe and catches a disease that in his own land doesn't exist."²⁹ Moravia's "decadence" is a sickness, but hardly a mortal one: a writer like himself, "desirous of experiences and free of Eurocentric prejudices," can recover from it and return whence he came. Under the right circumstances, he is capable of "forgetting" the illness of history: "I have the ability to forget Humanism, the Renaissance, the age of En-lightenment, everything that for centuries has represented the glory of Europe" (p. 80). The ludicrousness of Moravia's claim that he is free of "Eurocentric prejudices" need not concern us here.³⁰ What is more to the point is that his sanguine view of the "learned" writer's return to a "simple nature" (and his consequent reliance on the openly subjec-tive genre of the travelogue) is not, ultimately, one Pasolini can share.

The writer is for Pasolini a mediatory figure who, in his unavoidable attachment to history, cannot help rhetoricizing the prehistoric object; if this object is to speak for itself, the artist himself must be as absent as possible from his own work and yet somehow, to be sure, still pres-ent. Hence Pasolini's attraction to the cinema and its promise of direct representation and immediate capture of that exotic, prehistoric dif-ference from which the writer finds himself at a seemingly insuperable distance; as he will claim later in the decade, only the cinema allows him "to maintain contact with reality, a physical, carnal, I would even say sensual contact."³¹ The truth or falsity of this assertion need not be argued here; rather, in the remainder of this section, I will look at the (pseudo-)objective form of writing that prepares us for this "unedu-cated" encounter with the prehistoric—namely, the screenplay for what would have been Pasolini's most accomplished Third World work, *Il padre selvaggio*.* This screenplay (a project that was to have been shot in 1962 and to which Pasolini intermittently returned up un-til the very end of his life) provides perhaps the most vivid illustration of how the double problem of "prehistory" and revolutionary politics functions in Pasolini's own peculiar blend of *tiers-mondisme*.

The plot of *Il padre selvaggio* is indeed a simple one, which has the

* I will refer to two versions of this screenplay: an early draft (henceforth cited as *PS₁*), first published in *Film selezione* in 1962 and reprinted in Bertini, pp. 116–23; and a greatly expanded version (henceforth cited as *PS₂*), first published in 1967 in the journal *Cinema e film* (1.3: 377–82, 1.4: 500–509) and then brought out verbatim in 1975 as a book. For my purposes, I treat these versions as one work; however, a comparative analysis of the two texts would by no means be unprofitable.

Congo crisis of the early 1960's as its historical subtext. The new African State has just gained its independence: an idealistic European teacher arrives, buoyed up by his "democratic ideology" and hoping to guide his students away from the conformist colonial education they had received before the coming of independence. The results of this first academic year are mixed but promising. Comes the summer vacation and the students leave for the interior, returning to their respective villages; it is a time of political chaos, of civil war and neo-colonial machinations. The teacher's best and most sensitive student, Davidson, finds himself actively caught up in the tribal violence rampant in his part of the country: as Pasolini put it in a 1962 interview, the boy undergoes "a prehistoric experience, archaic, of savage life, even of cannibalism perhaps" ("un'esperienza preistorica, arcaica, di vita selvaggia, addirittura di cannibalismo forse").[32] This fall back into the "archaic," "prehistoric" world of his "savage father" traumatizes Davidson; upon his return to the school, he maintains an anguished and at times violently hysterical silence. Eventually, though, he snaps out of it. A poetic voice awakens inside of him; as a result of his traumatic experience he has become a poet and will create what in the 1962 interview Pasolini refers to as "poems whose content is profoundly democratic and rational" (p. 62). In the following paragraphs, I will briefly retell this story in the light of what we have already learned about Pasolini's *tiersmondisme*.

The central problem that Pasolini attempts to grapple with in this post-colonial story is the legacy of colonialism, and more specifically the presence of writing in the space of orality/alterity. The sudden fall, or leap, from orality to writing is, of course, among the most familiar of exoticist (and ethnographic) tropes; in *Il padre selvaggio*, this "passage from a fully oral language, pure of all writing—*pure*, innocent—to a language appending to itself its graphic 'representation' as an accessory signifier of a new type, opening a technique of oppression" has long since taken place.[33] Colonialism has brought the dubious gift of writing, inscription, and hierarchy to the erstwhile "innocent" space of the Other (most emphatically, we find it on the three doors of the public latrine where one can still discern "the signs carved out by the old colonialism. Section for Whites, section for Arabs, section for Blacks"; PS_2, pp. 21–22). The traditional continuum of the past has already been ruptured and, as a result, the students have come under the nefarious spell of "the conformism taught . . . by the previous colonialist professors" (PS_1, p. 116); much to the dismay of the "democratic professor," "the authority and the rhetoric of the colonialists" continues to exercise its unhealthy influence upon his charges (PS_2, p. 13).

The "esperienza drammatica" of the teacher does not, however, form the central focus of the screenplay. Indeed, Pasolini ends up taking a certain ironical distance from the teacher's well-intentioned efforts, even though he is in many ways a projection of the author himself. We are told, for instance, that his idealism is "always a little ingenuous and inconsequent" and are referred to "the idealistic and romantic limbo of his new teaching" (PS_2, pp. 9, 25). (It should be noted, however, that in the earlier version Pasolini shows little or no such irony toward the teacher's "sincere and democratic" pedagogy.) Pasolini's distance from this figure, I would argue, stems in large part from his sense that the teacher's project of pedagogical decolonization only furthers the process of assimilation inaugurated by colonialism— a process another sort of intellectual might well have condoned under the very different name of "authentic" hybridization.* Because from his perspective it could result only in a hybrid state of affairs more compatible with global capitalism than with an emancipatory Resistance, Pasolini will both conjure up and yet defer the success of this project. Under "normal," peaceful circumstances, we are told (PS_1, p. 120), the teacher's efforts would result in the diffusion of democratic culture not just among his students but through them into the very heart of the new nation, but it is precisely this moment of peace that is, and must be, absent from the text in order for a more extreme dialectical solution to arise.

---

*See, e.g., Michel Leiris's seminal "L'ethnographe devant le colonialisme" (1950), collected in *Brisées*, pp. 125–45. According to Leiris, however nefarious the colonialist enterprise may be, it has not destroyed anything essential, since the very idea of cultural essence is no more than a false lure in a world that is inevitably historical. One must, he advises, abandon the idea of a supposed integrity, "for it is very clear that the societies under our jurisdiction have never known this integrity, even before being colonized" (p. 128). This rejection of cultural "integrity" is, however, immediately followed by a new "hybrid" version of the same old purist story: it is, Leiris continues, precisely those who have undergone the most changes who should be of especial interest to the ethnographer. The most "authentic" Africans turn out to be those most affected by capitalism and colonialism and who, therefore, are best able to combat these evils; Leiris would valorize those who, "having a full awareness of what their condition as colonized men of color involves and tolerating with ever greater difficulty the capitalist oppression introduced by Europeans, have become the instigators of liberation [*se sont faits les promoteurs de l'émancipation*]" (p. 139). In the name of a post-colonial "liberation," Leiris privileges an "authentic" hybridity, thereby repeating, in a different key, exoticism's ideological embrace of purity.

The time of Pasolini's story is one of crisis, a state of war that allows for the dissolution of "civil" society ("everything that is historical, civilized, seems to dissolve"; PS_1, p. 20) and the "reflowering" of savagery that is the necessary condition of the Other's emergence, on its own terms and out of its own ground, into history. Only an apocalyptic return to the very "heart of Africa" can ensure the Other's revolutionary difference from the world of the Same. Davidson and the reader-viewer will be "reprecipitated" into "the prehistoric world of an Africa that has just made its appearance on the scene of history" ("il mondo preistorico dell'Africa, appena affiorato alla storia"; PS_1, p. 120); an archaic darkness becomes a "black light" ("negra luce") whose continued presence troubles the dominion of that "enlightened" and writing culture to which the author himself remains tied.

The spectacle of the prehistoric Other is twofold, as we might have guessed from Moravia's definition: the double vision of a natural landscape and of a primitive culture. Returning home, Davidson's first revelation of his prehistoric origin comes when he reaches the forest that surrounds his native village; he sees for the first time "the prehuman anxiety that reigns there, with its death-like peace" (PS_2, p. 32). This vision of a "prehuman" nature—innocuous in itself and entirely compatible with Davidson's newly acquired "conscience"—is quickly supplemented, however, by its human corollary: tribal society at its most savage, "the ancient and bestial fury of men born in the forest" (PS_1, p. 120). Davidson will lose his post-colonial identity in the radical alterity of the Other's "archaic soul": at first remaining on the margins of tribal violence, he is eventually absorbed back into his own culture. Forgetting both himself and his "civic" education, Davidson becomes one with "the Blacks with their prehistoric fury" (PS_1, p. 121); "in his dark gracious eyes," we are told, "now trembles a forgetful inebriation, a terrible light" (PS_2, p. 36).

This violent resurgence of an irrational "prehistory" ultimately makes possible a new leap forward into a truly rational history, one that has rid itself of the recent colonial past and thereby been freed from the process of global rationalization that colonialism at once exemplifies and provokes; the return to a savage origin interrupts the script of modernity and prepares the way for an entirely different sort of writing grounded in an Other, truly autochthonous voice. Davidson eventually overcomes his trauma and as a consequence comes into his own; the influence of the European teacher, who had formerly been for him "the sole voice of culture," gives way to the inspiration of his own "interior voice" (PS_2, pp. 23, 55). This voice will "dictate" the words of an authentically African poem to him—one that looks out upon the "confused but happy future" (PS_1, p. 123) from which, as we recall, European poetry has perforce turned away.

It is with this "POEM," and a series of related cinematic images, that *Il padre selvaggio* ends. Or was to have ended. The film, as I said, was never shot: standing in the place of what was to have inaugurated an Other future is nothing but the word "POEM" itself, a word without content, pointing mutely forward. A rather meager result, one might venture, for all the emotional investment that Pasolini put into this work, not to mention the curious, and degrading, dialectical machine that he had to construct in order to achieve even that much. A meager result, yes, but in its helpless reticence, like the ellipsis at the end of "Frammento alla morte," a perfect emblem of Pasolini's own truncated encounter with the Third World.

In a 1965 article on oral language, Pasolini recapitulates the *tiers-mondiste* position that he was unable to put into literary practice. "The 'oral' word," he admits, "is . . . like a phantasm. And, indeed, it is a phantasm, since we are dealing with a linguistic category that is only real at the limit (savage peoples)."[34] This slippage between a phantasmic and real object is, as we have seen, the enabling condition of Pasolini's *tiers-mondisme*. The oral word remains a potent force, despite (or because of) the fact that its "reality" is situated only "at the limit." A "savage" voice that "belongs, at the limit, to a different human moment of civilization, to an *other culture*" can still be heard amid the cacophonous hue and cry of the modern world. There exists, furthermore, a continuity between our world and this "other culture": his young friend Nino's ingenuous exclamation at first seeing snow can thus, for instance, be interpreted as "a vocality due to a *memoriel, which joins together in an uninterrupted continuum* the Ninetto of today at Pescasseroli to the Ninetto of Calabria, marginal and conservative sphere of Greek civilization, to the pre-Greek, purely barbaric, Ninetto who stamps his heels on the ground as do today the prehistoric, naked Denka in the lower Sudan" (pp. 73–74). Pasolini's claim for this "uninterrupted continuum" between the Nino of today and his "barbaric" predecessor depends, though, upon the real existence of this savage, oral past in the here and now: were it not for the abiding presence in the lower Sudan of "prehistory" and its "savage limit," the claim could never amount to anything more than a hypothesis. We would have no true idea of just what it was that Nino was re-enacting.

This state of undecidability, I have maintained, is the inescapable consequence of a modernity that, in its worldwide hegemony, allows for no such "uninterrupted" relation to the past. What has preceded us is no more than a "representation of language," a darkness that our own enlightenment presupposes but can never recover. For the adversaries of modernity, this disappearance of everything that came before it is an unremitting source of melancholy. "To his horror," as Benjamin once said of Baudelaire, "the melancholy man [*der Schwermütige*] sees the earth revert to a mere state of nature. No breath of prehistory [*Vorgeschichte*] surrounds it: there is no aura."[35] The melancholic "holds in his hands the scattered fragments of genuine historical experience [*Erfahrung*]," but there is now nothing "genuine" about these "fragments": whatever truth they embodied has been lost, has seeped back into the ground ("a mere state of nature") upon which we no longer stand; what remains in our possession has been falsified by the "passing moment [*Erlebnis*]"—veiled over, once and for all, by its light without meaning. Such is the saturnine disposition of Pasolini's earlier work, which he will abandon in his attempt at investing the Third World with an aura and breathing back into it the promise of "prehistory," the hope of a new beginning.

The decadentist position argued for in this book takes the impossibility of Pasolini's "auratic" promise as its starting point. Alternatives to a disenchanted modernity are irrevocably absent from our world even (and especially) at the "savage limit"; they can be for us no more than metaphors, phantasms powerless in the face of the present that denies them. Caught between a past that is no longer ours and a future to which in our impotency we cannot give birth, our "tragic" condition in a way calls to mind Sartre's famous characterization of the Negritude movement: "Because it is this tension between a nostalgic Past into which the [B]lack no more completely enters and a future where it will give way to new values, Negritude fashions itself in a tragic beauty which finds expression only in [p]oetry."[36] Of course, in his *tiersmondiste* polemic with modernity, Sartre affirms that this "tragic" state of tension will be resolved: "new values" will take the place of those that have been lost with the dissolution of traditional ways of life. But this call to the future is, I would suggest, no more than a symptom of the very malaise that the strong-thinking Sartre wants to cure: modernity demands the possibility of a future, and of "new values"; horizons are its beginning and not its end.

It is perhaps time to settle for a "tragic beauty," to live with the impossibility of our desire for an end to modernity. At an abyssal distance from our world, only the past—in all its irremediable discontinuity with the present—compels us to think this impossibility through. It is that which comes to us only in the light of the present day—a light that cannot fail to erase it from the face of the earth and thereby reveal it for what it is: unreal. A politics that has its (lack of a) ground in this unreality is no longer one of truth but of metaphor. During the last decade of his life, it is toward this politics of the impossible that Pasolini will unwillingly set his intellectual course.

The Place of the Other: Toward the Rhetoric of Exoticism in Late Pasolini

> . . . al posto dell'Altro
> per me c'è un vuoto nel cosmo
> un vuoto nel cosmo
> e da là tu canti.*
> —P. P. Pasolini, "Timor di me?"

By the end of the 1960's, Pasolini's hopes for a positive, scandalously dialectical resolution to the encounter of "prehistory" and history have given way to the bleak vision of a Third World in the process of being absorbed by the neo-colonial Same that it was meant to have renewed: "Neo-capitalism is the great object toward which the African countries are drawing without uncertainties; a socialist Third World is no more than a legend. The Third World is heading toward an industrialization that is identifiable with the neo-capitalist model, even where the governments declare themselves to be socialist and pro-communist."[37]

Pasolini's later writings abound with similar-minded assertions: the cultural integrity of traditional societies has been despoiled through their contact with a now ineluctably global capitalism; those new revolutionary values in which he had once placed his faith have failed to materialize. The bourgeoisie, he laments, "is triumphing, bourgeoisifying the workers on the one hand and the ex-colonial *contadini* on the other. In short, through neo-capitalism, the bourgeoisie is becoming the human condition. Whoever is born in this entropy, can in no way, metaphysically, be outside it. It's all over."[38] The workers and *contadini* of the Third World are—"despite the mythologization performed upon them by Marcusian and Fanonian intellectuals, myself included, but

---

*". . . in the place of the Other / for me there is an emptiness in the universe / an emptiness in the universe / and from there you sing."

A Postscript to Transgression

ante litteram"[39]—going the way of all modern flesh: toward the horrendous, and unsightly, universe of consumerism where "relations are no longer between one individual [*singolo*] and another but between individual and masses."[40] Pasolini now sees himself as the victim of a "myth": the relative good humor of the Courneau episode has given way to an at times virulent recantation of "a Third World idealized stupidly by the rhetoric of a Left that has read only Fanon."[41]

Commenting on this change of heart in a 1968 interview, Pasolini remarks, "Years ago, I dreamed of *contadini* coming up from the Africas with the banner of Lenin, taking with them the Calabrians and marching toward the West. Today I'm in the process of changing my mind. Once it was right to have those feelings. It was right to have those visions, or previsions, ten, five years ago. . . . Today it seems to me an idea that ought to come to a better reckoning with historical reality, with reality, with the truth."[42] As I have attempted to show in this book, the "time" in which such feelings were "right" (validated by "historical reality") was not just some five or ten years in the past. Since the age of the New Imperialism, if not before, the exoticist project had been patently vacant: the fin de siècle inheritors of this nineteenth-century literary tradition had already been forced to confront the inadequacy of geopolitical panaceas when it came to treating the ills of a modernity no longer limited to parts of the globe but coextensive with it. The exotic was a dream for them, as was that "single" individual who was to have bridged the gap between a degraded colonial world and its more authentic alternative(s). Only by failing to acknowledge the legacy of this superseded tradition can Pasolini maintain that his own *tiers-mondiste* ideology was ever adequate to "la realtà storica, la realtà, la verità." To have confessed his attachment to this "idea without a future" would have been to confront the fact that, from the beginning, his ideological beliefs were hollow, and to take this essential weakness as a point of departure rather than as the motive for an embittered abjuration.

It is this inability to come to terms with his literary precedents that makes of Pasolini, to use Paolo Valesio's forceful distinction, a "symptom" rather than a "sign" of his times: he is a writer who "expresses the situation but without controlling it—on the contrary, he is its victim."[43] As Valesio argues in his analysis of Pasolini's journalism, the merely symptomatic writer is one who has not reconciled himself to the genealogy of his own writing—who has not, that is, taken into account its attachment to a previous act of writing and thereby revealed the rhetorical ground of the ideology to which he is giving voice. The writer as "sign" has taken up the burden of the past, actively encouraging the tradition that in any case speaks through him to speak through him: "No one better than the writer (when he is fully that) takes into account, and accounts for, the fact that it is always in the final analysis the dead who have hold of the living" (p. 35). The writer's apprehension of the present is always mediated by what has come before him; the genealogical perspective presupposes this lack of immediacy, motivated as it is by an awareness that "to read men, and speak about them . . . it is not enough to look at them directly; indeed, it is not possible to look at them directly. Books are the indispensable mediation" (p. 40). Circling back to what he can neither escape nor truly recuperate, the writer as "sign" engages with his predecessors in an act of mediation that we call literature.

But this absence of genealogy—the rock upon which his neo-exoticist project founders—by no means characterizes all of Pasolini's later work: indeed, as his dream of unmediated contact with an Other way of life collapses, he will come more and more to (re)adopt, at least in his poetry, a perspective that is in some ways remarkably similar to the genealogical one Valesio argues for. In *Trasumanar e organizzar* (1971) and *La nuova gioventú* (1975; a parodic rewriting, or *rifacimento*, of his now decades-old *La meglio gioventú*), the melancholic insight of his early work into the mediated, purely written nature of the poet's relation to the realm of value returns—albeit this time in a mode more ironical than tragic. Pasolini rediscovers his poetic vocation but now also confronts what he calls its essential "vacancy": although, he writes in "Lungo le rive dell'Eufrate" (1969), he has "refound the poetic vein," it is "something that is in any case entirely useless / for what future has he in front of him?"[44] The author of *Trasumanar e organizzar* finds himself (once again) situated at an abyssal distance from the once and future worlds that he had briefly thought it possible to embrace:

> Ahi, non so il romanesco se non rivivendolo;
> non posso direttamente rivolgermi a loro,
> un'arringa non vale una manata sulla spalla,
> un pamphlet non vale un vaffanculo.
>
> ("Mirmicolalia," p. 571)

> (Ah! I don't know Roman dialect unless by reliving it;
> I can't directly address them,
> a harangue isn't worth a slap on the shoulders,
> a pamphlet isn't worth a "fuck you.")

His relation to the world of the Roman periphery, and a fortiori to the Third World, is no longer one of living but of reliving—a posthumous enterprise that must forgo all that is "worth" more than a mere oration or pamphlet, more than just words. The poet of the last years has re(-)signed himself to the melancholic position of his earlier work: to write is always to come after the object of one's desire, to postscript that which one would have prefaced.

It is not my purpose here to follow up on the intricacies of Pasolini's later, self-consciously literary work (which often touches upon greatness, especially in his six tragedies). Rather, in this brief epilogue I will say a few words about the fate of the exotic in Pasolini during the last decade of his life, since his reaction to its dissolution provides a particularly vivid example of the contrast between "strong" and "weak" thinking that I have been considering throughout this book. On the one hand, he will try to overlook the inadequacy of his *tiers-mondiste* ideology, continuing to posit alterity in "strong" terms—although to do so he must have recourse to increasingly extreme positions. On the other hand, Pasolini will give voice to an unbridled pessimism that, although it must seem only the fruit of "a desperately non-historical and non-class vision" to those who still fancy themselves capable of thinking beyond the confines of modernity,[45] clears the way for the beginning of a strategic recuperation, as rhetoric, of the very ideology that he can no longer believe in. Although never explicitly formulated, it is toward this second, "weak" way of thinking that his later work tends in its evaluation of alterity in general and of the Third World in particular.

During the 1960's, the primary source of Pasolini's "strength" will derive from his work in film. The cinema still held out to him the hope of what he had come to see as absent from literature and its mediatory language: namely, the possibility of radical change, of transgression, of direct contact with the reality of the Other. Discussing another never-completed but long-contemplated film about the Third World, the *Poema sul Terzo Mondo*, he remarks that his primary purpose is to "make of the film itself a revolutionary action."[46] This meeting of art and action is possible because moviemaking allows for an immediate capture of reality; unlike literature, which inevitably metaphorizes and hence debilitates its object, the cinema establishes contact with the outside world. As he exuberantly puts the case to one interviewer, "Reality doesn't need metaphors to express itself. If I want to express you, I express you through yourself. I couldn't use metaphor to express you.

In the cinema it is as though reality expressed itself with itself, without metaphors, and without anything insipid and conventional and symbolic."[47]

Pasolini was nonetheless aware that inserting this simple reality within the context of a fictional narrative would necessarily problematize it—a difficulty he had already encountered in his work on *Il padre selvaggio*. It is for this reason, no doubt, that his projected *Poema* was to be "a sort of documentary, an essay. . . . I could only conceive of it in this form."[48] If he could conceive of this movie project, however, he would never complete it (although parts of it were filmed and shown as *Appunti per un film sull'India* [1968] and *Appunti per un'Orestiade africana* [1970]). Although he attributed this fact to a gradual realization that the film would have no audience, a more likely reason, I think, lies in the very nature of his own cinematic practice—a practice built around an entirely different poetics than the one we just saw him theorizing, a poetics of *contamination* that runs counter to his professed cult of a truly documentable reality.[49]

Here is not the place to pursue the plausible argument that Pasolini's films do not aspire to the absence of metaphor that his theory proclaims and that the "insipid and conventional and symbolic" are all emphatically, and often willfully, present in his cinematic work. What needs emphasizing, rather, is the theoretical necessity of this simple "reality" for a Pasolini who could no longer avoid acknowledging the global stature of neo-capitalism. It functions as a last, extremist stronghold of authenticity, an as yet inviolate material base upon which stands a cultural superstructure now entirely given over to the horrendous universe of neo-capitalism. Pasolini's cult of "reality" is similar, in a way, to the erotic attachment with nature that the hero of *Le mariage de Loti* tried to effect; all that is left for him to valorize is what appears to be at a total distance from the realm of an already degraded culture. During his last decade, Pasolini will insist on the absolute division between body and conscience, between biological existence and human history; he will no longer treat them as necessary elements in the dialectical progress toward a new future but as mutually incompatible categories. As he says in a 1971 interview, "My dialectic is no longer ternary but binary. There are only oppositions, irreconcilable. Thus no more 'sun of the future,' no 'better world.'"[50] Cut off from the future, limited to a corporeal present, his revolutionary outlook transforms itself into a vitalist, depoliticized aestheticism—as, for instance, in a 1969 article in *Nuovi argomenti* on "the grace of the Eritreans" ("casting a comprehensive look down a street in Asmara, one does not see a single ugly person," and so on).[51]

As with Loti, however, Pasolini's exasperated attempt at preserving the integrity of the alternative that he desires does not succeed. No sooner has he set up this positive libidinal subject in response to the Other's neutralization as a political force (a move that finds significant echoes in other works of the period, such as Jean-François Lyotard's *Economie libidinale* [1974]), then it, too, begins to show damaging cracks; the simple "reality" of the body and of physical existence proves as subject to the malaise of neo-capitalism as had that of the "better world" he once prophesied. Pasolini's discovery that even this outpost of alterity has fallen to the enemy will result in ever more violent critiques of what he once praised—negative portrayals of the Other's body, which serve to reinforce those he has already devoted to its increasingly unoriginal culture. Revisiting Eritrea in 1973, for instance, his initial admiration for the natives' physical "grace" is transformed into a scathing critique of their "true nature" ("their grace hides a sick and aberrant sensitivity," and so on)—a nature now entirely determined by their subservient relation to modernity.

The most dramatic instance of this recantation of corporeal "reality" and the alternative present it seemingly offered is undoubtedly his "Abiura dalla *Trilogia della vita*" (June 1975).[52] Only a year before he had spoken in euphoric terms about making that triptych of films (*Il Decameron*, *I racconti di Canterbury*, and *Il fiore delle Mille e una notte* [1971–74]): "At Naples and in the East I knew no limits; I could let loose around me this language of the earth, of things, of volcanos, of palms, of nettles, and above all of the people."[53] In the "Abiura," though, he speaks with unsuppressed bitterness about the futility of his attempt at giving a positive representation of eros and the (predominantly Third World) body. Appealing to the irreconcilable opposition between biological existence and cultural history that we have been examining, he explains that his efforts in the *Trilogia* were justified at the time because he was then filming a "human sphere" that was "still physically present" in Naples and the Near East, even though it was already, if only just, "surpassed by history" and hence disabled as a political force (p. 72): "The degenerating present was compensated for both by the objective survival of the past and, as a consequence, by the possibility of recalling it" (p. 73). But, he continues, since that time the situation has changed dramatically; there is no longer any room for this anachronistic "survival" in the degraded present of consumerism and techno-fascism. What lived on as a physical if not political reality has itself acceded to the corrupting force of neo-capitalism. Indeed, he adds, "The degeneration of bodies and sexual members has assumed a retroactive import." If, that is, what he once valorized is now human filth, this means that even then it was potentially so: "The collapse of the present also implies the collapse of the past. Life is a pile of insignificant and ironical ruins" (p. 73).

This abjuration of an existential present that would differ from its degraded, historical double also, significantly, implicates the past in which this difference supposedly obtained—a past to which Pasolini in his later years felt himself more and more drawn. As he noted in a 1973 interview, "Nowadays, I prefer to move around in the past, because I believe that the only force capable of contesting the present is, precisely, the past: it is an aberrant form, but all those values that were the values in which we were formed, with all their atrocities, their negative aspects, are the ones that can put the present into crisis."[54] For Pasolini, in fact, the simple material "reality" of things and of people was never enough in itself: lacking the dimension of depth that the future and its revolutionary horizon had once provided, the irreconcilable opposition between existence and history that he had come to champion ran the risk—one that he was acutely aware of even as he himself often fell prey to it—of promoting merely a sterile aestheticism. Late Pasolini's preoccupation with the past thus emerges as an attempt at avoiding this danger, at providing the alternative realm of the body with a cultural ground and a political raison d'être.

Now, clearly, this affirmation of the past as a repository of values capable of putting the present in crisis is yet another instance of Pasolini's "strong" way of thinking: the past that he valorizes remains for him an efficacious, if aberrant, "force." Indeed, granting such power to the past allows him to engage the same historicist scenario that we saw to be at the heart of Conrad's *Nigger of the 'Narcissus'*: the eventual outcome of this crisis, Pasolini will suggest, could be a real return to the realm of value, a final solution to the malady of our own worth-less time. Such a possibility is broached, for instance, in a passage from the *Scritti corsari* (1975) discussing the significance of his return to writing in Friulan dialect: "Perhaps we have already reached the summit of this aberrant history—even though we dare not hope it— and now the descending parabola is beginning. Men must perhaps re-experience their past, after having artificially surpassed and forgotten it in a sort of fever, a frenzied lack of conscience" (p. 225). The figure of the parabola allows Pasolini to contemplate a world from which the "artificial" has disappeared and where what has been "forgotten" shall have been truly restored. To be sure, he adds, "for a long time the recuperation of such a past will be an abortion: an unhappy mixing of new comforts and old miseries." This hybrid situation is, however, no more than the strait gate through which we must pass, the unhappy prelude to another life; it is the necessary condition, as he says, of "beginning everything from the beginning again."

This renewed vision of the past is what Pasolini will rule out in the "Abiura" when he acknowledges the "retroactive import" of modernity's hegemony. All that is left for him now, he asserts, is "to adapt to the degradation," "to accept the unacceptable" (p. 75): for this reason, he concludes, "I am in the process of forgetting how things were *before*" ("sto dimenticando com'erano *prima* le cose"; pp. 75–76). But it is precisely at this point, here at the end of the line, when all real alternatives—past, present, or future—to the horrendous universe of neocapitalism have been closed off for him, that we can begin to discern in Pasolini the elements of a "weak" approach to the past and the values that ensure its alterity.

Unfolding a logical contradiction in the "Abiura" will help us get a sense of what this approach involves. The contradiction is generated by Pasolini's claim that the possibility of recalling the past he so valued depends upon its objective survival in the present. By this logic, we must assume that once that past's anachronistic presence disappears then so too will the possibility of remembering it. And yet in the "Abiura," which he emphatically situates after the definitive and "genocidal" elimination of what he would valorize, Pasolini nonetheless continues to invoke the very world that he claims has now disappeared for good. This amounts to an admission that the vision of the past he puts forward in the "Abiura" depends not upon the objective survival of that past but upon his own, necessarily subjective, capacity for recreating it. The writer who recreates the past is one who has, for good or ill, already "adapted" to the degradation of the present; his work testifies that things as they were before have been well and truly forgotten. This forgetting is the condition of his memory: a memory that can come into its own only after the real disappearance of its object; a memory that must establish itself at a posthumous distance from what it records—the distance of (a pious) fiction. This is the "weak" vision of the past that Pasolini's logical contradiction allows us to glimpse in the "Abiura"—and, as I have suggested, it is this vision that, against the "strong" if ever more desperate grain of his theory, guides the greater part of his more properly artistic output during the final decade of his life.

To be sure, even in the last and most pessimistic years of his life, Pasolini never explicitly embraced what we have seen to be implicit in the "Abiura"—namely, the "weakness" of his presentation of the past and its difference from the degraded present of neo-capitalism. But it is certainly fair to say that he was beginning to confront the need for a re-evaluation of his parti pris in favor of "strong thinking": his attempts at capturing the reality of the Other had by this time all fallen through, each having failed to live up to the promise that, in theory, it held out. The more hopeless this situation becomes, the more Pasolini shows himself willing to open up (again) the question of literature and its resolutely mediated relation to the realm of value—a relation that, since the end of the 1950's, he had been intent upon surpassing. At the end of his ideological line, Pasolini begins to consider in a more positive light the (im)possibilities offered by a form of representation that he had consistently identified, and criticized, as merely "conventional."

One extremely relevant instance of this (re)turn to literature is the account he gives in the *Lettere luterane* of a recent film shoot in Yemen. He first rehearses his now familiar distinction between "strong" and "weak" perceptions of the world: "Whereas in a literary man things are destined to become words, that is, symbols, in the expression of a director things remain things: the 'signs' of the verbal system are thus symbolic and conventional, whereas the 'signs' of the cinematographic system are precisely the things themselves in their materiality and their reality" (p. 38). One's impressions of a place, he adds, depend entirely upon which of these two ways of seeing, "conventional" or "realistic," one has adopted: "If I had gone to Yemen as a literary man, I would have returned with an idea of Yemen completely different from that which I got having gone there as a director." The writer would return "with the idea—exalting and static—of a country crystallized in a historical situation that is medieval" (pp. 38–39), whereas the director sees "in the midst of all this, the horrible 'expressive' presence of modernity [*la presenza 'espressiva,' orribile, della modernità*]"—a modernity that has, among other things, turned the people of Yemen "into buffoons physically" (p. 40).

However, Pasolini goes on to affirm, and here his argument starts moving in an entirely less familiar, more ambivalent, direction, that these two visions cannot be hierarchically situated with respect to one another. The "exalting and static" literary vision now takes its place for Pasolini alongside the sordid "reality" of modern Yemen. He is, he admits, unable to tell which of these two visions, the "conventional" or the "realistic," is more true; what confronts him, rather, is "the coexistence of two semantically different worlds, unified in one babelic expressive system" (p. 39). But to have identified the possible equivalence of these two worlds, to have posed the question of whether "things themselves in their materiality and their reality" are more true or less true than the patently mediated vision of the literary man, is to have already taken the side of "weakness" against "strength" in representing the exotic and those political and cultural differences it should embody. If Yemen offers an alternative to modernity, it is one that will henceforth be accessible only to those who have taken the literary perspective as their point of departure, promoting and engaging in a necessarily fictional, "symbolic" construction: such is the conclusion toward which Pasolini points his reader.

In this article, then, Pasolini begins laying the theoretical foundation for a literary re-vision of what he claims has "really" been desecrated once and for all. It is this same poetics, and politics, of re-vision that we saw him actively, if only implicitly, putting into practice in the "Abiura." What is thus everywhere prepared for in the work of Pasolini's last years is a direct confrontation with the real absence of the Other worlds he has consistently been positing, and abjuring, over the past two decades; by the end of his life, he appears to have ruled out every possible alternative to the fallen world of neo-capitalism. Whether Pasolini would ever knowingly have taken the path that we have seen him hesitantly venturing toward, however, is a matter for fruitless speculation: how far he would have been willing to accept the insight that he broaches in his article on Yemen is a question that his untimely, if poetically just, death renders forever undecidable.

Fittingly, only a few days before that death, Pasolini would compose a speech that vividly evokes the continued tension in his thinking with regard to the political and cultural alternatives he so wished to embrace.[55] The speech that he was to have delivered, as a representative of the Italian Communists, to the congress of the Radical party is an ardent, eloquent appeal to the "real revolutionary alterity" for which, he asserts, his own party has always fought and will continue to fight. But the conditions in which this fight can be maintained, he adds, are on the point of dissolving: with the imminent and definitive victory of techno-fascism, the space for this real alterity will be "restricted to utopia or memory," thus reducing the function of all Marxist parties to a merely social-democratic contestation of—that is to say, compliance with—the world of neo-capitalism. For this reason, "one must fight for the conservation of all the forms, alternate and subaltern, of culture" (p. 192). Considered in and of itself, this call for the conservation of cultural alternatives would seem yet another banal appeal to those few remaining islets of solid ground yet to be engulfed by the neo-capitalist swamp. But placed in the context of that long trajectory of decline away from the realm of value that we have been chronicling here and whose absolute nature Pasolini himself comes to acknowledge in his last years, however grudgingly, however implicitly, his words here take on a special pathos. They are spoken by a man who has come to the conclusion that perhaps there is nothing left now to conserve of that alterity of which he once dreamed. Coming as it does at the very end of Pasolini's ideological decline, this conservative appeal seems to point us in quite another, rhetorical direction. One must fight for the conservation of what no longer exists, of what is now irrevocably absent and yet absolutely necessary: that, I think, is the covert imperative guiding Pasolini's last writings, despite their overt and, in the light of this imperative, hypocritical appeal to a "strength" they no longer possess.

It is this conservative position that Pasolini prepares us for and that I have argued is central to the decadentist imagination of such writers as Segalen, Conrad, and D'Annunzio. The reality of the exotic is no longer an issue for these writers; it is an alternative that has passed away, once and for all, but that they will nonetheless continue to invoke. In conserving this unreal alterity, they create a space between what no longer exists and the marmoreal present that is their point of departure as writers. This is the intermediate space of memory, and of genealogy. It is the allegorical space of the fetish, as described by Giorgio Agamben, which "continually refers beyond itself toward something that can never really be possessed"[56]—a referring (*rimandare*) beyond that is always also a sending again, and a sending back. Back again—not only to an alternative world that is forever behind us but also to the one and only world that we can never leave behind, to a present that denies us any real contact with that which we desire. To approach this space between the two worlds of the living and the dead is to begin to explore the poetic dimensions of what, in "Le ceneri di Gramsci," Pasolini once called with great beauty and even greater theoretical precision, "la tregua in cui non siamo" ("the reprieve in which we are not"). It is also to begin to engage a politics of absence—a politics that in the persistent "weakness" of its conservatism, the acknowledged impossibility of its confrontation with the present, forces us to reconsider our every idea of politics and the very idea of change itself in a world where, as Leopardi put it so long ago, "tutto è simile, e discoprendo, solo il nulla s'accresce."

To inhabit this space is, finally, to put oneself in the place of the Other: to take as one's own the burden of an emptiness that can never be possessed—that emptiness from which alone a song comes forth, and another who sings it.

Reference Matter

NOTES

For complete author names, titles, and publication data for the items cited here in short form, see the Works Cited, pp. 245–53.

CHAPTER 1

1. For the contrasting representations of Australian and New Zealand indigenes, see the Intégrales Jules Verne edition (1977) of *Les enfants du capitaine Grant*, pp. 292–300 and 358–71, respectively.
2. For relevant accounts of Weber, see Jameson, "The Vanishing Mediator: Narrative Structure in Max Weber," in *Ideologies of Theory*, 2: 3–34; and Berman, pp. 14–54.
3. Quoted in Derrida, *Of Grammatology*, p. 136.
4. Benjamin, *Illuminations*, p. 159 ("On Some Motifs in Baudelaire," 1939). For a brilliant gloss on this aspect of Benjamin's thought, see Giorgio Agamben's essay "Infanzia e storia: Saggio sulla distruzione dell'esperienza," in his *Infanzia e storia*, pp. 3–62.
5. Girard, pp. 28–29.
6. Segalen, *Essai*, p. 46.
7. Valesio, "The Beautiful Lie," p. 175.
8. Tocqueville, p. 675.
9. Benjamin, *Charles Baudelaire*, p. 75 ("The Paris of the Second Empire in Baudelaire," 1938).
10. Moretti, *Signs Taken for Wonders*, p. 265. For a detailed discussion of this "compromising" literary form, see idem, *Way of the World*, where Moretti portrays the bildungsroman as an attempt at representing the fusion of external (social) compulsion and internal (individual) impulses: there, "one's formation as an individual in and for oneself coincides without rifts with one's social integration as a simple *part of the whole*" (p. 16). Moretti goes on to add that the "dialectical synthesis" effected by this sort of "formative encounter with reality, assimilation of the new, incessant reorganization of a developing personality"—one typified by Goethe's *Wilhelm Meisters Lehrjahre* (1796) and Austen's *Pride and Prejudice* (1813)—gives way in the subsequent generation of bildungsroman writers (Stendhal, Pushkin) to a radical discontinuity between the individual and his world, between the private and public spheres of human activity.

11. By the end of the eighteenth century, Green asserts in his *Dreams of Adventure*, "English literature had organized itself into a system, of which the central seriousness was hostile to the material of adventure and therewith of empire and frontier" (p. 65).
12. Hulme, pp. 182–84. For a detailed study of the idea of adventure and its changing meanings, see Nerlich.
13. See Simmel's classic account of the differences between eighteenth- and nineteenth-century views of the individual, "Individual and Society in Eighteenth- and Nineteenth-Century Views of Life: An Example of Philosophical Sociology" (1917), in Simmel, pp. 58–84.
14. For an exhaustive account of Enlightenment thought on these matters, see Duchet and, in the particular context of Africa and the Caribbean, Cohen, pp. 60–180.
15. Moretti, *Way of the World*, p. 181.
16. For Schlegel's definition of "project," see Lacoue-Labarthe and Nancy, pp. 42–43.
17. Wordsworth, *Poetical Works*, p. 104 (ll. 832–34).
18. For a recent and thorough survey of exotic motifs in the literature of Victorian England, see Brantlinger, *Rule of Darkness*; on the strategic procedures of French exoticism at this time, see Terdiman's probing analysis of Flaubert's voyage to the Orient, "Ideological Voyages: On a Flaubertian Dis-Orient-ation," in his *Discourse/Counter-discourse*, pp. 227–57.
19. Doyle, p. 345.
20. Speech given before the Royal Colonial Institute in March 1893; quoted in Semmel, pp. 54–55.
21. For an absorbing consideration of the economic and geopolitical differences between nineteenth-century colonialism and its twentieth-century national and multinational successors, see Arrighi.
22. Segalen, *Journal des îles*, p. 115.
23. Conrad, *Collected Letters*, 2: 159–60, and 161 for the translation (letter of 8 Feb. 1899).
24. Said, "Kim," p. 61.
25. For an historical assessment of this process, see J. M. Mackenzie.
26. Nandy, p. 70.
27. Benjamin, *Gesammelte Schriften*, p. 666.
28. For an elaboration of this distinction between ideology and rhetoric, which is based on ideas put forward in Paolo Valesio's *Novantiqua*, see my "*Contro il male del tempo*." (I take this opportunity to note that the article's bibliographical and footnote apparatus was badly mangled by the journal's editors.)
29. Lyotard, p. xxiv and *passim*.
30. For an effective account of Vattimo's thought, see Snyder's introduction to *End of Modernity* (pp. vi–lviii); and Ferraris, esp. pp. 21–39, 109–24, 141–52.
31. Vattimo, "Dialettica," p. 22.
32. Vattimo's *Andenken* calls to mind, albeit in a *weak* and non-dialectical way,

the "unique experience" of the past that characterizes "historical materialism" as Benjamin conceived it: the historical materialist's proper object is the "dialectical image"—shards of the past that flare up into the "now" of re-cognition, thereby "blasting open the continuum of history" in a revolutionary encounter of the oppressed past and the messianic present that redeems them both. See Benjamin, "Theses on the Philosophy of History" (1940), in *Illuminations*, pp. 253–64. For a *strong*, and admirable, reading of Benjamin's "dialectical image" in the specific context of colonial discourse, see Taussig.

33. Vattimo, *La fine della modernità*, p. 185 (this passage is not in the English-language edition).
34. Agamben, *Idea della prosa*, p. 60.
35. For an example of Jameson's surprisingly reductionistic approach to the "Third World," see his "Third-World Literature."
36. For a detailed elaboration of this argument, see Severino.
37. See, e.g., Spivak's "Can the Subaltern Speak?" in Nelson and Grossberg, pp. 271–313.
38. Spivak, *In Other Worlds*, p. 207.
39. Parry, "Problems," pp. 34–35. The Spivak-Parry debate has become an obligatory point of reference for discussions of colonial and post-colonial discourse; see, e.g., Sharpe, pp. 138–39.
40. Spivak, "Interview," p. 89.
41. Bellamy, p. 732.
42. Vattimo, "Dialettica," pp. 27–28.

CHAPTER 2

1. Quoted in Bluche, p. 338. For an extended historical discussion of despotism, see Anderson, esp. pp. 195–235.
2. Macaulay, p. 139.
3. Mill, 3: 167–68.
4. Darby, p. 39.
5. Betts, p. 72.
6. The various debates from February through May 1876 are recorded in *Hansard's Parliamentary Debates*, 3rd series, vols. 227–29 (London, 1876). References in the text cite volume and page numbers.
7. Koebner and Schmidt, p. 194.
8. Steins, p. 75.
9. Eagleton, p. 135.
10. Fleishman, p. 68.
11. Conrad, *Collected Works*, 14: 288. This and all subsequent citations of Conrad, unless otherwise noted, refer to the Medallion Edition of the *Complete Works* and will be given in the text by page number only.
12. Conrad, *Collected Letters*, 2: 139–40.
13. Watt, p. 216.
14. The theoretical justification for this combination of terms (or *combinatoire*) derives from the semiotics of A.-J. Greimas, although I do not wish to insist

upon his structuralist procedure here. For an excellent technical application of Greimas's system to literature in general and to Conrad in particular, see Jameson, *Political Unconscious*, esp. pp. 46–49, 166–68, and 253–
57.

15. Oliva, p. 51.
16. Daniell, p. 141.
17. For an example of a similar mediation at work in contemporary theory, see
    Deleuze and Guattari's portrait of the Barbarian Despotic Machine: "the
    common horizon for what comes before and what comes after it," that is
    to say, for "savagery" and "civilization." In their study "Savages, Barbar-
    ians, Civilized Men" (*Anti-Oedipus*, pp. 139–271), Deleuze and Guattari
    distinguish between capitalist and primitive representation. The former
    involves such things as the universal circulation of abstract signs (most
    prominently, money) and the unlimited transmission of information via
    non-immanent media. The latter is marked by a limited exchange of ma-
    terial goods (barter) and the inscription of bodies in a theater of cruelty as
    a means of conveying information (for instance, tattooing). The emergence
    of the despot from primitive society marks the foundation of the State but
    also anticipates a new, capitalist State from which he will be excluded.
    Primitive society is subsumed by capitalism and ceases to exist in itself.
    Deleuze and Guattari's polemical return to this pre-capitalist world is a
    purely rhetorical gesture that matches Conrad's own re-presentation of the
    despotic and the savage in *Heart of Darkness*.
18. Vámbéry, p. 487.
19. L. F. Kostenko, quoted in D. Mackenzie, p. 727.
20. Fieldhouse, p. 334.
21. See the introduction to Alexis de Levchine, *Description des hordes et des
    steppes des Kirghiz-Kazaks ou Kirghiz-Kaïssaks*, trans. Ferry de Pigny (Paris,
    1840).
22. The novel, originally entitled *Le courrier du Csar*, was first published in *Le
    magasin d'éducation et de récréation*, a periodical run by Verne's editor Jules
    Hetzel. It has been most recently translated into English by I. O. Evans
    (Westport, Conn., 1959), but the translations given here are my own and
    refer, as do all my citations from the *Voyages extraordinaires*, to the Inté-
    grales Jules Verne edition of his works put out by Hachette. For a recent
    and very interesting study of Verne's work as a whole, see Martin.
23. Watt, p. 140.
24. C. L. Miller, p. 172.
25. See Chesneaux, pp. 184–85.
26. Macherey, p. 177.
27. Prendergast, p. 87.
28. Chesneaux, p. 166.
29. According to Virilio, the nineteenth century saw the emergence of *speed* as
    a basic category of social life; with the Industrial, or *dromocratic* (from *dro-
    mos*: race), Revolution, the age of the brake gave way to the age of the ac-
    celerator. See Virilio, esp. pp. 42–45.

30. Moscovici, p. 254.
31. Vierne, *Le roman initiatique*, pp. 122–29.
32. For the association of all plotted narratives with boundary crossing, see Lotman, pp. 231–39; on *Michel Strogoff* as a typical adventure novel, see Tadié, pp. 76–93.
33. On actantial performance and competence, see Greimas's essay "Actants, Actors, and Figures," in idem, *On Meaning*, pp. 109–10.
34. Said, *Beginnings*, p. 146.
35. Given Verne's *reticentia*, this identification must be regarded as no more than a tendentious, if commonsense, interpretive move. Strictly speaking, only one passage in the text bears it out: "The Czar had the right to utter these words with real pride, for *he has often shown*, by his clemency, that Russian justice knew how to pardon" (p. 25; my italics).
36. Gillard, p. 120.
37. Morris, p. 71.
38. Allworth, Introduction, p. 10.
39. Becker, p. 13.
40. Jules-Verne, pp. 205–6. Verne's response to Turgenev reveals another political dimension of *Michel Strogoff* that, though of immense interest, cannot be expanded on here: "Only the invasion seemed improbable [*invraisemblable*] to him. And [the Prussian invasion of France in] 1870, he found that probable?" (quoted in Jules-Verne, p. 207)
41. Vierne, *Une vie*, p. 50.
42. Hellwald, pp. 304–5.
43. Delabroy, "*Michel Strogoff*," p. 158. For an extension of this argument, see also idem, "Jules Verne."
44. For another extremely relevant study of the relation between dialectical thinking and exoticism, see Vero.
45. Soriano, pp. 134–35.
46. Huet, p. 124; see also pp. 82, 129.
47. Chesneaux, p. 76.
48. Mill, 1: 172.

CHAPTER 3

1. Gauguin, *Lettres à sa femme*, p. 222.
2. Ibid., p. 219 (letter of July 1891).
3. For the definitive version of Gauguin's *Noa Noa*, pruned of his literary collaborator Charles Morice's stylistic revisions and additions, see Loize's 1966 edition.
4. Segalen, *Gauguin*, p. 30.
5. Collected in Segalen, *Gauguin*, pp. 81–124.
6. See Agamben's *Stanze*, esp. pp. 39–43, 167–80.
7. Andersen, p. 184.
8. Gauguin, *Lettres à sa femme*, p. 238.
9. Gauguin, *Lettres à Georges-Daniel de Monfreid*, p. 165 (letter of 14 Feb. 1897).
10. I take this phrase from Timothy Mitchell's recent, and remarkable, *Colon-*

ising Egypt, p. 13. The perspective Mitchell adopts in his book is similar to my own inasmuch as he too considers colonialism one manifestation of a peculiarly modern, and global, form of power that emerges in the nineteenth century and "in which we are still caught up." This power, which enforces a division of the world "into a realm of mere representations and a realm of 'the real'; into exhibitions and an external reality; into an order of mere models, descriptions or copies, and an order of the original" (p. 32), necessarily problematizes our relation to all prior forms of ordering the world, as he makes clear in his nice analysis of the differences between the colonial "model village" and the manner of dwelling it replaced and, more generally, between the modern world and any other world whose order "is not an order of appearance" (pp. 48–62). The "strong," Foucauldian drift of Mitchell's argument, however, which apparently permits him to step beyond the very "historical practice" that constitutes "us" ("we inhabitants of the world-as-exhibition"; p. 51), pushes his work in a rather different ethico-political direction from my own.

11. Blanch, p. 175. For another detailed biographical study, see Quella-Villéger.

12. All references to *Aziyadé* and *Le mariage de Loti* (1880) are to the first volume of the (never completed) *Oeuvres complètes* and those to *Le roman d'un spahi* (1881) to the second. A paperback edition of *Aziyadé*, containing a great deal of interesting bibliographical material, was published in 1989 by Flammarion, and an edition of the *Mariage* is also forthcoming there; somewhat antiquated translations of these two novels were reissued by Kegan Paul International in 1989 and 1986, respectively.

13. Baumgart, p. 34.

14. Thornton, *Imperial Idea*, p. 62.

15. For a useful counterpoint to the following reading of time(s) in the beginning of *Aziyadé*, see Johannes Fabian's engaging *Time and the Other*.

16. Benveniste, p. 208.

17. Gladstone, p. 14.

18. On the distinction between *historical utterance* and *discourse*, see Benveniste, pp. 205–15.

19. Barthes, pp. 105–21.

20. Simpson, p. 112.

21. Highlighting the idea of discontinuity between texts in the corpus of a writer (for example, Loti's shift from anonymity to authorship) is admittedly a problematical interpretive strategy, although it is one that I make frequent use of in this book. As Dominick LaCapra has remarked, this strategy depends upon a "simple model of intelligibility," like those of "linear development" and "dialectical synthesis"; such categories, he adds, are surely "too simple for interpreting the functioning of both a complex text and the corpus of complex texts" (pp. 55–56).

22. The Duke of Argyll, quoted in Millman, p. 229.

23. Clayton, p. 123.

24. Hargreaves, pp. 45–67.

25. Quoted in Annie Joly-Segalen's Introduction to Segalen's *Journal des îles*, p. 9.
26. Loutfi, p. 25.
27. See Fanoudh-Siefer, pp. 51–110.
28. Bhabha, esp. pp. 161–62.

CHAPTER 4

1. Segalen, *Trahison fidèle*, pp. 119–20. For a thorough, book-length introduction to Segalen's work, see Hsieh.
2. Bouillier, p. 295.
3. Segalen, *Thibet*, p. 90.
4. In a note written for the *Essai* on 21 Oct. 1911, Segalen explicitly returns to this first entry in a withering gloss: "Bernardin de Saint-Pierre! Read only here at Tientsin seven years later. Doubtless cited [an illegible word] contempt for his insipidity. Loti? Already outdistanced" (p. 57).
5. Lebel, pp. 75, 82.
6. On the "tragic" quality of Segalen's exoticism, see Licari, pp. 39–40.
7. For more details on this proposed collection, though presented from a perspective very different from my own, see Gilles Manceron's introduction to the Livre de Poche edition (Paris, 1986) of the *Essai*, pp. 23–25.
8. Zecchi, *Drago*, p. 65.
9. Zecchi, "Romanzo," p. 104. This strategy will not, however, fully take shape until some years later; given this fact, one should note Gérard Macé's useful suggestion in *Ex libris* (p. 139) that Segalen's first, and unfinished, novel about China, *Le Fils du Ciel* (1910–11), was initially conceived as an Oriental version of the *Immémoriaux*.
10. Quoted in Bouillier, pp. 263–64.
11. Zecchi, "Romanzo," p. 105.
12. Baudelaire, p. 694.
13. Bouillier's reading, as the following quotation makes clear, is determined by the idea of the *grand artiste* that founds Segalen's own dream of an "absolute exoticism": "We, who are familiar with *Stèles, Peintures, Equipée, René Leys*, can recognize that if the *Immémoriaux* is not to be situated at the same level, it nonetheless contains in germ the gifts and the personal vision of a great writer. One sees in it very clearly the promises that will be kept. For, at bottom, what gives a unity of tone to this book is that it is the discovery by an artist of his chosen field" (p. 142). Good criticism of Bouillier's dismissive attitude toward the *Immémoriaux* is scattered throughout Zecchi, *Drago*.
14. Gozzano, p. 145.
15. Said, *Orientalism*, p. 93.
16. Sanguinetti, p. 46.
17. See Grisay, as well as the thoroughgoing introduction and philological apparatus in Cudini's edition of Gozzano's Indian stories.
18. For a discussion of the *Derniers jours* in the context of Segalen studies, see White, pp. 38–40. The phrase "oeuvre de la conquête abominable" is from

one of the dialogues in Octave Mirbeau's *Jardin des supplices* (p. 205), an extraordinary fin de siècle mélange of libertinism and orientalism.

19. Segalen, *Lettres de Chine*, p. 206.
20. Bird, p. 11.
21. Voisins, 1: 86.
22. Thornton, *Imperialism*, p. 200.
23. Kidd, p. 82.
24. Leroy-Beaulieu, p. x.
25. On the central role of vision in the construction of *récits de voyage*, see Hartog, esp. pp. 260–309; for scathing critiques of "visualism," see Fabian, pp. 105–41; and Tyler.
26. Segalen, *René Leys*, p. 239. The novel has been translated into English by J. A. Underwood (Chicago, 1974), but the translations given here are my own. In order to facilitate close reading, I have also cited most of the longer passages in the original French. (Unless otherwise indicated, ellipses are Segalen's.)
27. Voisins, 2: 190–91.
28. See Segalen, *Lettres de Chine*, pp. 101–2.
29. Manceron, p. 86.
30. Verrier, pp. 342–43. Despite its predilection for "textuality," Verrier's article remains—along with those of Bougnoux; and Zecchi (*Drago*, pp. 123–85)—one of the best readings of *René Leys*.
31. The articles are reprinted in Segalen, *Dossier*, pp. 19–35, 59–67.
32. For a good reading of the novel as a meditation on the problematical status of ethnographical knowledge, see Jamin; and the brief but effective portrait of Segalen in Clifford, pp. 152–64.
33. Though suggestive, my identification of the two voices would require a careful documentation to be fully convincing. An ambiguous bit of information that needs to be looked at is *Segalen*'s extremely curious affirmation that Yüan backed the Emperor Kuang-hsü during his aborted reform movement of 1898 (p. 86). Segalen, one would assume, knew as well as everybody else that Yüan's support of the Empress Dowager Tz'u-hsi was one of the major reasons behind the failure of this movement. On Segalen's cult of the *chef*, see his letter of 20 June 1915 to Henry Manceron (*Trahison fidèle*, pp. 202–3).
34. This phrase is taken from a letter of 25 Aug. 1910 (*Lettres de Chine*, p. 148) in which Segalen divulges the story line of what was to have been the *Fils du Ciel*.
35. For details of Agamben's argument, which combines a Derridean view of writing as the scene of supplementarity with a Heideggerian sensitivity to the immemorial provenance of written culture, see "L'origine et l'oubli."

CHAPTER 5

1. Letter of 25 June 1920, quoted in Clark, p. 380.
2. Horkheimer, p. 139. For a useful survey of nineteenth- and twentieth-century perceptions of the masses, see Brantlinger, *Bread and Circuses*.

3. For stimulating accounts of the turn exoticism takes during the *entre-deux-guerres*, see Licari; and Leenhardt, pp. 157–200.
4. See Goldmann, pp. 18–131.
5. Quoted in Najder, p. 471.
6. Le Bon, p. 184.
7. Quoted in Karl, p. 738.
8. Simpson, p. 119.
9. Goonetilleke, p. 93.
10. Jenkins, p. 138.
11. Simpson, p. 99.
12. Wordsworth, *Prelude*, p. 236 (ll. 128–29).
13. Watt, p. 37.
14. The term is the guiding motif of Bruffee's *Elegiac Romance*; in its general outlines, his account of the development of Conradian narrative in the early novels and stories is similar to the one put forward here, although to very different ends (see pp. 73–95). For another interesting argument about a shift in Conrad's thinking at the time of *Heart of Darkness* and *Lord Jim*, see Hunter, pp. 108–20.
15. Karl, p. 401.
16. Conrad, *Collected Letters*, 1: 381 (letter of 6 Sept. 1897).
17. See, e.g., Benita Parry's excellent account in *Conrad and Imperialism*, pp. 60–75.
18. For an interesting interpretation of this passage from *Lord Jim*, see J. H. Miller, pp. 26–30; for a good discussion of the early short stories as a whole and their links to the longer fiction, see Fraser.
19. Said, "Kim," p. 61. Said's account of "The Return" in his *Joseph Conrad* (pp. 104–11) remains one of the most thoughtful discussions of this story.
20. Sertoli, p. 407.
21. Arac, p. 84.
22. Conrad, *Collected Letters*, 1: 430 (letter of 23 Dec. 1897).
23. Watt, p. 115. Although Watt has stated (pers. comm.) that he doubts Conrad ever read Le Bon, Najder suggests that the origin of Conrad's fear of "anarchistic destructive rabble" can probably be traced "not only to the historical and sociological books he had read (Taine, Gustave Le Bon) or to conservative political propaganda, but also to his own experiences with the urban and port mobs he later described with contempt in *The Nigger of the 'Narcissus'*" (pp. 88–89).
24. Le Bon, p. 29.
25. Le Bon's pessimism, on the other hand, is palliated by a belief that "the genius [*âme*] of the race exerts a paramount influence upon the dispositions of a crowd" (p. 158). Whereas "the substitution of the unconscious action of crowds for the conscious activity of individuals is one of the principal characteristics of the present age" (p. 3), the distinction between "primitive, inferior, middling, and superior races" serves as a more or less efficacious counter to this homogenizing process. On this point, see especially his *Lois psychologiques de l'évolution des peuples* (1894).

26. See, e.g., Bruffee, pp. 79–80.
27. Conrad, *Collected Letters*, 2: 25 (letter of 23 Jan. 1898).
28. Valesio, "Declensions," p. 403.
29. Quoted in Najder, p. 373.
30. Jameson, *Political Unconscious*, pp. 211–12.
31. Hartog, pp. 335–36.
32. My comments here obviously assume a theory of tragedy that, for reasons of space, I have sketched out only in the most cursory of terms. For a detailed analysis of "tragic form" and its relation to the dissolution of organic society, see Franco Moretti's provocative essay on the Elizabethan theater in his *Signs Taken for Wonders* (pp. 42–82); on the problem of secularization, see Walter Benjamin's discussion of the difference between tragedy, whose object is myth, and *Trauerspiel*, whose object is history, in *German Tragic Drama*, esp. p. 62.
33. For a more extended consideration of the intimate connection between ironical and allegorical responses to modernity, see my "Fathers and Sons." For a relevant comparative study of Flaubert and Conrad, see Conroy.
34. D'Annunzio, 1: 1065–231. For an interpretation of this play that situates it directly in the context of colonial literature, see Tomasello, pp. 25–31.
35. "La tragedia impossibile di Corrado Brando," in Bàrberi Squarotti, pp. 107–51.
36. No longer a *polis*, the modern city has become a *metropolis*: as Maurizio Ferraris argues, unlike the polis "the metropolis does not set itself up against its opposing foundation: nature, origin, being. It refers simply to itself and communicates exclusively with other metropolises: it is *causa sui* and *index sui*; it is an all-inclusive and boundless space, without intervals. The metropolis communicates with the metropolis, and there is nothing outside of this" (p. 95).
37. Jameson, *Political Unconscious*, pp. 253–57.
38. See Anderson's article, "Modernity and Revolution," in Nelson and Grossberg, pp. 317–33.
39. Rella, *Asterischi*, p. 112.

CHAPTER 6

1. Pasolini, *Uccellaci e uccellini*, pp. 65–111; a first version of this episode can be found in idem, *Belle bandiere*, pp. 321–24. For a general introduction to Pasolini and his work, see Siciliano, *Pasolini*.
2. "Where colonialism," Bruckner argues, "posited as an absolute the relationship of master and pupil, *tiers-mondisme* has inverted the dialectic and turned the pupil into the master of the master" (p. 241).
3. The most theoretically sensitive commentary on Pasolini's literary encounter with the Third World is scattered throughout Rinaldo Rinaldi's magisterial *Pier Paolo Pasolini* (hereafter *PPP*), esp. pp. 201–11.
4. The Courneau episode itself bears witness to this absence at the heart of Pasolini's *tiers-mondisme*: although filmed, it was omitted from the final

version of *Uccellacci e uccellini* and survives only as part of the published screenplay.

5. Pasolini, *Belle bandiere*, p. 117 (11 Mar. 1961); for another extremely relevant statement on neo-decadentism, see "L'irrazionalismo cattolico di Fellini" (1960), collected in idem, *Con Pier Paolo Pasolini* (hereafter *Con PPP*), pp. 129–40.

6. Rinaldi, *PPP*, p. 15; for another interesting critical analysis of Pasolini's Friulan poetry, see Santato, pp. 1–26.

7. Pasolini, *Passione e ideologia*, p. 196 ("La poesia popolare italiana," 1955).

8. In a much later interview, he will call the Friuli an "ex-colony" of Venice and Austria; see Pasolini, *Sogno*, p. 29.

9. Rinaldi, *PPP*, p. 189.

10. Agamben, *Infanzia e storia*, p. 37; for a detailed, and brilliant, analysis of Pasolini's Roman novels, see Rinaldi, *PPP*, pp. 144–80.

11. Brevini, p. 414. For a good selection of mainstream Italian criticism of Pasolini, see Martellini; for an evaluation of this body of criticism, see Rinaldi, *PPP*, pp. 399–423.

12. Pasolini, *Poesie*, p. 18. Unless otherwise noted, all references to Pasolini's poetry are to this edition.

13. Giorgio Agamben, for one, argues that negativity—the absence of an "originary force"—is the founding "mythologeme" of both poetry and metaphysics: see his *Linguaggio e la morte*, especially the discussion of Leopardi's "L'infinito" (pp. 93–102).

14. On both the conceptual and syntactical absence of a future tense in the *Ceneri*, see Rinaldi (*PPP*, p. 125), who in turn cites Vincenzo Mannino, *Il 'discorso' di Pasolini: Saggio su 'Le ceneri di Gramsci'* (Rome, 1973), p. 116.

15. Pasolini, *Belle bandiere*, p. 170.

16. Pasolini, *Empirismo eretico*, p. 138 (recently translated by Ben Lawton and Louise K. Barnett as *Heretical Empiricism* [Bloomington, Ind., 1988]). This "renunciation of the novel," we should add, is matched by a scathing critique of the literary avant-garde: Pasolini will argue throughout the 1960's that, far from effecting a break with capitalism, the avant-garde's linguistic experiments are in perfect accord with the world of neo-capitalism; they are carried out (although perhaps unwittingly) in the name of "homo technologicus."

17. Golino, pp. 241–43.

18. Foucault, *Language*, p. 33.

19. See Derrida, *Writing and Difference*, pp. 31–63.

20. For an interesting account of Sartre's preface to Léopold Senghor's groundbreaking anthology of Black poetry, see Mudimbe, pp. 83–87.

21. Pasolini, *Belle bandiere*, p. 120.

22. Aijaz Ahmad has noted a similar imperative at work in Fredric Jameson's recent attempts at defining the paradigmatic Third World text ("all third-world texts are necessarily . . . *national allegories*"). In Jameson's totalizing approach, "difference between the first world and the third is absolutised as an Otherness, but the enormous cultural heterogeneity of social for-

mations within the so-called third world is submerged within a singular identity of 'experience'" (Ahmad, p. 10).

23. This banal piece of journalism has nonetheless found its way into a handsome English-language paperback edition—*The Scent of India* (London, 1984)—despite the fact that many of Pasolini's major writings remain untranslated; the commercial feasibility of this translation in the travelwriting-hungry 1980's itself merits an extended sociological analysis.

24. Rinaldi, "Dell'estraneità," p. 98.

25. Moravia, *Intervista*, p. 81. For additional remarks of this nature, see also the final pages of his interview in Camon, pp. 11–32, as well as his own Indian travelogue, *Un'idea dell'India* (Milan, 1962).

26. Moravia, *Tribe*, p. 8.

27. Moravia, *Intervista*, p. 82.

28. Siciliano, *Moravia*, p. 221. For Moravia, Africa functions as a real-life alternative to the ineluctably decadent world of his novels, where, as Margaret Brose has elegantly pointed out, "The leap into *kairotic* time, into the fullness of some epiphanic presence, is everywhere desired but everywhere denied" (Brose, p. 64).

29. Moravia, *Intervista*, p. 132.

30. For a scathing criticism of Moravia's African writings, see Pratt, "Conventions of Representation."

31. Pasolini, *Sogno*, p. 25. In all fairness, however, one should point out that Pasolini's notorious definition of the cinema as "the *written* language of reality" (see, e.g., *Empirismo eretico*, pp. 202–30) itself undermines his own more extremist claims for the unmediated, sensual nature of filmic representation.

32. Pasolini, *Con PPP*, pp. 61–62.

33. I am quoting here from Derrida's critique of Lévi-Strauss's reliance on this "epigenetist" account of orality's fall into writing (*Of Grammatology*, p. 120).

34. Pasolini, *Empirismo eretico*, p. 64.

35. Benjamin, *Illuminations*, p. 185.

36. Sartre, p. 63.

37. Pasolini, *Corpi e luoghi*, p. 47 ("In Africa tra figli obbedienti e ragazzi moderni," 1970).

38. Pasolini, *Empirismo eretico*, pp. 161–62.

39. Pasolini, *Con PPP*, p. 103.

40. Pasolini, *Empirismo eretico*, p. 163.

41. Pasolini, *Descrizioni di descrizioni*, p. 302.

42. Camon, p. 115.

43. Valesio, "Pasolini come sintomo," p. 32.

44. Collected in Pasolini, *Medea*, p. 121.

45. Ferretti, p. 88.

46. Pasolini, *Corpi e luoghi*, pp. 36–37 ("Appunti per un poema sul Terzo Mondo," 1968).

47. Pasolini, *Pasolini on Pasolini*, p. 38.

48. Pasolini, *Sogno*, p. 108 (ellipsis in original); as he says in the interview with Oswald Stack, the *Poema* "would be an essay, not a narrative film, because I am not a vulgarizer" (p. 140).

49. For just one example of this poetics, compare Pasolini's description of how he made the *Gospel According to Saint Matthew*: "A double series of figurative worlds were projecting upon my imagination, often interconnected: the physiological, brutally alive, world of biblical times as it had appeared to me in my voyages in India or on the Arabian coasts of Africa, and a world reconstructed out of the figurative culture of the Italian Renaissance, from Masaccio to the *manieristi neri*." From an article in *Il giorno* (6 Mar. 1963), reprinted in *Il Vangelo secondo Matteo*, p. 14.

50. Pasolini, *Con PPP*, p. 99.

51. For this piece, along with Pasolini's subsequent recantation of it, see *Corpi e luoghi*, pp. 50–58.

52. Collected in Pasolini, *Lettere luterane*, pp. 71–76. (For an English translation, see *Lutheran Letters*, trans. Stuart Hood [Manchester, 1983], pp. 49–52.)

53. Interview of Aug.–Sept. 1974, in *Con PPP*, p. 111.

54. Pasolini, *Con PPP*, p. 105.

55. Collected in Pasolini, *Lettere luterane*, pp. 185–95.

56. Agamben, *Stanze*, p. 41.

WORKS CITED

Agamben, Giorgio. *Idea della prosa*. Milan, 1985.
———. *Infanzia e storia: Distruzione dell'esperienza e origine della storia*. Turin, 1978.
———. *Il linguaggio e la morte: Un seminario sul luogo della negatività*. Turin, 1982.
———. "L'origine et l'oubli: Parole du mythe et parole de la littérature." In *Regard, espaces, signes: Victor Segalen*. Paris, 1979, pp. 169–79.
———. *Stanze: La parola e il fantasma nella cultura occidentale*. Turin, 1977.
Ahmad, Aijaz. "Jameson's Rhetoric of Otherness and the 'National Allegory.'" *Social Text* 17 (1987): 3–25.
Allworth, Edward, ed. *Central Asia: A Century of Russian Rule*. New York, 1967.
Andersen, Wayne. *Gauguin's Paradise Lost*. New York, 1971.
Anderson, Perry. *Lineages of the Absolutist State*. London, 1979.
Arac, Jonathan. "Romanticism, the Self and the City: *The Secret Agent* in Literary History." *Boundary* 2 9.1 (1980): 75–90.
Arrighi, Giovanni. *The Geometry of Imperialism: The Limits of Hobson's Paradigm*. Trans. Patrick Camiller. London, 1978.
Bàrberi Squarotti, Giorgio. *Il gesto improbabile: Tre saggi su Gabriele D'Annunzio*. Palermo, 1971.
Barrès, Maurice. *L'oeuvre de Maurice Barrès*, vol. 2, *Du sang, de la volupté et de la mort*. Paris, 1965.
Barthes, Roland. *New Critical Essays*. Trans. Richard Howard. New York, 1980.
Baudelaire, Charles. *Oeuvres*. Ed. Y.-G. Le Dantec. Paris, 1954.
Baumgart, Winfried. *Imperialism: The Idea and Reality of British and French Colonial Expansion, 1880–1914*. Oxford, 1982.
Becker, Seymour. *Russia's Protectorates in Central Asia: Bukhara and Khiva, 1865–1924*. Cambridge, Mass., 1968.
Bellamy, Richard. "Post-modernism and the End of History." *Theory Culture & Society* 4 (1987): 727–33.
Benjamin, Walter. *Charles Baudelaire: A Lyric Poet in the Era of High Capitalism*. Trans. Harry Zohn. London, 1983.
———. *Gesammelte Schriften*, vol. 1. Ed. Rolf Tiedemann and Hermann Schweppenhaüser. Frankfurt, 1972–74.
———. *Illuminations*. Trans. Harry Zohn. New York, 1969.
———. *The Origin of German Tragic Drama*. Trans. John Osborne. London, 1977.

Benveniste, Emile. *Problems in General Linguistics.* Trans. M. E. Meek. Coral Gables, Fla., 1971.

Berman, Russell A. *The Rise of the Modern German Novel: Crisis and Charisma.* Cambridge, Mass., 1986.

Bertini, Antonio. *Teoria e tecnica del film in Pasolini.* Rome, 1979.

Betts, Raymond F. *The False Dawn: European Imperialism in the Nineteenth Century.* Minneapolis, 1975.

Bhabha, Homi K. "The Other Question: Difference, Discrimination and the Discourse of Colonialism." In *Literature, Politics, and Theory: Papers from the Essex Conference, 1976–84.* Ed. Francis Barker et al. London, 1986, pp. 148–72.

Bird, Isabella. *The Yangtze Valley and Beyond.* London, 1985.

Blanch, Lesley. *Pierre Loti: The Legendary Romantic.* San Diego, Calif., 1983.

Bluche, François. *Le despotisme eclairé.* Paris, 1968.

Bongie, Chris. "*Contro il male del tempo*: The Dream of Gabriele D'Annunzio." *Quaderni d'italianistica* 8 (1987): 23–41.

———. "Fathers and Sons: The Self-revelations of Flaubert and Céline." *Romanic Review* 77 (1986): 428–47.

Bougnoux, Daniel. "Dix-neuf, et un, gongs pour boômer *René Leys*." *Silex* 1 (1976): 98–127.

Bouillier, Henry. *Victor Segalen.* Rev. ed. Paris, 1986.

Brantlinger, Patrick. *Bread and Circuses: Theories of Mass Culture as Social Decay.* Ithaca, N.Y., 1983.

———. *Rule of Darkness: British Literature and Imperialism, 1830–1914.* Ithaca, N.Y., 1988.

Brevini, Franco. "Pier Paolo Pasolini." *Belfagor* 37 (1982): 407–38.

Brose, Margaret. "Alberto Moravia: Fetishism and Figuration." *Novel* 15 (1981): 60–75.

Bruckner, Pascal. *Le sanglot de l'homme blanc: Tiers Monde, culpabilité, haine de soi.* Paris, 1983.

Bruffee, Kenneth A. *Elegiac Romance: Cultural Change and Loss of the Hero in Modern Fiction.* Ithaca, N.Y., 1983.

Camon, Ferdinando. *Il mestiere di scrittore.* Milan, 1973.

Chesneaux, Jean. *Jules Verne: Une lecture politique.* Paris, 1982.

Clark, Ronald W. *The Life of Bertrand Russell.* New York, 1976.

Clayton, G. D. *Britain and the Eastern Question: Missolonghi to Gallipoli.* London, 1971.

Clifford, James. *The Predicament of Culture: Twentieth-Century Ethnography, Literature, and Art.* Cambridge, Mass., 1988.

Cohen, William B. *The French Encounter with Africans: White Response to Blacks, 1530–1880.* Bloomington, Ind., 1980.

Conrad, Joseph. *Collected Letters of Joseph Conrad*, vols. 1–2. Ed. Frederick R. Karl and Laurence Davies. Cambridge, Eng., 1983, 1986.

———. *Collected Works.* Medallion ed. 22 vols. London, 1925–28.

Conroy, Mark. *Modernism and Authority: Strategies of Legitimation in Flaubert and Conrad.* Baltimore, 1985.

Daniell, David. "Buchan and 'The Black General.'" In *The Black Presence in English Literature*. Ed. David Dabydeen. Manchester, 1985, pp. 135–53.

D'Annunzio, Gabriele. *Tragedie, sogni e misteri*. 2 vols. Milan, 1939, 1940.

Darby, Phillip. *Three Faces of Imperialism: British and American Approaches to Asia and Africa, 1870–1970*. New Haven, Conn., 1987.

Delabroy, Jean. "Jules Verne, ou le procès de l'aventure et de son livre." In *L'aventure dans la littérature populaire au XIXe siècle*. Ed. R. Bellet. Lyon, 1985, pp. 127–37.

———. "*Michel Strogoff* ou le sacrifice du spectacle." *Revue des lettres modernes* 669–74 (1983): 149–60.

Deleuze, Gilles, and Félix Guattari. *Anti-Oedipus: Capitalism and Schizophrenia*. Trans. R. Hurley, M. Seem, and H. R. Lane. Minneapolis, 1983.

Derrida, Jacques. *Of Grammatology*. Trans. Gayatri Chakravorty Spivak. Baltimore, 1976.

———. *Writing and Difference*. Trans. Alan Bass. Chicago, 1978.

Dostoyevsky, Feodor. *Diary of a Writer*. Trans. Boris Brasol. Salt Lake City, Utah, 1985.

Doyle, Michael W. *Empires*. Ithaca, N.Y., 1986.

Duchet, Michèle. *Anthropologie et histoire au siècle des lumières: Buffon, Voltaire, Rousseau, Helvétius, Diderot*. Paris, 1971.

Eagleton, Terry. *Criticism and Ideology*. London, 1978.

Fabian, Johannes. *Time and the Other: How Anthropology Makes Its Object*. New York, 1983.

Fanoudh-Siefer, Léon. *Le mythe du nègre et de l'Afrique noire dans la littérature française*. Paris, 1968.

Ferraris, Maurizio. *Tracce: Nichilismo, moderno, postmoderno*. Milan, 1983.

Ferretti, Gian Carlo. *Pasolini: L'universo orrendo*. Rome, 1976.

Fieldhouse, D. K. *The Colonial Empires: A Comparative Study from the Eighteenth Century*. 2nd ed. London, 1982.

Fleishman, Avrom. *Conrad's Politics: Community and Anarchy in the Fiction of Joseph Conrad*. Baltimore, 1967.

Foscolo, Ugo. *Opere* [*Ultime lettere di Iacopo Ortis*]. Ed. Mario Puppa. Milan, 1966.

Foucault, Michel. *Discipline and Punish: The Birth of the Prison*. Trans. Alan Sheridan. New York, 1979.

———. *Language, Counter-memory, Practice*. Trans. D. F. Bouchard and Sherry Simon. Ithaca, N.Y., 1977.

Fraser, Gail. *Interweaving Patterns in the Works of Joseph Conrad*. Ann Arbor, Mich., 1988.

Gauguin, Paul. *Lettres de Gauguin à sa femme et à ses amis*. Paris, 1946.

———. *Lettres de Paul Gauguin à Georges-Daniel de Monfreid*. Paris, 1920.

———. *Noa Noa*. Ed. Jean Loize. Paris, 1966.

Gillard, David. *The Struggle for Asia, 1828–1914: A Study in British and Russian Imperialism*. London, 1977.

Girard, René. *Deceit, Desire, and the Novel: Self and Other in Literary Structure*. Trans. Yvonne Freccero. Baltimore, 1965.

Gladstone, W. E. *Bulgarian Horrors and the Question of the East*. London, 1876.

Goldmann, Lucien. *Towards a Sociology of the Novel*. Trans. Alan Sheridan. London, 1975.

Golino, Enzo. *Pasolini: Il sogno di una cosa—Pedagogia, eros, letteratura dal mito del popolo alla società di massa*. Bologna, 1985.

Goonetilleke, D. C. R. A. *Developing Countries in British Fiction*. Totowa, N.J., 1977.

Gozzano, Guido. *Un natale a Ceylon e altri racconti indiani*. Ed. Piero Cudini. Milan, 1984.

Green, Martin. *Dreams of Adventure, Deeds of Empire*. New York, 1979.

Greimas, A.-J. *On Meaning: Selected Writings in Semiotic Theory*. Trans. P. J. Perron and F. H. Collins. Minneapolis, 1987.

———. *Structural Semantics: An Attempt at a Method*. Trans. D. McDowell, R. Schleifer, and A. Velie. Lincoln, Nebr., 1983.

Grisay, Aletta. "L'India di Guido Gozzano e quella di Pierre Loti." *La rassegna della letteratura italiana*, 7th ser., 71 (1967): 427–37.

Hargreaves, Alec G. *The Colonial Experience in French Fiction: A Study of Pierre Loti, Ernest Psichari and Pierre Mille*. London, 1981.

Hartog, François. *The Mirror of Herodotus: The Representation of the Other in the Writing of History*. Trans. Janet Lloyd. Berkeley, Calif., 1988.

Hellwald, Frederick von. *The Russians in Central Asia: A Critical Examination down to the Present Time of the Geography and History of Central Asia*. Trans. Theodore Wirgman. London, 1874.

Horkheimer, Max. *Eclipse of Reason*. New York, 1974.

Hsieh, Yvonne Y. *Victor Segalen's Literary Encounter with China: Chinese Moulds, Western Thoughts*. Toronto, 1988.

Huet, Marie-Hélène. *L'histoire des "Voyages extraordinaires": Essai sur l'oeuvre de Jules Verne*. Paris, 1973.

Hulme, Peter. *Colonial Encounters: Europe and the Native Caribbean, 1492–1797*. London, 1986.

Hunter, Allan. *Joseph Conrad and the Ethics of Darwinism*. London, 1983.

Huysmans, Joris-Karl. *Oeuvres complètes*, vol. 7, *A rebours*. Geneva, 1972.

Jameson, Fredric. *The Ideologies of Theory: Essays, 1971–1986*. 2 vols. Minneapolis, 1988.

———. *The Political Unconscious: Narrative as a Socially Symbolic Act*. Ithaca, N.Y., 1981.

———. "Third-World Literature in the Era of Multinational Capitalism." *Social Text* 15 (1986): 65–88.

Jamin, Jean. "Une initiation au réel: A propos de Segalen." *Cahiers internationaux de sociologie* 66 (1979): 125–39.

Jenkins, Gareth. "Conrad's *Nostromo* and History." *Literature and History* 6 (1977): 138–78.

Jules-Verne, Jean. *Jules Verne*. Paris, 1973.

Karl, Frederick R. *Joseph Conrad: The Three Lives*. New York, 1979.

Kidd, Benjamin. *The Control of the Tropics*. London, 1898.

Koebner, Richard, and H. D. Schmidt. *Imperialism: The Story and Significance of a Political Word*. Cambridge, Eng., 1964.

LaCapra, Dominick. *Rethinking Intellectual History: Texts, Contexts, Language.* Ithaca, N.Y., 1983.

Lacoue-Labarthe, Philippe, and Jean-Luc Nancy. *The Literary Absolute: The Theory of Literature in German Romanticism.* Trans. Philip Barnard and Cheryl Lester. Albany, N.Y., 1988.

Lebel, Roland. *Histoire de la littérature coloniale en France.* Paris, 1931.

Leblond, Marius-Ary. *Après l'exotisme de Loti: Le roman colonial.* Paris, 1926.

Le Bon, Gustave. *The Crowd: A Study of the Popular Mind.* Ed. Robert K. Merton. New York, 1960.

Leenhardt, Jacques. *Lecture politique du roman: "La jalousie" d'Alain Robbe-Grillet.* Paris, 1973.

Leiris, Michel. *Brisées.* Paris, 1966.

Leroy-Beaulieu, Pierre. *La rénovation de l'Asie: Sibérie-Chine-Japon.* Paris, 1900.

Lévi-Strauss, Claude. *Tristes tropiques.* Paris, 1955.

Licari, Anita. "Lo sguardo coloniale: Per una analisi dei codici dell'esotismo a partire dal *Voyage au Congo* di Gide." In Licari et al., pp. 27–62.

Licari, Anita; Roberta Maccagnani; and Lina Zecchi. *Letteratura, esotismo, colonialismo.* Bologna, 1978.

Loti, Pierre. *Les derniers jours de Pékin.* Paris, 1902.

———. *Oeuvres complètes,* vols. 1–2. Paris, 1893.

Lotman, Jurij. *The Structure of the Artistic Text.* Trans. Ronald Vroon and Gail Vroon. Ann Arbor, Mich., 1977.

Loutfi, Martine Astier. *Littérature et colonialisme: L'expansion coloniale vue dans la littérature romanesque française, 1871–1914.* Paris, 1971.

Lukes, Steven. *Individualism.* Oxford, 1973.

Lyotard, Jean-François. *The Postmodern Condition: A Report on Knowledge.* Trans. Geoff Bennington and Brian Massumi. Minneapolis, 1984.

Macaulay, Thomas Babington. *The Works of Lord Macaulay,* vol. 8. Ed. Lady Trevelyan. London, 1879.

Maccagnani, Roberta. "Esotismo-erotismo—Pierre Loti: Dalla maschera erotica alla sovranità coloniale." In Licari et al., pp. 63–99.

Macé, Gérard. *Ex libris.* Paris, 1980 .

Macherey, Pierre. *A Theory of Literary Production.* Trans. Geoffrey Wall. London, 1978.

Mackenzie, David. "Russian Expansion in Central Asia (1864–1885): Brutal Conquest or Voluntary Incorporation? A Review Article." *Canadian Slavic Studies* 4 (1970): 721–35.

Mackenzie, John M. *Propaganda and Empire: The Manipulation of British Public Opinion, 1880–1960.* Manchester, 1984.

Manceron, Gilles. "Aux origines de *René Leys*: Textes et prétextes." *Europe* 696 (1987): 79–88.

Martellini, Luigi, ed. *Il dialogo, il potere, la morte: Pasolini e la critica.* Bologna, 1979.

Martin, Andrew. *The Mask of the Prophet: The Extraordinary Fictions of Jules Verne.* Oxford, 1990.

Mill, John Stuart. *Dissertations and Discussions: Political, Philosophical, and Historical.* 3 vols. London, 1867.

Miller, Christopher L. *Blank Darkness: Africanist Discourse in French*. Chicago, 1985.

Miller, J. Hillis. *Fiction and Repetition: Seven English Novels*. Cambridge, Mass., 1982.

Millman, Richard. *Britain and the Eastern Question, 1875–1878*. Oxford, 1979.

Mirbeau, Octave. *Le jardin des supplices*. Paris, 1899.

Mitchell, Timothy. *Colonising Egypt*. Cambridge, Eng., 1988.

Moravia, Alberto. *Intervista sullo scrittore scomodo*. Ed. Nello Ajello. Bari, 1978.

———. *Which Tribe Do You Belong To?* Trans. Angus Davidson. New York, 1974.

Moretti, Franco. *Signs Taken for Wonders: Essays in the Sociology of Literary Forms*. Rev. ed. Trans. S. Fischer, D. Forgacs, and D. Miller. London, 1988.

———. *The Way of the World: The "Bildungsroman" in European Culture*. Trans. Albert Sbragia. London, 1987.

Morris, Peter. "Russian Expansion into Central Asia." In *Africa, America and Central Asia: Formal and Informal Empire in the Nineteenth Century*. Ed. Peter Morris. Exeter, Eng., 1984, pp. 63–82.

Moscovici, Serge. *L'âge des foules: Un traité historique de psychologie des masses*. Rev. ed. Paris, 1985.

Mudimbe, V. Y. *The Invention of Africa: Gnosis, Philosophy, and the Order of Knowledge*. Bloomington, Ind., 1988.

Najder, Zdzislaw. *Joseph Conrad: A Chronicle*. New Brunswick, N.J., 1983.

Nandy, Ashis. *The Intimate Enemy: Loss and Recovery of Self Under Colonialism*. Delhi, 1983.

Nelson, Cary, and Lawrence Grossberg, eds. *Marxism and the Interpretation of Culture*. Urbana, Ill., 1988.

Nerlich, Michael. *Ideology of Adventure: Studies in Modern Consciousness, 1100–1750*. 2 vols. Trans. Ruth Crowley. Minneapolis, 1987.

Oliva, Renato. "Dalla commedia della luce alla tragedia della tenebra, ovvero l'ambigua redenzione di Kurtz." In idem and Alessandro Portelli, *Conrad: L'imperialismo imperfetto*. Turin, 1973, pp. 7–70.

Parry, Benita. *Conrad and Imperialism: Ideological Boundaries and Visionary Frontiers*. London, 1983.

———. "Problems in Current Theories of Colonial Discourse." *Oxford Literary Review* 9.1–2 (1987): 27–58.

Pasolini, Pier Paolo. *Le belle bandiere: Dialoghi, 1960–65*. Ed. Gian Carlo Ferretti. Rome, 1977.

———. *Il Caos*. Ed. Gian Carlo Ferretti. Rome, 1979.

———. *Con Pier Paolo Pasolini*. Ed. Enrico Magrelli. Rome, 1977.

———. *Corpi e luoghi*. Ed. Michele Mancini and Giuseppe Perrella. Rome, 1981.

———. *Descrizioni di descrizioni*. Turin, 1979.

———. *Empirismo eretico*. Milan, 1972.

———. *Lettere luterane*. Turin, 1976.

———. *Medea*. Milan, 1970.

———. *L'odore dell'India*. Milan, 1962.

———. *Il padre selvaggio*. Turin, 1975.

———. *Pasolini on Pasolini: Interview with Oswald Stack*. London, 1969.

———. *Passione e ideologia (1948–1958)*. Milan, 1960.

―――. *Le poesie*. Milan, 1975.
―――. "La Resistenza negra." In *Letteratura negra: La poesia*. Ed. Mario De Andrade. Rome, 1961, pp. xv–xxiv.
―――. *Scritti corsari*. Milan, 1975.
―――. *Il sogno del centauro*. Ed. Jean Duflot. Trans. Martine Schruoffeneger. Rome, 1983.
―――. *Uccellaci e uccellini*. Milan, 1966.
―――. *Il Vangelo secondo Matteo: Un film di Pier Paolo Pasolini*. Milan, 1964.
Pratt, Mary Louise. "Conventions of Representation: Where Discourse and Ideology Meet." In *Contemporary Perceptions of Language: Interdisciplinary Dimensions*. Ed. Heidi Byrnes. Washington, D.C., 1982, pp. 139–55.
―――. "Fieldwork in Common Places." In *Writing Culture: The Poetics and Politics of Ethnography*. Ed. James Clifford and George E. Marcus. Berkeley, Calif., 1986, pp. 27–50.
Prendergast, Christopher. *The Order of Mimesis: Balzac, Stendhal, Nerval, Flaubert*. Cambridge, Eng., 1986.
Quella-Villéger, Alain. *Pierre Loti l'incompris*. Paris, 1986.
Regismanset, Charles, and Louis Cario. *L'exotisme: La littérature coloniale*. Paris, 1911.
Rella, Franco. *Asterischi*. Milan, 1989.
―――. *Metamorfosi: Immagini del pensiero*. Milan, 1984.
Rinaldi, Rinaldo. "Dell'estraneità: Tra il giornalismo e il saggismo dell'ultimo Pasolini." *Sigma* 2–3 (1981): 95–124.
―――. *Pier Paolo Pasolini*. Milan, 1982.
Russell, Bertrand. *The Problem of China*. New York, 1922.
Said, Edward W. *Beginnings: Intention and Method*. New York, 1985.
―――. *Joseph Conrad and the Fiction of Autobiography*. Cambridge, Mass., 1966.
―――. "Kim, the Pleasures of Imperialism." *Raritan* 7.2 (1987): 27–64.
―――. *Orientalism*. New York, 1979.
Sangari, Kumkum. "The Politics of the Possible." *Cultural Critique* 7 (1987): 157–86.
Sanguinetti, Edoardo. *Tra liberty e crepuscolarismo*. Milan, 1961.
Santato, Guido. *Pier Paolo Pasolini: L'opera*. Vicenza, 1980.
Sartre, Jean-Paul. *Black Orpheus*. Trans. S. W. Allen. Paris, 1963.
Seeley, John. *The Expansion of England: Two Courses of Lectures*. London, 1884.
Segalen, Victor. *Dossier pour une fondation sinologique*. Mortemart, 1982.
―――. *Essai sur l'exotisme: Une esthétique du Divers (notes)*. Montpellier, 1978.
―――. *Gauguin dans son dernier décor et autres textes de Tahiti*. Montpellier, 1975.
―――. *Journal des îles*. Papeete, 1978.
―――. *Lettres de Chine*. Paris, 1967.
―――. *René Leys*. Paris, 1971.
―――. *Thibet*. Ed. Michael Taylor. Paris, 1974.
―――. *Trahison fidèle: Correspondance Victor Segalen–Henry Manceron, 1907–1918*. Paris, 1985.
Semmel, Bernard. *Imperialism and Social Reform: English Social-Imperialist Thought, 1895–1914*. Cambridge, Mass., 1960.
Serres, Michel. *Jouvences sur Jules Verne*. Paris, 1974.

Sertoli, Giuseppe. "Una negazione testuale: Frammento di lettura da *The Nigger of the 'Narcissus'* di Joseph Conrad." *Nuova Corrente* 61–62 (1973): 382–412.

Severino, Emanuele. *La tendenza fondamentale del nostro tempo*. Milan, 1988.

Sharpe, Jenny. "Figures of Colonial Resistance." *Modern Fiction Studies* 35 (1989): 137–55.

Siciliano, Enzo. *Alberto Moravia: Vita, parola e idee di un romanziere*. Milan, 1982.

———. *Pasolini*. Trans. John Shepley. New York, 1982.

Simmel, Georg. *The Sociology of Georg Simmel*. Ed. and trans. K. H. Wolff. Glencoe, Ill., 1950.

Simpson, David. *Fetishism and Imagination: Dickens, Melville, Conrad*. Baltimore, 1982.

Soriano, Marc. *Jules Verne (le cas Verne)*. Paris, 1978.

Spivak, Gayatri Chakravorty. *In Other Worlds: Essays in Cultural Politics*. London, 1987.

———. "Interview." *Stanford Humanities Review* 1.1 (1989): 84–97.

Steins, Martin. "Entre l'exotisme et la négritude: La littérature coloniale." *L'Afrique littéraire* 58 (1981): 71–82.

Tadié, Jean-Yves. *Le roman d'aventures*. Paris, 1982.

Taussig, Michael. "History as Sorcery." *Representations* 7 (1984): 87–109.

Terdiman, Richard. *Discourse/Counter-discourse: The Theory and Practice of Symbolic Resistance in Nineteenth-Century France*. Ithaca, N.Y., 1985.

Thornton, A. P. *The Imperial Idea and Its Enemies: A Study in British Power*. 2nd ed. London, 1985.

———. *Imperialism in the Twentieth Century*. Minneapolis, 1977.

Tocqueville, Alexis de. *Democracy in America*. Trans. George Lawrence. New York, 1966.

Tomasello, Giovanna. *La letteratura coloniale italiana dalle avanguardie al fascismo*. Palermo, 1984.

Tyler, Stephen. "The Vision Quest in the West or What the Mind's Eye Sees." *Journal of Anthropological Research* 40 (1984): 23–40.

Valéry, Paul. *Oeuvres*. 2 vols. Ed. Jean Hytier. Paris, 1957–60.

Valesio, Paolo. "The Beautiful Lie: Heroic Individuality and Fascism." In *Reconstructing Individualism: Autonomy, Individuality, and the Self in Western Thought*. Ed. T. C. Heller, M. Sosna, and D. E. Wellbery. Stanford, Calif., 1986, pp. 163–83.

———. "Declensions: D'Annunzio After the Sublime." Trans. Marilyn Migiel. *New Literary History* 16 (1985): 401–15.

———. *Novantiqua: Rhetorics as a Contemporary Theory*. Bloomington, Ind., 1980.

———. "Pasolini come sintomo." *Italian Quarterly* 21–22.82–83 (1980–81): 31–43.

Vámbéry, Arminius. *Travels in Central Asia*. New York, 1865.

Vattimo, Gianni. "Dialettica, differenza, pensiero debole." In *Il pensiero debole*. Ed. Gianni Vattimo and Pier Aldo Rovatti. Milan, 1983, pp. 12–28.

———. *The End of Modernity: Nihilism and Hermeneutics in Post-modern Culture*. Trans. Jon R. Snyder. Baltimore, 1988.

———. *La fine della modernità: Nichilismo ed ermeneutica nella cultura post-moderna.* Milan, 1985.

Verne, Jules. *Voyages extraordinaires.* Les Intégrales Jules Verne ed. Paris, 1977– .

Vero, Gianpiero de. "Esotismo e dialettica." In *Esotismo e crisi della civiltà.* Ed. Berta Cappelli and Enzo Cocco. Naples, 1979, pp. 205–31.

Verrier, Jean. "Segalen lecteur de Segalen." *Poétique* 27 (1976): 338–50.

Vierne, Simone. *Jules Verne et le roman initiatique.* Paris, 1973.

———. *Jules Verne: Une vie, une oeuvre, une époque.* Paris, 1986.

Virilio, Paul. *Pure War.* Trans. Mark Polizotti. New York, 1983.

Voisins, Gilbert de. *Ecrit en Chine.* 2 vols. Paris, 1923.

Watt, Ian. *Conrad in the Nineteenth Century.* Berkeley, Calif., 1979.

White, Kenneth. *Segalen: Théorie et pratique du voyage.* Lausanne, 1979.

Wordsworth, William. *The Fourteen-Book "Prelude."* Ed. W. J. B. Owen. Ithaca, N.Y., 1985.

———. *Poetical Works*, vol. 5. Ed. E. de Selincourt and Helen Darbishire. Oxford, 1949.

Zecchi, Lina. *Il drago e la fenice: Ai margini dell'esotismo.* Venice, 1982.

———. "Il romanzo della colonizzazione e il cadavere dell'esotismo: *Les Immémoriaux* di Victor Segalen." In Licari et al., pp. 101–39.

INDEX

In this index an "f" after a number indicates a separate reference on the next page, and an "ff" indicates separate references on the next two pages. A continuous discussion over two or more pages is indicated by a span of page numbers, e.g., "57–59." *Passim* is used for a cluster of references in close but not consecutive sequence.